By Her Own
BOOTSTRAPS:

A Saga of Women in North Carolina

by ALBERT COATES
Professor Emeritus in the Law School
The University of North Carolina
at Chapel Hill

THIS BOOK IS DEDICATED
TO GLADYS HALL COATES

I saw her for the first time in the summer of 1923, after her junior year at Randolph-Macon Woman's College (she graduated there in 1924), was engaged to her in 1925, and brought her to Chapel Hill as a bride in 1928, while the Institute was taking form. As we passed in review before students standing on the Law School building steps, one student observed: "There goes tidewater Virginia and rainwater North Carolina."

Shortly after coming to North Carolina, she got acquainted with the location of cities and towns of the state and with many officials by filing thousands of early Institute of Government letters. She stuffed, sealed, and stamped envelopes; worked up mailing lists and addressed early issues of *Popular Government;* entertained prospective staff members and found them places to live in Chapel Hill; cooked meals for officials and visitors who came to give advice and counsel; discussed programs and policies with me throughout the years and chauffeured me on countless trips crisscrossing the state while I prepared for the next day's law classes. She helped plan both Institute buildings and superintended the furnishing and decoration of them when they were built.

She has edited nearly everything I have ever written—cutting out purple passages, frying off fat, and adding insult to injury by improving the final product in ways which could not be denied.

There was the time I spelled out the story of the Institute of Government. I wrote it in the glow of creation, carried forward by the momentum of my feeling about it, with commas, colons, semicolons, dashes, and periods incidental to the movement—as indeed they were. I thought I was turning over to her a perfect thing. I recall the words of the little boy whose teacher asked him what was 2 x 2; "Four," he replied and the teacher said, "Very good." "Very good, hell," the boy said, "it's perfect." When the manuscript came back to me, every page was blemished by unseemly marks. Whole sentences were marked out and here and there a paragraph entire. Deflation did not describe my feeling. Nor did dehydration. That night I went to bed in worried sleep. Some hours later she woke me up—entranced by Thomas Hardy's description of Eustacia Vye as Queen of the Night in *The Return of the Native*. It was a glorious description full of the same sort of curlicues and hyperboles and figures of speech she had just cut out of my pages. Half awake and in dead earnest, I replied: "It's a god's blessing that Thomas Hardy got his manuscript to the printer before you got hold of it."

She has done independent research on her own. Her largest venture was a study of the structure and workings of student government in the University of North Carolina at Chapel Hill. I stated the scope and character of her work in accepting the Di Phi award for public service in 1951: "A five-year quest led her through a hundred and fifty years of trustee minutes, faculty minutes, Dialectic and Philanthropic Society minutes; through the pages of the *University Magazine* from its beginning in the 1840s, the *Tar Heel* from its beginning in the 1890s, the college humor publications from their beginning in the early 1900s; state newspapers of the various periods of University history, the *Yackety-Yacks* and the *Hellenians;* the University catalogues and other formal records; diaries of students and writings of faculty members, and the priceless recordings of Cornelia Phillips Spencer. In this five-year vigil and epic of research she uncovered and tracked out a story of governmental evolution on this campus which I believe to be without parallel in this country or any other. I could not say more without violating her own canons of propriety and good taste. I could not say less without losing my own self-respect."

Most of this work was done in the North Carolina room of the University library where the records were kept. I got into the habit of dropping in for a few minutes conference with her around the middle of the morning. The young lady at the library desk observed these tête-à-têtes and feared an "affair" was in the making—as indeed it was. Later she came up to the lady in research and said with a smile: "Now I know who you are. For a long time I thought you were his secretary and I felt so sorry for his wife."

Another cooperative venture was the history of the University Law School. I stated the scope and character of her work in the special issue of the *North Carolina Law Review:* "This story could not have been told without the underpinning of three months of meticulous and painstaking research by my wife, Gladys Hall Coates, in the Colonial and State Records, the James Sprunt Historical Publications, the files of the North Carolina Bar Association, the North Carolina Historical Review, the diaries and correspondence, private papers and biographies of personages involved, nineteenth century newspapers, and many other sources and documents in the North Carolina and Southern Historical Collections in the University Library, together with the minutes of the Trustees and Faculty of the University of North Carolina, the University and the Law School catalogues, and the reports of the President and Chancellor for a hundred and twenty-three years."

She has lit up the path we have traveled with music and art and many a heartening observation. Once, when we were driving over a river and the wind had stirred the water into ripples which caught and reflected the morning sun, she said: "It looks like a place where bright angels' feet have trod." In the middle of ups and downs and numberless frustrations I heard her say: "All these woes shall serve for sweet discourses in our time to come." And then again: "These are they which came out of great tribulation."

She has not been above the protective use of astringents. I do not believe she ever forgot a thing I ever said that she could use to advantage later on. I once told her that as a five-year-old boy I won fifty-two brightly colored celluloid butterflies for walking two miles to Sunday School and not missing a single Sunday for a year. A long while later, when I was about to win an argument on some religious point, she blurred my argument with the observation that it was a pity I had not gotten something out of Sunday School besides celluloid butterflies. In forty-seven years of married life, I do not believe I have ever won an argument she did not want to lose.

There was the time when she went to the library to read Macaulay's essay on Samuel Johnson in the *Encyclopedia Britannica* and was so entranced by the editor's note at the beginning of the essay that she copied it down, brought it home to me, and said with great glee that it was a perfect description of her husband! Here is what it says: "We have left Lord Macaulay's essay on Samuel Johnson intact except at those points where Macaulay's invincible love of the picturesque has drawn him demonstrably aside from the dull line of veracity."

In 1952, I accepted the O. Max Gardner Award on the common law theory that man and wife are one and the man is the one, saying: "I am sure this was the understanding of the givers of this good and perfect gift; and in that understanding I share the credit with the distaff side and commit the cash *in toto* to her keeping. For if a grateful heart is privileged to miss a beat in the catching of the breath that comes with this award, and in that breathless moment I confess this recognition satisfies a human longing for the only sort of fame I want, then in a spirit that vaunteth not itself, is not puffed up, and would not behave itself unseemly, I will put my feeling in its proper setting and clothe it with a poet's words:

O fame; If I e'er took delight in thy praises,
'Twas less for the sake of thy high-sounding phrases,
Than to see the bright eyes of the dear one discover
She thought that I was not unworthy to love her.
There chiefly I sought thee, there only I found thee;
Her glance was the best of the rays that surround thee;
When it sparkled o'er aught that was bright in my story,
I knew it was love, and I felt it was glory."

I repeat that statement now.

Contents

By Her Own
BOOTSTRAPS

I
The Married Woman's Fight To Own and Control Property

THE WEDDING CEREMONY AND THE COMMON LAW

In the Church of England *Book of Common Prayer*, this vow, among others to be taken by the bridegroom in the wedding, was long prescribed: "With all my worldly goods I thee endow." This vow was taken "according to God's holy ordinance." It was not according to the common law of England. Perhaps the difference is explained by Blackstone: "Our law considers marriage in no other light than as a civil contract. The holiness of the matrimonial state is left to the ecclesiastical law...."

The single woman at the common law had the same capacity as a man to own property, to make contracts, to go into business, to sue in her own name for injuries done to her, to be sued by others for injuries she did to them, and to be indicted in her own name for her own crimes.

But when she went to the altar with her prospective husband, she lost most of these capacities by uttering the words prescribed in the *Book of Common Prayer* in 1662: "I take thee to be my wedded husband, to have and to hold from this day forward, for better for worse, for richer for poorer, in sickness and in health, to love, cherish, and to obey, till death do us part; according to God's Holy ordinance, and thereto I give thee my troth." She thus became a party to the greatest property conveyance in English history.

She may have gone to the altar as the greatest propertied heiress in England, but with the pronouncement of those magic words (or the equivalents in another church or in a civil ceremony), the sorcery of the common law transferred most, if not all, of her lands, chattels, and choses in action—intangible property, such as promissory notes, bonds, stocks, and legal claims against another—to her husband. The hand was quicker than the eye.

Let me illustrate my meaning:

The Property Transfer

1.) All of the tangible personal property in her possession, or held for her by another, went to her husband absolutely, in the twinkling of an eye. It was his to keep, to sell, to give away to any other of his choosing, without the knowledge or consent of his wife, and even against her will. If he did not dispose of it during his lifetime, it went to his personal representatives at his death. His creditors could take it while he was living, or after he was dead, and there was nothing his wife or his children could do about it . . . with one exception: her "paraphernalia," including such articles of wearing apparel, personal ornament, or convenience as were suitable to the wife's rank and condition! But all of these, except her "wearing apparel," could be taken by her husband's creditors to pay for his debts if nothing else was left in his estate. This exception was perhaps a concession to the sentiment against indecent exposure.

Her intangible property, including her choses in action—such as promissory notes and mortgages or other debts owing to her on contracts or leases, or her claims for damages for injuries to person or property—went to her husband if, as, and when, he made a move to take it in her lifetime. A token move to reduce them to the possession was enough to satisfy the common law. If he did not make that token move, he had no one to blame but himself. Nothing and nobody could keep him from making this move. All of the personal property accruing to her from any source went through her to her husband without any visible trace of its passage.

2.) The use of the wife's lands at the time of the marriage and all lands which she acquired thereafter during their married lifetime went to the husband. The possession was his, the rents were his, the profits were his, during their married lifetime, and he could convey these lifetime rights during his wife's lifetime, without her knowledge, consent, or approval, and in spite of all that she could do to prevent it.

If no child of the marriage was born alive, and the wife died before

[4]

the husband, the husband's rights in his wife's lands ended at his wife's death. But if a child was born alive, capable of inheriting the wife's estate, the husband's rights in his wife's lands continued after her death for as long as he lived. His children meant a lot to him—they did not extend his life, but they extended his life estate. In these cases the husband was called a tenant by the curtesy—curtesy initiate during the wife's life, and curtesy consummate after her death. If one cares to play with words it might be said that both curtesies were by the courtesy of the wife, or of the common law, or both, and that the last courtesy was consummate indeed.

3.) When land was conveyed to the husband and wife at common law, they took it as tenants by the entirety—a metaphysical conception growing out of the fact that the common law looked on the husband and wife as one; neither the husband, nor the wife, nor the creditors, could do away with this estate, and the survivor took it all. But even here, the husband had the same rights to the possession and the use of this land, and the rents and the profits, during their married life, as he had in her other landed estates.

The wife had this advantage in outliving her husband: the common law gave her the right to dower—a life estate in one-third of the lands of the husband acquired during their married life. This did not automatically give the surviving wife a life estate in these lands, but merely a chose in action—a right to claim a life estate and to have it assigned to her.

By way of summary, before the woman was married, she was as free as a man to go into business for herself, to make contracts and commitments for which she could be held responsible, to go into court in her own name, to sue and be sued—for breach of contract, or for torts committed by or against herself—to pay out damages if she lost, to take in damages if she won, to put the money in the bank in her own name, and pay it out by her own check. She could invest her own money in her own name and the returns on the investment would be her own.

As soon as she was married, she became a "kept" woman: kept by the status of marriage at the common law; kept by her husband with the marriage laws of England solidly behind him. She could no longer do any of those things which she had done before. She could not use her own name; she had exchanged it for her husband's name. Her contracts were his contracts. Her torts were his torts. And, within limits,

[5]

her crimes were his crimes. She was a "picked" chicken and in many ways a "smothered" chicken. There was more truth than poetry in the observation that man and wife were one, and the man was the one—at the common law.

The change was sudden, violent, and well nigh absolute: she had no incentive to do any of the things which she had done before. The day before she was married, she could make a contract and put the profits in her own pocket—the day after, the profits went into her husband's pocket. The day before she was married, she could sue in her own name for damages for a broken leg and keep the money for herself; the day after, the husband could sue in his name for the damages to her leg, because her leg was his leg, and her name was his name, and her money was his money. She had taken the veil—a wedding veil.

Shakespeare, in the 1590s, had it just about right when he put these words into the mouth of the husband in *The Taming of the Shrew:*

... I will be master of what is mine own. She is my goods, my chattels; she is my house, my household stuff, my field, my barn, my horse, my ox, my ass, my anything."

There was more truth than poetry in those words, too.

The Other Side of the Coin

But there was another side to the coin. While giving the husband these rights to his wife's property, the common law imposed on him certain responsibilities, whether she brought any property to her husband or not, including: the duty to pay all debts accumulated by the wife prior to the marriage, including claims against her for damages for torts or breach of contract; the duty to support the wife and children born of the marriage to the best of his abilities, in a manner becoming her rank and station; the duty to pay any claims for damages against her for injuries she inflicted on third persons after marriage; and the duty to pay any fines and costs assessed against her in criminal proceedings.

This was done partly on the theory that, if the husband took over the property of the wife at the time of the marriage and all that she acquired thereafter, it was only fair for him to take on her liabilities before and after, though it should be added that he took on these liabilities even if she brought no property to the union and acquired none thereafter. The taking was "for better or for worse"—partly on the theory that man and wife were one and the man was the one, and

[6]

partly on the theory that the wife was presumed to be under the control of the husband so that she did what she did under his coercion (though this presumption could be rebutted).

Of course, it was more likely that in most cases the wife had not incurred any debts, or committed any torts (legal wrongs) or crimes, but these circumstances did not do away with the fact that the common law rules transferred the woman's property to the husband as here outlined. After all, she might have incurred all these liabilities—and she still might.

EQUITY TEMPERS THE WIND TO THE SHORN LAMB

Equity followed slowly on the heels of the common law. The king was looked on as the fountainhead of justice. He settled disputes arising between his subjects, at first according to whim or fancy or caprice, and later according to more or less flexible rules which could be relied on. As disputes increased, the king ran out of time, appointed judges, and sent them throughout the land to hold courts "in the name of the king." The common law, growing out of these procedures and decisions of the judges in the courts, tended to become a set of rigid rules.

But the king retained a residuary right to relieve his subjects from the rigors of the common law in hardship cases.

As this work increased, the king appointed persons to act for him in relieving against the rigors of the common law, and to do what, in conscience, ought to be done. This person came to be the king's chancellor—known as the keeper of the king's conscience. In this fashion rules of equity grew up, somewhat after the manner in which the rules of the common law had grown up, developing the principles according to which the chancellor could settle hardship cases.

In the swing of the centuries, people would go into equity courts to ask relief against the hardships imposed on married women by the rigid rules of the common law. To illustrate: Suppose a wealthy father saw his daughter falling in love with a young man who was a spendthrift, and wanted to protect his daughter from the consequences of marriage to a wastrel. Suppose the young man was "worth a million dollars," but did not have a penny.

It was natural for the father to go to his lawyer and ask him what could be done about it. It was natural that his lawyer would go to the chancellor in a court of equity to present this hardship case, and find out what the chancellor would be willing to do.

It was natural that the lawyer would present the chancellor with a plan by which the father, or somebody else, with the approval and guidance of the court of equity, could give his property to his daughter for her "sole and separate use and benefit," independent of the control of her husband, so that she could do with it as she pleased after marriage. And it was natural that if, as, and when, this plan (or something like it) was approved, the court of equity would put the will and power of the king behind it. But it had to be clear that the father, or other person giving the property, intended to give the property to the wife to the exclusion of her husband, that the husband shouldn't have anything to do with it.

COMMON LAW AND EQUITY COME TO NORTH CAROLINA

The rules of the common law and equity came to North Carolina from England by way of the charter from the crown in 1663, the beginning of organized government on this soil. The General Assembly in 1711 recognized that "the laws of England are the laws of North Carolina," including the rules of law and equity governing the rights of married women, and this recognition continued throughout colonial days.

The rules continued to be the law of the land in North Carolina after the Declaration of Independence in 1776 proclaimed that the thirteen colonies "are, and of right ought to be, free and independent states."

Here in North Carolina the courts continued to enforce the common law rule that the vows of the wedding ceremony gave all the tangible personal property of the wife to the husband—including livestock, farm machinery, household furniture, other earthly possessions, and all that she thereafter acquired as long as the marriage continued. There was one exception: her wearing apparel, which was protected under the sentiment against indecent exposure.

The courts also continued to enforce the common law rules giving all of the intangible personal property of the wife to the husband—

including bonds, shares of stock, and claims against all others, provided he made at least a token effort to reduce these choses in action to his possession.

In addition, the courts continued to enforce the common law rules giving to the husband the possession and rents and profits of all the lands the wife owned at the time of the wedding ceremony, and all that she thereafter acquired as long as the marriage continued, including the tenancies by curtesy initiate and curtesy consummate, depending on whether a child was born alive and capable of inheriting.

They continued to enforce the common law rules of dower as amended from time to time by statute.

The courts even went so far as to say that if the woman fiancé secretly transferred her property to another in advance of the wedding day, as a woman once did to her children by a former marriage, this was done in fraud of her prospective husband, and the second husband could sue in court to get it back. In this case, decided in 1845, the court spelled out the doctrine in all its raw reality and put it on the line:

> The law . . .conveys the marital rights [in the wife's property] to the husband, because it charges him with all the burdens, which are the consideration which he pays for them; and therefore they are rights on which a fraud may be committed. Out of that right arises a rule of law, that the husband shall not be cheated, on account of his consideration. . . . They are prospective rights—those that the husband expects to enjoy upon the contemplated marriage by the law of the land.
>
> A husband, being bound to pay his wife's debts and to maintain her during coverture, and being chargeable by the law with the support of the issue of the marriage, and bound by the ties of natural affection also to make provision for the issue, it is the nature of things, as a matter of common discretion, that a woman's apparent property should enter materially, if not essentially, into his inducements for contracting the marriage, and incurring those onerous obligations.
>
> It is also to be assumed by a man proposing this relation to a woman, that she too has a view to their means of livelihood after marriage, and feels an interest in the provision that, between their joint stocks, can be made a family. Every woman therefore must suppose, that the man, who is about to marry her, expects she will not put away her fortune, at least the visible part of it, and thereby diminish his ability to discharge his duties and legal obligations to herself, her creditors, and her future family. And if she, after allowing him to form such expectations, deliberately defeats them by a conveyance of her property, and draws him

[9]

into marriage by a deception on that point, it would seem, that it could be nothing less than a fraud on the husband. He is disappointed of what the law promised him, and of what she held out to him, he would get. . . .

His opinion of his intended wife's feelings towards him would have so changed, and the gross imprudence of contracting a marriage, when he had nothing but a trade, and she had conveyed all her property of any value, would have presented itself in so glaring a light, that he must not only have hesitated, but stopped short.

And that was that.

In North Carolina, as in England, the courts continued to enforce the rules creating the married woman's separate estate in equity. But here, as in England, the instrument creating this separate estate had to make it abundantly clear that the property was being transferred to the wife for her "sole and separate use," and to the total exclusion of her husband, and that the husband was to have nothing to do with it.

It was for the court to decide whether the instrument of transfer had made this intent clear beyond the shadow of doubt. It was natural that different judges in the same court in North Carolina would differ on whether this had been done. It is natural that different courts in different periods would differ on whether this had been done. It was natural that some courts would be strict constructionists, favoring the husband, and that others would be liberal constructionists, favoring the wife. But over the years I think it may be fairly said that if any personal bias or predilection entered into the processes of judicial reasoning it was more than likely to favor the concepts of the common law.

THE TURNING OF THE TIDE: ARTICLE X, SECTION 6

In the 1800s, the General Assembly of North Carolina began to nibble away some of these harsh exactions of the common law. It took three nibbles in 1837:

1) It provided that if a husband wanted to convey any part of his wife's land to a third person, the deed of conveyance had to be executed jointly by husband and wife, that the wife must undergo a private examination, and this "privy examination" had to be conducted out of the presence of the husband so as to make sure that her consent

was voluntary and of her own free will.

2) It provided that the wife could keep for herself any property acquired after a divorce from "bed and board" (a form of legal separation and limited divorce) and that this after-acquired property was free from the power, domination, and control of the husband, and was not liable for his debts. The creditors could not reach it as they could before.

3) It provided that the husband could no longer lease any part of the lands of the wife without her consent and joining in the conveyance, and that he could no longer under any circumstances transfer the rents from her property for a longer period than their married life.

In 1848, the General Assembly went still further and provided that the husband could no longer lease any part of his wife's lands for the term of his own life, or for any shorter period, without the consent of his wife ascertained by a privy examination; and it prohibited creditors of the husband from selling under execution against him any interest he might have in his wife's lands.

These statutory inroads on common law rules were carried forward in a watershed amendment to the North Carolina Constitution in 1868, providing in Article X, section 6:

> The real and personal property of any female in this state, acquired before marriage, and all property, real and personal, to which she may after marriage, become in any manner entitled, shall be and remain the sole and separate estate and property of such female, and shall not be liable for any debts, obligations or engagements of her husband, and may be devised or bequeathed, and, with the written assent of her husband, conveyed, by her as if she were unmarried.

What did this amendment mean? And how far did it go?

THE MEANING OF ARTICLE X, SECTION 6

As to Property Acquired before and after 1868

To begin with, the court made it clear that Article X, section 6, applied only to property acquired by the wife after the 1868 amendment, not to property acquired before.

To illustrate: In the case of *Hackett* v *Shuford*, 86 N.C. 144 (1882), where the wife acquired the property *before* 1868, the court held that under Article X, section 6, the common law was still in effect and gave the property to the husband.

In the case of Holliday v McMillan, 78 N.C. 315 (1875), the wife acquired the property after 1868, and the husband's creditors tried to reach it to satisfy debts against him. The creditors argued that the marriage contract prior to 1868 gave the husband a vested right to property the wife then owned, or might thereafter acquire, and that neither statute nor constitution could impair the obligation of the contract.

The court held that the husband's claim to property acquired by the wife after 1868 was not a "vested" right but at best a mere "expectancy," a "possibility of future acquisition," and that the wife took the after-acquired property as her "sole and separate estate," free from the "debts, obligations, or engagements of her husband," as the constitution provided.

After 1868 the woman could go to the altar to the strains of Lohengrin and come away to the strains of Mendelssohn, with the satisfying assurance that Article X, section 6, of the Constitution had pulled the teeth of the common law to the extent that her property was now intact, and that all her property, real and personal, tangible and intangible, was free from the "debts, obligations, or engagements of her husband." The wedding ceremony had ceased to be a conveyance of property, and, for the woman at least, had become more of a celebration and less of a sacrifice. From now on, as far as property was involved, her husband would have to talk to her with more of persuasion and less of command.

To illustrate: In the case of *Kirkman* v *Bank of Greensboro*, 77 N.C. 394 (1877), a lawyer collected money due a married woman as heir of an estate, deposited it in the bank, and the bank paid the money to the woman. At her death, the husband sued the bank to recover the money, on the ground that she could not "convey" any of her property without her husband's "written assent." The Court held that the "written assent" of the husband was required only for conveyances of the wife's real property; that Article X, section 6, did not prevent the wife from receiving money which was personal property; that the bank simply owed her a debt, and paid it to her, that was all; and that what she did with the money after she got it was none of the business of the bank, or of the court, or of the husband.

The court made it clear that Article X, section 6, gave the husband no marital rights at all in his wife's personal property—tangible or intangible, chattels or choses in action—and that the wife did not need her husband's assent, written or otherwise, in order to sell it, give it away, or otherwise dispose of it.

THE "WRITTEN ASSENT" OF THE HUSBAND

Article X, section 6, put one limitation only on the power of the married woman to dispose of her real property after 1868. The property was hers all right, but she could not "convey" it without "the written assent of her husband," and her deed without this "written assent" was, said the Court, "wholly inoperative and totally void."

In 1871 the General Assembly added a further limitation: that the wife should undergo a "private examination separate and apart from her husband" in order to determine "her free consent" to "any conveyance of any freehold estate in her property."

In the case of *Ferguson* v *Kingsland*, 93 N.C. 337 (1885), the court faced the question whether the added statutory requirement of a private examination was a valid requirement. The Court held that this was not an "added" requirement, but merely "a legislative direction as to the manner in which" the "written assent" may be exercised.

This additive had not been put in fine print. It had been written with invisible ink, which came into view with the light and heat of a court proceeding.

Eight years later, the case of *Strouse* v *Cohen*, 113 N.C. 350 (1893), gave Justice Clark an opportunity to take a crack at this statutory provision by observing that the Constitution of 1868 did not intend to "throw additional shackles around married women in the management of their separate property," but to "emancipate them from most of the restrictions formerly existing."

In 1964, Article X, section 6, was amended by providing that "every married woman may exercise powers of attorney conferred upon her by her husband, including the power to execute and acknowledge deeds to property owned by herself and her husband or by her husband."

"The chief purposes of the 1964 amendment," says Professor Robert E. Lee, "were to remove the former constitutional provision which required the assent of the husband for a conveyance of the wife's real property and to empower the General Assembly to enact statutes relative to the wife's conveyances of her real property and the disposition by will of both her real and personal property."

The 1965 General Assembly exercised this power by amending Chapter 52 of the General Statutes to apply to "married persons" instead of "married women." By this act it abolished the disparity between the property rights of married men and married woman by demanding the same requirements of both sexes. In other words, it took out the provision requiring the married woman to have the "written assent" of her husband in order to convey her real property, and put in the provision that the real property of a married woman may be "conveyed by her subject to such limitations as the General Assembly may prescribe."

Statutes still provide that in *conveyances between husband and wife*, the married woman must undergo a privy examination, but it is within the power of the General Assembly to abolish this requirement whenever it sees fit.

The 1964 amendment and the 1965 General Assembly had restored to married women in fact, if not *in toto*, the freedom that the General Assembly in 1871–72, and the Supreme Court in 1885, had taken away.

II
The Married Woman's Fight to Remove Business Restrictions

THE FIGHT FOR POWER TO ENTER INTO CONTRACTS

While Article X, section 6, referred to a married woman's power to "convey" her property, with the "written assent" of her husband, it made no specific mention of her power to enter into binding contracts with third parties.

Whatever the intent of the writers of the 1868 amendment to the Constitution, there is no doubt about the restrictive intention of the General Assembly in the 1871–72 statute in providing:

> No woman during her coverture shall be capable of making any contract to affect her real or personal estate, except for her necessary personal expenses, or for the support of the family, without the written consent of her husband, unless she be a free trader, as hereinafter allowed.

Four years later, the case of *Pippen* v *Wesson*, 74 N.C. 437 (1876), raised the question whether a married woman could, with the written assent of her husband, enter into an executory contract for breach of which she could be sued for damages and her property subjected to sale. In this case the court was more restrictive than the statute, and held that no such power to make executory contracts was given to a married woman by Article X, section 6; that the constitution had merely turned the equitable separate estate of a married woman into a statutory separate estate, with the husband as the trustee.

Justice Rodman firmly stated the majority position of the court in the case of *Fowles* v *Fisher*, 77 N.C. 437 (1877): "No one can reasonably rely upon the contract of a married woman or on a representation of her intentions which at best is in the nature of a contract, and by which must be presumed to know that she is not legally bound."

And this position was confirmed six years later, in *Dougherty* v *Sprinkle*, 88 N.C. 300 (1883), where the court held that the contract of a married woman "is still as void as it ever was, with no power in any court to proceed to judgment against her *in personam.* . . ."

But the tide was beginning to turn. The court would not allow this doctrine to be used in order to perpetrate a fraud. For in the case of *State* v *Lanier*, 89 N.C. 517 (1883), a man tried to escape from liability on a contract he had made with a married woman by claiming that she had no power to contract and that her effort to do so was null and void. The court would not permit this. One year later in *Burns* v. *McGregor*, 90 N.C. 222 (1884), a married woman contracted to trade land and to pay the difference in value, received the land, was sued for this difference, and tried to escape her liability by claiming she was a married woman and had no power to enter into a contract. Justice Merrimon replied: "She repudiates her contract, and desires to obtain the fruit of so much of it as is beneficial to herself. . . .This the law will not tolerate. . . .She must observe and keep her engagements, or else return the property."

The tide was speeded by the language of the Court in *Bell* v *Pacquin*, 140 N.C. 83 (1905) , saying:

> The decisions, while not in all respects harmonious, indicate a movement of the court towards bringing the law in this respect into harmony with our social and industrial and commercial conditions. The legislature has to some extent responded to this demand. In so far as it is within our province to do so, we desire to express our opinion that it is desirable that the legislature simplify the subject by giving to married women full power to enter into executory contracts, binding their property, real and personal, 'as if unmarried'—removing all doubt and uncertainty either as to the form of the contract, its execution, or remedy for breach.
>
> We hope that the subject of the powers and rights of married women in respect to their property and contracts, may attract the attention of the General Assembly and be brought into harmony with the best modern thought and conditions.

Five years later in *Bushard* v *Barnett*, 153 N.C. 564 (1910), Chief Justice Clark, in a dissenting opinion, appealed to the General Assembly, saying:

> In *Bell* v *Pacquin, supra* ...and in other cases, this court has
> suggested that the legislature bring the status of the law as to
> married women into conformity with the spirit and the letter of
> the Constitution of 1868. After 42 years, it is to be hoped that this
> will be done, in view of the anomalous condition of the law on
> the subject and repeated suggestions of the court.

The General Assembly responded to this appeal in 1911, in the Martin Act, authorizing the married woman

> to contract and deal so as to affect her real and personal property
> in the same manner and with the same effect as if she were unmarried ....

The first judicial enforcement of the Martin Act came with the case of *Lipinsky* v *Revell*, 177 N.C. 508 (1914), in a suit to recover payment from a married woman for merchandise sold and delivered to her by the plaintiff. The woman claimed that her husband should be liable instead of herself, even though she made the contract, as the goods purchased were allegedly "necessaries." The court held that as this debt was contracted in 1912 and thus subsequent to the Martin Act of 1911, the married woman was liable, because "that act completely emancipates the married woman," in cases of this sort.

This act of the General Assembly was held constitutional and valid by the court in the case of *Warren* v *Dial*, 170 N.C. 406 (1915).

"FREE TRADER" EXCEPTIONS TO COMMON LAW RULES

In his casebook dealing with the rights of married women, Compton points out that "at common law, a married woman had no power or capacity to contract and her attempted contracts were completely void," with two exceptions for obvious reasons: 1) where the husband was "exiled," and 2) where he had "abjured the realm." In such cases the disability of coverture (the married status) was removed, and the married woman had the powers of a single woman to enter into contracts as though she were unmarried.

The concept of a married woman as a "free trader" was introduced into North Carolina statutes with the enactment of the Marriage Act of 1871–72, permitting her to become "a free trader as hereinafter allowed." (Ch. 69, sec. 17, *Battle's Revisal* for 1973.)

The precise mechanics for becoming a free trader were outlined as follows:

1. The married woman must be at least twenty-one years old.
2. She must have the consent of her husband.
3. There must be a specified written agreement signed by both spouses, acknowledged by them, approved by the officer authorized to probate deeds, and filed with the register of deeds.

A married woman could also become a free trader:

1. By docketing a judgment of divorce from bed and board by registering such a judgment.
2. If abandoned by her husband, or if he maliciously turned her out.

In 1890, the first case arose challenging the constitutionality of these sections. The court in *Hall* v *Walker*, 118 N.C. 377 (1890) decided that sec. 24, which deemed a married woman a free trader if her "husband had abandoned or shall abandon her, or shall maliciously turn her out of doors," was constitutional and in keeping with the spirit of Art. X, sec. 6. As the court said, this provision "was not intended to disable her, but to protect her."

The Court reiterated this fact once again in 1942. In *Campbell* v *Campbell*, 221 N.C. 257 (1942), the defendant refused to accept a deed from a woman whose husband had abandoned her, because the deed did not carry the husband's joinder. The court merely said the woman was a free trader and, by statute, could convey a valid deed without her husband's joinder therein.

Except for these few cases, the Court did not deal with the question of free trader status very much after 1911. In that year, the Martin Act was passed, which in effect made all married women "free traders." In fact, the "free traders" statutes were repealed by Session Laws 1945, Ch. 635 (29).

THE FIGHT TO KEEP
EARNINGS AND SERVICES

Here in North Carolina, as in other states, the husband was entitled to his wife's earnings and services at the common law.

Article X, section 6, of the 1868 Constitution, did not specifically mention the wife's earning and services, and the courts held that they continued to belong to the husband. To illustrate: in the case of *Syme* v *Riddle*, 88 N.C. 463 (1883) Justice Ruffin said:

Unquestionably, it was the well settled principle, both of law and equity, as understood and enforced in this state prior to the adoption of the constitution of 1868, and the "marriage act" of 1871–72, that the husband was entitled absolutely and in his own right to the services of the wife, and likewise to the fruits of her industry, whether exerted in his own affairs or in those of a stranger.

These rights were given to the husband, because of the obligation which the same law imposed upon him, to provide for her support and that of her offspring; and it would seem to be but just that they should continue unimpaired, so long as the obligation rests upon him . . . .

There is certainly nothing, either in the constitution or the statute, which, in terms or by a necessary implication, secures to a married woman her separate earnings; and by nothing short of a plain expression of such an intention could this court be induced to give them that construction. If certified, as a matter of right, to her own earnings, then she must be entitled to the time and opportunity necessary to make them, and, that is to say, that she may, at her own election, and without the consent of her husband, forsake her domestic duties and go out to labor for another for the purpose of acquiring earnings for her separate use. There can be no middle ground taken in the matter; for the one right, if admitted, necessarily draws to it the other, and we cannot suppose that those who framed the organic law or the statute intended to introduce any such anomalous conditions into the law regulating the relations of husband and wife in this state. . . .

Doubtless a husband may consent that the fruit of his wife's toils shall be her own, and constitute her separate estate; but in such case her title will rest upon his consent and not upon the law; and the validity of the gift, against his creditors, will depend upon the same rules which govern other conveyances from him to her. Nothing of the sort, however, is pretended to have been done in the present case, so as to take it out of the general rule and the court, therefore, holds, as did the court below, that the debt created by the services rendered to the plaintiff's intestate was due to the husband.

Circumstances could alter cases, as the court suggested, and had already done so. In *Kee* v *Vasser*, 37 N.C. 553 (1843), the husband had allowed his wife to keep the money she made from her needlework, and that which she received from the sale of fowls, eggs, butter, and vegetables from the garden. He had always recognized the money as hers, and she managed to save $350 which she loaned out in her name. They kept separate store accounts and when people came to borrow money of him, he would say he had none to lend, but that his wife did. Upon the husband's death, his executor sued the wife for this money. The court dismissed the doctrine of pin-money, finding that the husband had made a valid gift of the money to the wife.

According to the court in this case, "they had separate accounts at the stores of their neighboring merchants—when a borrower of money applied to him for a loan, he said he had none to lend, but his wife had .... The husband himself also borrowed money of his wife.... The proofs in the case, in our opinion, come up to these requirements . . .by some clear and distinct act . . .by which he divests himself of the property."

In 1962, the Court said, in the case of *Rushing* v *Polk*, 258 N.C. 256, it had become a "well-established" principle that the "wife's earnings are her sole and separate property."

THE FIGHT FOR THE RIGHT TO SUE AND RECOVER FOR INJURIES TO HER PERSON

At the common law, as we have seen, the wedding ceremony gave to the husband all of the choses in action belonging to her before marriage, and all of the choses in action she acquired after marriage, and during their married life—provided he would make at least a token move to reduce them to his possession.

Injuries Inflicted by Third Persons

Here in North Carolina, as in other states, these choses in action included 1) the wife's claims against third persons for damages for breach of contract, 2) her claims for compensation for her services and earnings, and 3) her claims for compensation for injuries to her person. Her body was his body. Her suffering was his suffering. Her name was his name. And he was allowed to sue and recover for her injuries in his own name and put the money in his own pocket. Let me illustrate my meaning:

In the case of *Crump* v *McKay*, 53 N.C. 32 (1860), the wife suffered injuries from being thrown by the defendant into the Cape Fear River from his boat. Chief Justice Pearson held that the husband could sue in his own name, recover the damages, and keep the money for himself.

Article X, section 6, of the 1868 Constitution did not specifically mention the wife's claims against third persons for injuries to her person, as it did not mention her claims for damages for breach of contract, or her claims for compensation for earnings and services; the courts continued to hold that they belonged to her husband.

To illustrate: In the case of *Hollerman* v *Howard*, 119 N.C. 150 (1896), a druggist sold laudanum to the wife, knowing she was using it as a beverage, over the protest of the husband. The wife became "a mental and physical wreck," and the Court allowed the husband to sue in his own name for damages, saying that the wife owed the husband companionship and services in the home, that the husband was entitled to earnings from her services, that the wife was now incapable of rendering these services, and that whoever destroyed the husband's rights was liable to him in damages. In the words of the court:

> A married woman still owes to her husband, notwithstanding her greatly improved legal status, the duty of companionship and of rendering all such services in his home as her relation of wife and mother require of her. The husband, as a matter of law, is entitled to her time, her wages, her earnings, and the products of her labor, skill, and industry. He may contract to furnish her services to others, and may sue for them, as for their loss, in his own name. And it seems to be a most reasonable proposition of law that whoever willingly joins with a married woman in doing an act which deprives her husband of her services and her companionship is liable to the husband in damages for his conduct. . . .
>
> There is no difference between the principle involved in this action and the principle upon which a husband can recover from a third person for assault and battery upon his wife.

The court admitted that the General Assembly could change the common law rule whenever it saw fit.

This is illustrated in the case of *Brown* v *Brown*, 121 N.C. 8 (1897), where the wife's father-in-law had slandered the wife in the process of alienating the husband's affection, the husband had thereafter abandoned the wife, and the wife was allowed to sue and recover in her own name. The Court said:

> Our Constitution and statutes have made very material and important changes in the status of married women in this State, by extending protection to their person and separate property, and allowing them the privilege of free traders suing in their own

[21]

name, etc., in certain conditions.

Where there was no legislative change, the court continued to follow the common law rule, as illustrated in the case of *Kimberly* v *Howland*, 143 N.C. 399 (1906), where the defendant was blasting rock with dynamite, and by his negligence a twenty-pound rock crashed through the roof of the home, not hitting, but frightening, the wife who was lying in bed "heavy with child," shocking her nervous system to the point that "she has never recovered," and nearly causing a miscarriage. The court allowed the husband to sue in his own name and recover damages, saying:

> It is contended that the husband sustained no injury, and as to him the motion to nonsuit should have been allowed. It seems to be well settled that where the injury to the wife is such that the husband receives a separate loss or damage, as where he is put to expense, or is deprived of the society or services of his wife, he is entitled to recover therefore, and he may sue in his own name.
>
> The Court (below) further charged that if the injuries are permanent the husband could also recover such sum as will be a fair compensation for the future diminished capacity to labor on the part of the wife. This instruction we think is correct and supported by authority.

In 1913, the General Assembly responded to Chief Justice Clark's argument by providing that "any damages for personal injuries, or other torts sustained by her can be recovered by her suing alone, and such...recovery shall be her sole and separate property as fully as if she had remained unmarried."

The court made a slight advance from the common law rule in the case of *Price* v *Electric Co.*, 160 N.C. 450 (1912). The wife was injured through the fault of the company in a collision with its street car and the husband joined with the wife in suing for damages for her pain and suffering and her diminished capacity to provide services for her husband. The Court said that the cases had allowed the husband to sue alone for damages in such cases as this, but that by joining with his wife in this action, the husband had "formally renounced" his right in her favor, and this was held to "validate the recovery even if it could otherwise be questioned."

Chief Justice Clark went still further in a concurring opinion, arguing that the wife should be allowed to sue for her own diminished power to earn wages without the joinder of her husband as required by the majority. He cited the Constitution of 1868 and the Martin Act of 1911 as lending authority to the conclusion that such claims were "peculiarly her own."

He argued that the common law in this instance was "as a clog upon progressive legislation," and suggested that the General Assembly change the law, so that "progress and betterment should not be denied us by the dead hand of the past."

In 1945 the court said in *Helmstetler* v *Duke Power Company*, 224 N.C. 821: "Under statute providing that any damages for personal injuries or other torts sustained by the wife can be recovered by her suing alone and that such recovery shall be her sole and separate property as if she were unmarried, the husband has no separate right of action for loss of consortium or mental anguish sustained by him as result of injury to the wife." The wife's injury is her cause of action and hers alone.

In *Johnson* v *Lewis*, 251 N.C. 797 (1960) the court said that a wife could recover for any pecuniary loss for personal injuries sustained by her by reason of inability to perform labor or carry on household duties, and such a recovery shall be her sole and separate property as if she were unmarried. According to the court: "Our statute . . .is in accord with the realistic trend of the modern decisions, which recognize the fact that a wife, as an individual, has a personal right to work and earn money, whether she is gainfully employed at the time or engaged merely in the performance of household duties, and where her capacity to work and earn money is impaired by injury, she has suffered a definite and substantial loss."

Injuries Inflicted by the Husband

Suppose the husband inflicted injuries on the wife. Could the wife sue the husband? Not at common law, because husband and wife were one, the man was the one, and the man could not sue himself. Even if the common law had allowed the wife to sue the husband and recover damages, the money would be property acquired by the wife after marriage and would belong to her husband.

In the case of *Crowell* v *Crowell*, 180 N.C. 516 (1920), where the husband infected his wife with a venereal disease, the wife was allowed to sue the husband and recover damages. Chief Justice Clark pointed out that:

> At common law neither civil nor criminal actions could be maintained by the wife against the husband because of the alleged unity of persons of husband and wife, or rather the merger of the wife's existence into the husband's. . . .

[23]

In the case of *Young* v *Newsome*, 180 N.C. 315 (1920), the court held that a wife could sue her husband for slander of herself. And Chief Justice Clark, in a concurring opinion, put this decision in its setting in the law:

> The common law was formulated before there was any Parliament or when they were enacting very few statutes. It was created by judges who were for centuries Catholic priests only, and for centuries more they were all priests or laymen. It is not astonishing that under the influence of priests, who presumably knew little about such matters, it was laid down as a conclusive and irrebuttable presumption of law and fact that the wife acted solely under compulsion of her husband, and therefore that he was liable for her torts.

> A great writer, who was far better posted on such matter, in the last century presents that when Mr. Bumble was told that he was responsible for his wife's conduct, and that "indeed he was the more guilty of the two in the eyes of the law; for the law supposes that your wife acts under your direction," Mr. Bumble replied: "If the law supposes that, the law is a Ass—an idiot. If that's the eye of the law, the law's a bachelor; and the worst I wish the law is that his eye may be opened by experience." (*Oliver Twist* Ch. 51.)

> Priestly judges seem to have based their whole doctrine of the subjection of woman upon Genesis, 2:23–24 "And the man said, this is now bone of my bone and flesh of my flesh; ...and they twain shall be one flesh." But this is not the declaration of God, but of Adam, and is not a fact, and yet upon that false foundation was built a theory of the common law which has persisted in the minds of some down to the present day, much to the detriment of women whose legal rights have been far inferior to those of women in other civilized countries, and even to those living in semi-civilized countries under the domination of the Koran ...

> In view of the recent provisions recognizing the equality of the wife with her husband as to her property and rights of person, and especially the recent amendment to the U.S. Constitution recognizing the equality of women at the ballot box, it would seem common sense had overcome the common law as to the inequality of the sexes and that as a correlative, the husband should no longer be held liable for the torts of the wife, committed without his knowledge or concurrence.

Injuries Inflicted by the Wife on the Husband

Suppose the wife inflicted injuries on her husband. Could the husband sue the wife? In *Scholtens* v *Scholtens*, 230 N.C. 149 (1949), where the husband sued the wife for injuries due to the wife's negligent operation of an automobile, the court denied his right to sue, saying: "...there is no provision authorizing the husband to sue his wife in tort for injury inflicted upon him by her during coverture. Moreover, the provisions of this chapter G.S.52, in so far as the husband is concerned, constitute in the main abridgments of rights he had as to his wife's property under the common law, and do not purport to create in him, as against her, rights he did not have at the common law."

The General Assembly corrected this condition in 1951 by providing that "if husband and wife have a cause of action against each other [they can] recover damages sustained to their person or property as if they were unmarried."

In the case of *Shoe* v *Hood*, 251 N.C. 719 (1958), the court says: "A husband is not the agent of his wife merely because of the marital relationship, and neither a husband nor wife is ordinarily responsible for the torts of the other." However, in this case the negligence of the husband was imputed to the wife, not because of the marital relationship, but because the wife was the owner of the car and an occupant at the time of the accident. Negligence law requires the owner-occupant of an automobile to be imputed with the negligence of the driver at the time of any accident. In the court's words: "The test is this: Did the owner, under the circumstances disclosed, have the legal right to control the manner in which the automobile was being operated—was his relation to the operation such that he would have been responsible to a third party for the negligence of the driver?"

Thus, time marches on.

WHEN THE WIFE ACTS AS AGENT FOR HER HUSBAND

After the 1868 Constitution took away the common law rights of a husband to his wife's property, owned at the time of the marriage or acquired thereafter, the General Assembly was quick to provide in 1871–72 for the married woman's continuing "liability... for any debts owing or contracts made, or damages incurred, by her before her marriage." It made assurance doubly sure by providing that "no man by marriage shall incur any liability for any debts owing, or contracts made, or for wrongs done by his wife before the marriage" on

[25]

the theory that his assets ought not to be saddled with her liabilities.

But these statutes did not do away with the responsibility of a husband for acts of his wife while she was acting as his agent. His liability continued on common law doctrines of agency.

In the case of *Cox* v *Hoffman*, 20 N.C. 319 (1838), where the wife borrowed a mule from a third person and the mule was injured and died while in the wife's possession, the court said the husband "was liable for the injury done to the property of the plaintiff by the negligence, carelessness or unskillfulness of his servants in their performance of his business. The wife in the eye of the law is his servant, and the husband would be equally liable to third persons for her negligent and careless acts in doing his business as he would be for the acts of any other of his servants."

At the common law the husband was liable for torts committed by his wife while they were living together, on the theory she was acting as his agent, or under his control, and he was also liable for her torts when they were living apart, perhaps on the theory that he had acquired her assets by marriage. But when Article X, section 6, of the 1868 Constitution said that her property was no longer his, the General Assembly in 1871–72 passed a second statute providing that: "Every husband living with his wife shall be jointly liable with her for all damages accruing for any torts committed by her." What did this mean?

In the case of *Robert* v *Lisenbee*, 86 N.C. 136 (1882), the Court said:

> We think it more probable it was this principle of the common law, holding the husband responsible for the torts of the wife committed in his absence and without his knowledge or connivance that induced the legislature to enact that provision of the act of 1871–72 . . . which provides that "every husband *living with his wife* shall be jointly liable with her, for all torts committed by her." It was not intended to enlarge his responsibility, but to abridge his liability at the common law, so as to fasten responsibility upon him only so long as they should live together in the matrimonial relation, and as soon as that is terminated, whether by separation or the death of his wife, the liability should no longer exist.

In 1921 the General Assembly provided that "no husband shall be liable for damages accruing from any tort committed by his wife, or for any costs or fines incurred in any criminal proceeding against her." And this was the end of the common law rule making the husband liable for the torts of his wife to a third person.

[26]

III

The Married Woman's Fight for Freedom of her Person

THE CHANGING STORY OF HER LIABILITY FOR CRIMES

A single woman was responsible for her own crimes, committed of her own free will, at common law, and this responsibility continued after marriage with some exceptions, on the theory that she was under her husband's control and acting according to his directions. In 1871–72 the General Assembly provided that: "Every husband living with his wife shall be jointly liable with her . . . for all costs and fines incurred in any criminal proceeding against her."

In the case of *State* v *Williams*, 65 N.C. 398 (1871), the husband was indicted jointly with the wife for an assault and battery committed by the wife and the court was asked to instruct the jury that the wife was not guilty, as the offense had been committed with the knowledge and consent of the husband and in his presence. The court refused, saying:

It seems to be admitted by all the authorities, that if a wife commit any felony . . . in the presence of her husband, it shall be presumed, in the absence of evidence to the contrary, that she did it under constraint by him, and she is therefore excused.

It is generally agreed that treason and murder are exceptions to this rule; and some add to these, manslaughter, robbery, and perjury, although the last is not a felony . . . .

As has been seen, several eminent text writers confine the presumption to cases of felony. But the more recent cases, both English and American, extend it to misdemeanors as well; those cases excepted, which from their nature would seem more likely to be committed by women, such as keeping a bawdy house, etc. . . .

It is also conceded by all the authorities, that the presumption may be rebutted by the circumstances appearing in evidence, and showing that in fact, the wife acted without constraint; or by the nature of the offense. But in this case no circumstance appears tending to rebut the presumption which the law raises. . . .

Chief Justice Clark put the law succinctly in a later case, saying: "If the wife acted voluntarily, she ought to be held liable, whether her husband was present or not. If she acted under his compulsion, she ought to be exempt from punishment, not because of the marital relation, but like any one else acting under compulsion. At common law there was a presumption that when a crime was committed by the wife in the presence of her husband she acted under compulsion; but that presumption does not comport with twentieth-century conditions. The contention that a wife has no more intelligence or responsibility than a child is now out of date. No one believes it."

THE CHANGING STORY OF THE HUSBAND'S RIGHT TO DISCIPLINE HIS WIFE

According to Blackstone:

The husband . . . (by the old law) might give his wife moderate correction. For as he is to answer for her misbehavior, the law thought it reasonable to entrust him with this power of restraining her, by domestic chastisement, in the same moderation that a man is allowed to correct his apprentices or children; for whom the master or parent is also liable in some cases to answer.

This power was confined within reasonable bounds, and the husband was prohibited from using any violence to his wife, otherwise than lawfully and reasonably belongs to the husband for the due government and correction of his wife. The civil law gave the husband the same, or larger, authority over his wife; allowing him, for some misdemeanors, to beat his wife severely with scourges and sticks; for others only to use moderate chastisement.

But, with us, in the politer reign of Charles II, this power of correction began to be doubted: and a wife may now have security of the peace against her husband; or, in return, a husband against his wife. Yet the lower rank of people, who were always fond of the old common law, still claim and exert their ancient privilege: and the courts of law will still permit a husband to restrain a wife of her liberty, in case of any gross misbehavior.

Here in North Carolina in the case of *State v Black,* 60 N.C. 262 (1864), the husband was indicted for an assault upon his wife. The Court stated: "A husband is responsible for the acts of his wife, and he is required to govern his household, and for that purpose the law permits him to use towards his wife such a degree of force as is necessary to control an unruly temper and make her behave herself; and unless some permanent injury be inflicted, or there be an excess of violence, or such a degree of cruelty that shows that it is inflicted to gratify his own bad passions, the law will not invade the domestic forum, or go behind the curtain. It prefers to leave the parties to themselves, as the best mode of inducing them to make the matter up and live together as man and wife should."

In the case of *State v Rhodes,* 61 N.C. 453 (1868), the husband was indicted for an assault and battery upon his wife, Elizabeth Rhodes. Upon the evidence submitted to them the jury returned the following special verdict:

"We find that the defendant struck Elizabeth Rhodes, his wife, three licks, with a switch about the size of one of his fingers (but not as large as a man's thumb), without any provocation except some words uttered by her and not recollected by the witness." His Honor was of opinion that the defendant had a right to whip his wife with a switch no larger than his thumb, and that upon the facts found in the special verdict he was not guilty in law, saying:

Our conclusion is that family government is recognized by law as being as complete in itself as the State government is in itself, and yet subordinate to it; and that we will not interfere with or attempt to control it, in favor of either husband or wife, unless in cases where permanent or malicious injury is inflicted or threatened, or the condition of the party is intolerable. For, however great are the evils of ill temper, quarrels, and even personal conflicts inflicting only temporary pain, they are not comparable with the evils which would result from raising the curtain, and exposing to public curiosity and criticism, the nursery and the bed chamber. Every household has and must have, a government of its own, modeled to suit the temper, disposition and condition of its inmates. Mere ebullitions of passion, impulsive violence, and temporary pain, affection will soon forget and forgive, and each member will find excuse for the other in his own frailties. But when trifles are taken hold of by the public, and the parties are exposed and disgraced, and each endeavors to justify himself or herself by criminating the other, that which ought to be forgotten in a day, will be remembered for life.

[29]

The witness said there was no provocation except some slight words. But then who can tell what significance the trifling words may have had to the husband? Who can tell what had happened an hour before, and every hour for a week? To him they may have been sharper than a sword. And so in every case, it might be impossible for the court to appreciate what might be offered as an excuse, or no excuse might appear at all, when a complete justification exists. Or, suppose the provocation could in every case be known, and the court should undertake to weigh the provocation in every trifling family broil, what would be the standard? Suppose a case coming up to us from a hovel, where neither delicacy of sentiment nor refinement of manners is appreciated or known. The parties themselves would be amazed, if they were to be held responsible for rudeness or trifling violence. What do they care for insults and indignities? In such cases what end would be gained by investigation or punishment? Take a case from the middle class, where modesty and purity have their abode, but nevertheless have not immunity from the frailties of nature, and are sometimes moved by the mysteries of passion. What could be more harassing to them, or injurious to society, than to draw a crowd around their seclusion? Or take a case from the higher ranks, where education and culture have so refined nature, that a look cuts like a knife, and a word strikes like a hammer; where the most delicate attention gives pleasure, and the slightest neglect pain; where an indignity is disgrace and exposure is ruin. Bring all these cases into court side by side, with the same offense charged and the same proof made; and what conceivable charge of the court to the jury would be alike appropriate to all cases, except that they all have domestic government, which they have formed for themselves, suited to their own peculiar conditions, and that those governments are supreme, and from them there is no appeal except in cases of great importance requiring the strong arm of the law, and that to those governments they must submit themselves.

It will be observed that the ground upon which we have put this decision is not that the husband has the right to whip his wife much or little; but that we will not interfere with family government in trifling cases. We will no more interfere where the husband whips the wife than where the wife whips the husband; and yet we would hardly be supposed to hold that a wife has a *right* to whip her husband. We will not inflict upon society the greater evil of raising the curtain upon domestic privacy, to punish the lesser evil of trifling violence. Two boys under fourteen years of age fight upon the playground, and yet the courts will take no notice of it, not for the reason that the boys have the *right* to fight, but because the interests of society require that they should be left to the more appropriate discipline of the school room and of home. It is not true that boys have a right to fight; nor is it true that a husband has a right to whip his wife. And if he had, it is not easily seen how the thumb is the standard of size for the instrument which he may use, as some of the old authorities have said; and in deference to which was his Honor's charge. A light blow, or many light blows, with a stick larger than the thumb, might produce no injury; but a switch half the size might be so used as to produce death. The standard is the effect produced, and not the manner of producing it, or the instrument used.

In the case of *State* v *Oliver*, 70 N.C. 60 (1874), the defendant husband came home intoxicated one morning after breakfast was over, got some raw bacon, said it had skippers on it, and told his wife she would not clean it. He sat down and ate a little: then he threw the coffee cup and pot into the corner of the room and went out; while out he cut two switches, brought them in, and throwing them on the floor, told his wife that if he whipped her she would leave; that he was going to whip her, for she and her d—d mother had aggravated him near to death. He then struck her five licks with the two switches, which were about four feet long, with the branches on them about half way and some leaves. One of the switches was about half as large as a man's little finger; the other not so large. He had them in both hands, and inflicted bruises on her arm which remained for two weeks, but did not disable her from work.

One of the witnesses swore he struck as hard as he could. Others were present, and after defendant had struck four licks told him to desist. Defendant stopped, saying if they had not been there he would have worn her out.

Upon these facts the Court found the husband guilty, fined him $10, and upon appeal, the court said:

> We may assume that the old doctrine that a husband had a right to whip his wife, provided he used a switch no larger than his thumb, is not law in North Carolina. Indeed, the Courts have advanced from that barbarism until they have reached the position that the husband has no right to chastise his wife under any circumstances.
>
> But from motives of public policy, and in order to preserve the sanctity of the domestic circle, the Courts will not listen to trivial complaints.
>
> If no permanent injury has been inflicted, nor malice, cruelty nor dangerous violence shown by the husband, it is better to

draw the curtain, shut out the public gaze, and leave the parties to forget and forgive.

No general rule can be applied, but each case must depend upon the circumstances surrounding it.

Without adverting in detail to the facts established by the special verdict in this case, we think that they show both malice and cruelty.

In fact it is difficult to conceive how a man who has promised upon the altar to love, comfort, honor and keep a woman can lay rude and violent hands upon her without having malice and cruelty in his heart.

Let it be certified that the judgment of the Superior Court is affirmed.

In the case of *State* v *Edens*, 95 N.C. 693 (1886), the husband was charged with slandering an innocent and virtuous woman—his wife. He was convicted in the trial court, and the Supreme Court reversed the conviction, saying that in view of the policy against allowing the wife to sue her husband, and because of the fact that allowing one spouse to indict the other tended to cut off reconciliation "and forgiveness, the wife would not be allowed to indict her husband for slander," the court saying:

The changes made in the Constitution of 1868, and the enactments in pursuance of its provisions in reference to married women, are directed to the preservation and disposal of property, as separate estate, but do not materially affect the personal relations of the parties except as incidental to property and its use.

It may be suggested that an indictment might lie, while an action for damages would not, as in case of the assault and battery of the wife by the husband. But it is not correct to say that such an indictment may in all cases be maintained. It is only where the battery is so great and excessive as to put life and limb in peril, or where permanent injury to the person is inflicted, or where it is prompted by a malicious and wrongful spirit, and not within reasonable bounds, that the law interposes to punish. In other cases, short of these extremes, it drops the curtain upon scenes of domestic life, preferring not to take cognizance of what transpires within that circle, to the exposure of them in public prosecution. It presumes that acts of wrong committed in passion will be followed by contrition and atonement in a cooler moment, and forgiveness will blot it out of memory. So, too, the harsh and cruel word that sends a pang to the sensitive heart may be recalled, and relations that should never have been interrupted by an unkind or unwarranted expression, again restored. The unnumbered mischiefs that might flow from making an unguarded and false imputation upon the wife's chastity the subject of a public criminal proceeding, are so obvious that we cannot think the General Assembly intended such a possible result. Not only might this destroy the freedom and cordiality of marital intercourse, but it would tend to make a perpetual estrangement and severance, and cut off the reconciliation that may be expected to succeed a temporary difference and the atonement of a full repentance. Our law regards the marriage relation sacred and permanent, lifelong in its duration, and it leaves temporary differences and wrongs which one may do to the other to the corrective hands of time and reflection, in cases where they admit this remedy. We are not disposed, in carrying out the policy of separate properties, to break in needlessly upon that oneness of husband and wife, which is the fundamental and cherished maxim of the common law, by extending the act beyond all the beneficent purposes it was intended to subserve, to cover cases of slander.

Today, if a husband acts so as to put his wife in reasonable fear of immediate bodily harm, he may be convicted for assault—even though he does not touch her. If he goes on to touch her ever so lightly, he may be convicted of assault and battery. If he assaults her with intent to do serious bodily injury or to kill her, he may be convicted of those crimes. If he kills her, he may be convicted of murder in the first degree, murder in the second degree, or manslaughter, depending on the circumstances.

At the common law a husband has a legal right to sexual intercourse with his wife and therefore cannot be convicted of common law rape, which is "the unlawful carnal knowledge of a woman forcibly against her will." But if a husband forces his wife to have sexual intercourse with another against her will, he may be convicted for assault with intent to commit rape.

A vestige of the ancient notion that a husband and wife are one still hangs over in the common law that, being one, husband and wife cannot steal from each other.

THE PAST IS HISTORY AND THE FUTURE IS MYSTERY

Here in North Carolina, Professor Robert E. Lee of the Wake Forest University Law School, in his excellent and authoritative book on *North Carolina Family Law*, traces the evolution of the legal rights of women in North Carolina, the devolution of the legal rights of men, and the changing rights and privileges of men and women—not without the saving grace of humor. Here is a paraphrasing of some of the distinctions which make a difference in his mind: The law requires the husband to support the wife but not the wife to support her husband ....It is a crime for the husband to abandon the wife but not for the wife to abandon the husband....The primary responsibility for supporting minor children is on the father and not on the mother. ...A husband who marries and divorces one woman after another and marries again may have to support his first, second, and third wife at the same time, not so with a wife who marries and divorces one husband after another....If a man uses his money to buy land and has the deed made out to his wife there is a presumption that he intended a gift to his wife, but if a woman uses her money to buy land and has the deed made out to her husband there is a presumption that she intended to keep it for herself....

If a man dies insolvent and without children, his widow may claim up to a $1000 exemption from his creditors if she is not the owner of a homestead in her own right, but a widower may not claim a similar right in the estate of his deceased wife. ...

If a husband leaves his wife out of his will, his widow may in some circumstances dissent and take a specified share of the estate, but if a wife leaves her husband out of her will, the widower is left speechless....

A husband cannot execute a valid chattel mortgage on the household and kitchen furniture which he owns without the joinder of his wife, but the wife can execute a valid chattel mortgage on the household and kitchen furniture which she owns without the joinder of her husband. ...

If a wife is injured by the negligent act of a third person, her husband cannot recover for the resulting loss of his wife's services and the costs of nursing and medical care; the wife alone may recover for these things and do as she pleases with the money. ...

A woman prisoner cannot be forced to work on the public roads or streets, but a male prisoner can be....

A husband has to pay the funeral expenses of his wife, but a wife does not have to pay the funeral expenses of her husband. ...There are statutes limiting the hours of work for women but not the hours of work for men. ...It is a crime for a man to say that an innocent woman has engaged in sexual intercourse but it is not a crime for a woman to say that an innocent man has engaged in sexual intercourse. . . . It is a crime for a man to peep into the bedroom of a disrobing woman but not for a woman to peep into the bedroom of a disrobing man!

To make bad matters worse: The life expectancy of a woman is six years longer than the life expectancy of a man . . . . There are more men than women in mental institutions . . . . The suicide rate of men to women is ten to four . . . . Women have greater resistance to some diseases than men and recover more rapidly from diseases they have. . . . In the United States women own sixty to seventy per cent of the private wealth of the country and men only thirty to forty per cent. . . . Here and there in our law we find ancient relics to the effect that the husband is the head of the family, but all too often, like the King of England, he is a figurehead.

The Courts have not always looked with complacency on this bulldozing obliteration of the ancient landmarks. In 1872 the Supreme Court of Illinois said:

> The ancient landmarks are gone . . . . The foundations of the nuptial contract, and the maintenance of the marriage relation, are crumbling. The unity of husband and wife has been severed . . . . She no longer clings to and depends upon man, but has the legal right and aspires to battle with him in the contests of the forum; to outvie him in the healing art; to climb with him the steps of fame; and to share with him in every occupation . . . . His legal supremacy is gone, and the sceptre has departed from him.

In 1875, Bishop wrote about the rights of married women in Massachusetts:

> This is one of those States in which legislation, almost ever since the popular agitation of the subject of married-women laws commenced, has been travelling forward seeking rest and finding none . . . . [They leave little] to be complained of by the most ardent advocate of the policy which yields to wives the double advantages of matrimony and single bliss, and lifts from the shoulders of their husbands none of the burdens borne when the law gave them compensatory advantages. It remains only to add a provision compelling every young man to marry instantly the girl who chooses him, and the end of domestic woe will have come in Massachusetts. Then she can have, as she can have now if the man will submit to the marriage, for her sole and separate use, to accumulate till her husband dies, all that she owned before marriage, all that comes to her afterward, and all that she can acquire by her labor and skill; while he provides for her house room, meals, clothing, and other necessaries of life.

[35]

If these changes in the law brought cold chills to the men of Illinois and Massachusetts in the 1870s they would freeze to death on reading Professor Lee's account of the march of progress in North Carolina by the 1960s, and turn over in their graves to hear him describe the shape of coming events which are already casting their shadows before. Perhaps one of the most enlightening and lasting achievements of his book will be found in his suggested changes in the law and his projections for the future.

IV
The Woman's Fight for Education beyond the High School

EARLY ILLUSTRATIONS

In his 1970 brochure on *Higher Education in North Carolina* William S. Powell says: "The first higher education for women in the state was offered by the Moravians at Salem Female Academy in 1802 when arrangements were made to accept boarding students."

Between 1838 and 1860, Professor Powell continues, more than a dozen "colleges" for women were started, mostly church related, including:

- Greensboro Female College (Methodist) founded in 1838; opened in 1846.
- St. Mary's School (privately owned but Episcopal really) founded in 1842.
- Chowan Baptist Female Institute, 1848.
- Oxford Female College (Baptist), 1851.
- Concord Female College (Presbyterian), 1856.
- Davenport Female College (Methodist), 1857.
- Charlotte Female Institute (Presbyterian), 1857.

Guion Griffis Johnson, in her book on *Ante-Bellum North Carolina,* says, "After 1840 schools for women began to adopt the ambitious title of college although their courses of study were little more advanced than those offered in the female academies and boarding schools prior to that date."

Women were admitted to the University of North Carolina in the later 1890s.

A *Statistical Abstract of Higher Education in North Carolina* in the fall of 1973 records that there were 40,966 women registered on the 16 campuses of the University of North Carolina, 44,685 in community colleges and military centers, and 21,623 in private institutions, making a total of 66,308.

The *Abstract* records that a total of 83,953 men were registered in these institutions: 49,488 in the 16 University of North Carolina campuses, 56,693 in community colleges and military centers, and 27,260 in private institutions.

This article on *The Coming of Women to the University of North Carolina,* by Gladys Hall Coates, illustrates the prolonged fight of women in North Carolina for education beyond the high school.

THE COMING OF WOMEN TO THE UNIVERSITY OF NORTH CAROLINA BY GLADYS HALL COATES

"The Coming of Women to the University of North Carolina" grows out of a larger piece of research that I undertook for my husband some years ago. It began with his interest in the evolution of student government in the University.

My research led to the reading of the trustee and faculty minutes and records beginning in the latter part of the 18th century; the files of the University Magazine beginning in the 1840s; the files of the Tar Heel beginning in the 1890s; many diaries and letters of the same periods to be found in the Southern Historical Collection; the Yackety Yack and its forerunner, the Hellenian; and finally the comic magazines.

Perhaps the most interesting records of all were the minutes of the Dialectic and Philanthropic Literary Societies, or the Di and Phi, as they came to be known affectionately through the years. And what records they are! The Societies were founded in 1795, the same year the University opened, and their history, written in their minutes in great volumes, is one of the finest student records in our country. One can trace American history by their very topics for debate.

I became deeply interested in all of these records and found material relating not only to the subject that had been the original reason for my research but all sorts of other fascinating information as well—such as material relating to the building of the Society libraries which became the foundation of the University's splendid library; the collection of portraits of famous alumni and other distinguished Americans, portraits painted by some of the foremost artists of our country; and still other material concerning many facets of student life. Indeed, it was while delving in into these records that my interest was awakened in the part that women have played in the life of the University.

Women as Visitors

From the opening of the University and the attendance of Mary Leach Spaight, wife of the Governor of North Carolina, at the first public examination, women have shown an interest in the University's welfare and were among its earliest benefactors. The women of Raleigh in 1802 contributed a pair of globes and a compass; and in 1803, the women of New Bern, a quadrant. "Our sex," they wrote in the stately phrases of the period, "can never be indifferent to the promotion of science, connected as it is with the virtues that impart civility to manners and refinement to life. Nor can we suppress the emotions of (we hope) an honest pride, at the reflection that our native country boasts a seminary, where by the proper extension of Legislative patronage, its ingenuous youth might be taught to emulate the worth of their fathers . . . ."

From the beginning, women were welcomed to the University commencements, the dances, and all University occasions generally—but never as students. The first University tutor, Charles W. Harris, wrote that he had lately found "many good hints on education in a book entitled the rights of women—a book of very great merit, the production of an original genius—and penned in such a strong, masterly style that you would scarcely believe it the work of a woman—For we are taught by many able writers and tolerable accurate observers of mankind that the natural weakness of a woman's body extends to her mind, and becomes characteristic of her thoughts and words as well as of her actions. Miss Mary Wollstonecraft is the lady born effectually to rectify these misrepresentations from which so much evil has sprung. [Her] intention is to bring about a total reform in the education of women—." But it is doubtful that tutor Harris ever gave a thought to the entrance of women as students in the newly-created University.

Women in the Anterooms

A generation later, Ellen and Margaret Mitchell, daughters of Professor Elisha Mitchell, and Cornelia Phillips, daughter of Professor James Phillips, were occasional visitors to Dr. Mitchell's classes and welcomed there by the students. According to the reminiscence of one student of the period they sat in small classrooms adjoining the larger and heard the lectures. Truly this was feeding on the crumbs that fell from the table!

Another student of the same period, William Sidney Mullins, gives a graphic picture in his diary of the visits of these women to the classroom. According to him, the ladies seem to have been in the midst of things:

> July 21, 1841: This class convened in the Laboratory at half past eight and heard Dr. Mitchell's opening Lecture on the Science of Chemistry. Misses Margaret and Ellen Mitchell, and Miss Whitaker were also present, and perhaps drew off a little attention that should have been given to the Lecture.
>
> July 29, 1841: The Ladies of the Hill . . .attended our lecture on Wednesday morning, and it is useless to add the interest of the proceedings [was] greatly enhanced . . . .The lecture was not *very* interesting, however, and my eyes were on the fair faces oftener than on the experiments.
>
> August 4, 1841: The assembly of Ladies at the morning lecture was once more full, and we even had one exotic [slang of the time] in the lovely garden, Miss Wiley of Pittsboro, having come with Miss Hall, to whom she is now on a visit.
>
> August 11, 1841: For the first time this Session, Ladies were present at the afternoon lectures, and . . .as usual I basked in the lovely sunshine of their gaze! Sweet little Aula [Miss Hall], thy pouting lips and innocent glance would drive away study, and arouse love in temperaments less excitable than mine. I must beware, or ere I know my danger, I shall be completely the slave of this young nymph, and I have no reason to believe that she would make my servitude happy.

Faculty daughters, however, received the greater part of their education in their homes where they were taught by their professorial fathers with a thoroughness that made them the intellectual equal of any student in the University.

Woman as a subject for debate, composition, reading, and discussion was a frequent source of inspiration in society halls. In the early days of the 19th century students debated such topics as:

—Was woman made only for procreation?

—Should women receive a liberal education?

—Should women be admitted a share in the management of public affairs?

[40]

—Is the female sex inferior in intellectual faculties to the male sex?

—Ought the female to hold the reins of any government?

Captain Johnston Blakely, a naval hero of the War of 1812 and a student here in 1797, wrote an essay on the education of women. Hinton James, the first student to enter the University, read a passage from the history of women. Other members read on "ladies' headdresses" and debated the comparative effects of wine and women on students. Coeducation was not in the minds of these early students but woman was, and they frequently regretted the presence of so few women in the village of Chapel Hill. An editorial in the *University Magazine* of 1855 laments this state of affairs: "But if we are to regard the opinions of those who have learned wisdom by experience, it were well for us if we were not allowed so much as even to see those 'fairie nymphs' during our entire college sojourn; for we are told

Love ne'er haunts the breast where learning lies
Venus must set ere Mercury can rise.

But if we may be allowed to *amend somewhat* a very time-honored saying, we are decidedly of opinion that, 'A little *courting* now and then, is relished by the wisest men, *and women*, too.' "

Zebulon Baird Vance (Class of 1855), who later became the state's great war governor, evidently agreed with this sentiment when he wrote his fiancée that "the faculty are allways partial to the students who visit the ladies, and say that they are [the] most orderly young men and industrious students in College."

Women were so rare on campus in those days that when any were unexpectedly glimpsed, the cry would reverberate through the dormitories—"Angels on campus!" This was a real note of warning which, I suspect, had even more meaning in later years when the first baths on campus, and the only baths for several years, were installed in the basement of the library—the building now known as the Playmakers Theatre. Men in varying degrees of casual attire would cross the campus to and from the baths; "Angels on campus" was then sometimes, no doubt, a frantic cry of warning!

Students outdid themselves and the Societies vied with each other in their preparations for the one time of the year when women from all parts of the state were present on the Hill—commencement. At other times, students visited neighboring seminaries—Peace, St. Mary's, and Salem. One romance which grew out of these visits was that of James K. Polk (Class of 1818), later President of the United States, with Sarah Childress, a student at the Moravian Institute. He came with other students from the University to attend one of the "speaking nights" at Salem, where he met Sarah. According to college tradition, he was a frequent visitor while she was a student there.

The First Breakthrough

After the Civil War and the re-opening of the University, students began to take an interest in the subject of co-education. In 1877, the first summer normal school conducted by the University, said to be the first summer school in the United States connected with any university or college, was opened, and women as well as men were invited to attend. The invitation read somewhat condescendingly:

FEMALES

Although the law requires that the money paid by the State shall be devoted to the use of males, yet females are cordially invited to attend all the exercises of the school free of charge. . . .We earnestly appeal to every teacher and every man and woman in the State who desires to teach to come forward and attend this School.

Of the total number of 235 enrolled in the first summer school, 107 were women and 128 men.

The number and eagerness of the women teachers who grasped this opportunity impressed the students, and their observations are reflected in debates, editorials, and articles throughout the period. A *University Magazine* article in 1882 agreed that women should have a sound education but doubted the wisdom of co-education because of the supposed difference in the minds of men and women. An editor of the *Magazine* in 1883, however, came out strongly for the education of women and co-education as the solution to the problem because of the poverty of the state:

As early as 1795, North Carolina established a University for her boys. Ninety years, we may say, have elapsed and she has done nothing for her girls. Our people are growing tired of this discrimination. The State is expected to aid in female education. How must this be done? For those communities able to support a double system of colleges and universities, we prefer separate education, but for North Carolina, who is too poor to support a respectable system of public schools or give her University a shilling, we advocate Co-education.

In 1882, two women graduates of the Fayetteville Public Schools, prompted by their superintendent, Dr. Alexander Graham (father of

[42]

the late President Frank Graham) had applied for admission to the University. Etta May Troy and Fannie Watson took the entrance examinations but, though making higher grades than the boys applying from the same school, were not admitted. The girls, said their superintendent, came " . . . asking no quarter on account of age, sex, or previous condition of servitude [and] . . .were sent back to the bonne braes of Cumberland because they were girls."

When the summer normal school was discontinued in 1884, University students raised the question of admitting women to the University's teaching course in the regular session. The Dialectic Society passed a resolution heartily endorsing such an innovation, but the *Magazine* editor of that year, though declaring himself for the higher education of women, wondered if co-education was the answer.

There were mixed feelings throughout the student body at the possibility of women in the University. Some gallant students, said one writer, thought women would help "to polish boorish ways" and were favorable to their coming; others, fearful of falling in love, were against it.

When the summer normal school was re-opened in 1894, the *Magazine,* commenting on the great interest shown by women in their renewed opportunity, said: "Their attendance and interest was a sufficient answer to those who say that women would not take advantage of greater facilities for thorough culture."

The action of President Battle and the Board of Trustees inviting women as well as men to attend the University's first summer normal and the renewal of this invitation were long steps toward co-education in the University.

The Second Breakthrough

The second breakthrough came fifteen years later, in January, 1897, when President Alderman in his inaugural address said, "One whose mind is upon educational questions cannot longer hesitate to deal frankly with the duty of educational institutions to womanhood."

"I believe that this University at the earliest time practicable should open its post-graduate courses to the women of the State."

Within a month at a trustees' meeting the following resolution was offered on the recommendation of the President: "That the post-graduate courses at the University be opened to women, under such regulations as the faculty may prescribe."

[43]

At the same meeting, a trustee offered an amendment "that all the educational advantages of the University be opened to female pupils," but it was defeated and the original resolution adopted.

The trustees followed the suggestion of President Alderman with hope but some misgivings. The Visiting Committee reported that they had opened the University doors to women "to satisfy their demand, 'and to carry gentle peace to silence envious tongues,' and to place ambitious young women on an equality with their aspiring brothers." The Committee expressed

> ... no opinion as to the propriety or impropriety of this course. It is a departure from the time-honored policy heretofore pursued by the governors of the Institution. The proposition was thought to possess sufficient merit to warrant the Trustees in making the experiment. Other institutions of like character have tried the experiment and after testing its merit have continued it in operation. We express the hope that much good will result to the women of our country for this action of the Trustees, and that great good will result to the University; that the women of the State will honor the Institution as the Institution has honored them, and that hand in hand, they will march on to still greater achievements in the future. ...

It was indeed a revolutionary step for the trustees, and some of the papers of the State were decidedly opposed. "We are not Yankeeized enough in our ideas," wrote one editor, "to accept this mixing of sexes in universities and colleges. We have not reached the sublime altitude of gush and froth to advocate woman suffrage and office-holding, including the woman parson business also." He favored a separate state university for women.

Another wrote, "We hope the day is distant when the breed of ... unsexed bipeds shall be privileged to [romp] over the land to the shame of woman and the merriment of man."

Even the brilliant Cornelia Phillips Spencer, who, of course, favored the higher education of women, was not prepared to accept co-education as the proper method. In 1875, in her column in the *North Carolina Presbyterian*, she had written: "And as to sharing ...in any mode [of instruction] that would suggest or lead to co-education of the sexes, I am very sure all North Carolina would rise up against the project. In fact I do not believe any young woman in North Carolina could be induced to accept an education under such circumstances. And yet, I do long to put an opportunity into the hands of ...girls who stand helpless and sorrowful and longing."

[44]

She evidently remained unconvinced as late as 1887, when she is said to have remarked that "co-education will never do in these latitudes!"

The Third Breakthrough

In November of 1897, President Alderman reported to the trustees that five women had enrolled, that they had done very skillful work in the more difficult courses, and that their presence at the University demonstrated the feasibility of young women of maturity taking the higher courses. Although the amendment to open all University courses to women had failed, nevertheless the University's catalogue for 1897-98 stated that "...women are now admitted to all higher courses in the University and may be enrolled in the regular junior and senior classes in candidacy for undergraduate degrees." Behind this statement lies an interesting story of the interpretation of the trustee resolution.

President Alderman, who was a champion of co-education, felt the University's doors should be opened as far as possible to women, but he knew that few women had all the prerequisite training for post-graduate work. He, therefore, interpreted post-graduate work to mean further study for any qualified woman who had graduated from a woman's college or seminary. This meant that women could enter the junior and senior classes of the University, as most women's institutions offered only two years of college, if that.

The University was fortunate in its early women students. The first one to register was Mary S. McRae, the late Mrs. R. L. Gray, Sr. of Raleigh, a graduate of St. Mary's and mother of Frances Gray Patton of Durham. Dixie Lee Bryant, a graduate of the Massachusetts Institute of Technology, who had already served on the instruction staff of the University's summer normal, registered for graduate work in the summer of 1897. By the fall of that year they were joined by Sallie Walker Stockard, a graduate of Guilford, and Roanna Dodd and Julia Watkins.

I had the great pleasure of meeting Sallie Stockard Magness at commencement several years ago and talking with her about her student days. When I told her of my interest in the history of women on campus she promised to write down some of her recollections. She was quite an old lady then, but very alert and with a delightful sense of humor. Her eyes sparkled as she recalled that one of her fellow stu-

[45]

dents of that distant day declared that she was not going to take the Shakespeare course because she didn't want to be exposed to the unlicensed speech of Falstaff! But Sallie Stockard said she was going to study Shakespeare and Falstaff, too—and she did!

Misgivings Disappear

The *University Magazine* editor said in October, 1898, that the trustees' action in admitting women to the higher classes was "universally popular. Their work has been of the highest character and they have clearly proved that the women of our country deserve equal opportunities with their brothers along educational lines. . . ."

The Trustee Visiting Committee reported in 1900 that "while the members of the Committee are not agreed on the steps that should be taken in the future, we do agree that no mistake has been made in the privileges already granted to women at our University and we believe that the conduct and example of refined and intelligent associates of this class [have] not been without [their] influence in elevating the deportment of the whole student body, and giving some polish to 'Rough Diamonds.' "

The *Tar Heel*, referring in January of 1898 to a woman student of Cornell who had recently won a prize debate over the men of that institution, said "this great event in Cornell's history ought to serve as a warning to us. We too have 'co-eds,' who, although just admitted to the University this year, already rival the men in several departments and bid fair soon to outstrip them."

The prophecy was not long in being realized. Marcia Louise Latham (Class of 1900) walked away that year with the coveted Holt medal, the highest award in the Department of Mathematics. Major William Cain, head of the department, had remarked at the time women entered the University that his department, at least, would not be bothered with them because he knew none of them could pass higher mathematics. But when the unforeseen happened, he responded with great good humor, "Now I believe they can do anything!"

The first women students realized they had to establish themselves and that the future of other women entering the University depended on them. Though Mary McRae applied for, and was appointed to fill, a position on the *Tar Heel* staff as literary editor, and Sallie Stockard, the only woman in the senior class in 1898, cast the deciding vote in the election of the class president, they and the women students who followed them felt they were in the University by sufferance, as they undoubtedly were. They presented a thoroughly dignified appearance and attended classes in the most formal attire, wearing hats and gloves. When their pictures failed to appear in the annual with the year's graduating class and when diplomas were presented men graduates on the platform while theirs were given privately, they made no protest. One girl who was inclined to militant feminism wanted them to demand their rights, but the majority believed their salvation lay in making no demands.

Most of the men stood in awe of them and gave them a wide berth. A woman student wrote in the *Yackety Yack* of 1906: "One of the most remarkable things about being a co-ed is the amount of room you take up. You start towards an empty seat on the end of a bench and by the time you get there the whole row is vacant. . . .I advise any maiden who wants to be a co-ed to buy a parasol—it's lots of company at first."

An anonymous poem appearing in the *Tar Heel* of the period probably summed up the attitude of many of the men students. It was entitled:

THE VARSITY GIRL

She'd a great and varied knowledge
Picked up at a co-ed college
Of quadratics, hydrostatics and pneumatics
    Very vast.

She was stuffed with erudition
As you stuff a leather cushion
All the ologies of the college, and the knowledge
    Of the past.

She had studied the old lexicons
The Peruvians and Mexicans
Their theology, anthropology, and geology
    O'er and o'er.

She knew all the forms and features
Of the prehistoric creatures
Ichthyosaurus, plesiosaurus, megalosaurus
    And many more.

She knew all the mental giants
And the master minds of science
All the learning that was turning
    In the burning mind of man;

But she couldn't prepare a dinner
For a gaunt and hungry sinner

[47]

Or get up a decent supper
For her poor voracious papa
For she never was instructed
On the old domestic plan.

There was at least one "papa" in the United States who was determined not to be so victimized. The late Dean Alice Baldwin of Duke University told me that her father insisted that she learn to cook and keep house before he would allow her to go to college. And so the entire summer before she left for college in the fall was spent doing just that!

Another example of a determined father but with a slightly different twist comes to mind. This story involves tears, though I suppose that tears may have been a part of Dean Baldwin's experience, also. At any rate, this was the experience of the famous Carey Thomas, the second president of Bryn Mawr. Her father, too, was utterly opposed to her higher education. But her mother, realizing the unusual ability of her daughter, was just as determined in her quiet Quaker way that she should be given further opportunities. And so she said to her daughter, "Carey, thee and I must learn to cry, and we must cry day and night until thy father sees the light!" And cry they did, off and on for some weeks, and won their battle.

The number of women students at Chapel Hill did not increase rapidly at first. In 1912, fifteen years after their admission, President Battle wrote in his history of the University that the "experiment" had not met with much success, that though there were some brilliant students among the lot, the total number had averaged only about six a year—and this in a student body averaging 800. He attributed the lack of growth to the excellent "female" schools in the state and the founding of the Normal and Industrial School in Greensboro, later named the Woman's College, and now the University of North Carolina at Greensboro.

The Fourth Breakthrough

In 1917, President Edward Kidder Graham in his report to the trustees wrote:

In the twenty years that have passed since [the] admission [of women] in 1897, an average of less than ten a year have entered. For the most part they have been specially qualified students and their work has been uniformly excellent and in some cases highly distinguished. In the past few years women have registered in each of the professional schools of law, medicine, and pharmacy.

This year twenty-five women are registered in all departments—a considerable increase, but still the total number, owing to the fact that no dormitory provision has ever been made for them, nor other special encouragement given, is not a tenth of what it should be . . . .

The time has come, we believe, when the University authorities should give the matter serious attention and determine whether the University shall adapt itself to the education of women or not. To continue to admit them in a half-hearted way, and to furnish them with classroom instruction without the other features which make up college life, is a rather doubtful kindness to them. If it should be decided to make a place for women at the University, our aim should be to provide adequately for their physical and social welfare, as well as for their mental development.

In an article in the *Alumni Review* for October, 1917, entitled "A Woman's Building—A Magnificent Opportunity," President Graham expressed the hope that some person of insight and means would seize the opportunity to give the women of the state a dormitory at the University. In 1917, he appointed the first adviser to women on this campus, Mrs. Thomas W. Lingle, a former president of the North Carolina Federation of Women's Clubs, who served also on the staff of the University's Bureau of Extension as director of work with the women's clubs of the state.

President Graham was deeply appreciative of the great contributions that women had made in leadership and financial support of the University in the years following the Civil War. Cornelia Phillips Spencer, through her articles in the state papers and magazines and her correspondence and friendship with many leading University alumni, was largely responsible for the reopening of the University after it had been closed for five years in the tragic aftermath of the War. And other women—Mary Ann Smith, Mary Ruffin Smith, Mary Bryan Speight, and Mary Elizabeth Mason—through legacies had helped to keep it going after it was re-opened. In 1917, Mary Lily Kenan Bingham left to the University the largest sum of money it had ever received—one and a half million dollars, the interest from which is used today for enlarging and strengthening the faculty by the support of Kenan Professorships.

A woman's dormitory was sorely needed, for few of the proprietors of houses in Chapel Hill accommodating University students would even consider taking women. Most of the first women students found a haven in the same place—with Miss Sophia MacNider, whose house stood on the site of the present Franklin Street post office.

President Graham, whose untimely death occurred in 1918, did not live to see the dormitory he had envisioned, but his work in this venture was carried forward by his successor, Dr. Harry Woodburn Chase. President Chase appointed Mrs. Marvin Hendrix Stacy in 1919 to succeed Mrs. Lingle as a full-time adviser to women, and she immediately began a campaign for adequate housing. In her report for 1920, she stated that "the students are scattered from one end of town to the other, and lose much valuable time going back and forth. . . . They have few comforts and in their social life none of the finer things which come from contact with one another. . . ." By 1921, two houses, on adjoining lots and accommodating about forty-five of the sixty-five women, were provided by the University. Mrs. Stacy called this a makeshift arrangement, totally lacking in equipment for social and physical development. One small sitting room and five chairs and a table were all that were provided for the reception of callers.

Norma Connell (Mrs. Reece Berryhill) was a student in the University from 1923 to 1925 and recalls an experience during her sojourn in one of those houses. She and a roommate lived in Archer House over the kitchen. One cold and snowy day they realized there was not one stick of wood left to replenish the fire in the little tin stove, their only source of heat. They had previously notified the proper authorities that they needed fuel but no wood had been forthcoming. Deciding to take things in their own hands, and try another form of persuasion, they bundled up in all the coats and sweaters they could find, tied up their heads in scarves, making themselves look as much like refugees from Siberia as possible, and sallied forth to pick up broken branches from trees on campus. When they managed to find some near the President's office window, they were spotted and recognized by the President and his secretary, now a prominent banker and legislator. The secretary came out to see what was going on, and the girls told him. It goes without saying—a load of wood was delivered to their quarters that afternoon!

Archer House burned down shortly after this episode and the coeds who lived there were taken in by kindly faculty families. Perhaps the fire helped to forward plans for a woman's building.

The Battle of Spencer Hall

President Chase included a dormitory for women in the University's building program he presented to the General Assembly in 1921, but the appropriation for the biennium did not provide this building though it provided five dormitories for men.

In 1923, the next legislative year, the heaviest opposition that co-education at the University ever faced came to the front. When it was learned there was a strong probability that a woman's dormitory might be built, opponents on campus swung into action, and a controversy, later known as the "Battle of Spencer Hall," followed.

The president of the YMCA wrote: "If a co-ed dormitory is built it will simply mean the beginning of a flow of co-ed and other female species into the walls of our campus that will never stop until we are all 'flapperized.' "

An extra edition of the *Tar Heel* was issued for the avowed purpose of preventing the building of the dormitory. Two editorial blasts with the headings

Women Not Wanted Here

Shaves and Shines
but no Rats and Rouge

argued that co-education should be confined to residents of Chapel Hill, to graduate and professional students, and thus would not require a dormitory; that the state had provided a college for women in Greensboro which with other women's colleges in the state offered sufficient facilities without the invasion of Chapel Hill; that there were other co-educational institutions in the state where women desiring to be educated along with men might go; that money appropriated by the state for the University was needed for dormitories, classrooms, laboratories, and a gymnasium for men; that the idea of a woman's dormitory in this stronghold of men was simply the result of " . . . sentimental pleas from some of the women students now at the University and some of the politicians of the State who are seeking the favor of [the] women of North Carolina and have their eyes on some of the big jobs. . . ." Politicians of the state were indeed seeking the favor of the women of North Carolina, for women had been granted the right to vote three years before and were no longer to be ignored.

A campus vote held on the issue went overwhelmingly against the co-eds, but though the women lost the battle they won the war—for the Executive Committee endorsed the program outlined by the Building Committee favoring a woman's building, and in the fall of 1925 the Cornelia Phillips Spencer Dormitory, named in honor of one of the University's greatest friends, was opened.

The women had worked long and perseveringly for their goal. The Woman's Association of the University in 1921 had passed a resolution respectfully memorializing the Building Committee for a dormitory, and one co-ed, May Belle Penn (Mrs. Roger Jones), president of the Woman's Association, had spent most of one summer journeying to many parts of the state to talk to legislators about the need of a dormitory.

The coeds were not without help in their battles. A resolution that a woman's dormitory be constructed had been proposed by a prominent alumnus, Judge Francis D. Winston, at a meeting of the Alumni Association at the commencement of 1920. Influential alumni and friends throughout the state held meetings, wrote letters, and, together with women students, helped to raise funds for a dormitory. Nor were friends on campus wanting. The editor of the *Magazine* criticized the *Tar Heel* for its propaganda against a woman's dormitory and called such a policy a misuse of the paper. A previous *Magazine* editor had compiled student-faculty opinions regarding co-education and found that while the students were both for and against the question, the faculty were almost unanimously in favor of co-education.

President Chase spoke in chapel while the campus was in the midst of turmoil and declared himself in favor of equal opportunity for both men and women.

Dr. Frank Graham, then professor of history and later president of the University, was active in helping to organize the movement for a woman's dormitory, and he was joined by many prominent men and women in the state.

"I believe in co-education at the University of North Carolina," said Professor Graham, "because I believe that education in a University is not a sex right but a human right. Education was once a sex monopoly. Woman has established her rights to education in general against the inertia and hostility of slow-changing opinion. The right of co-education is as logical as the progress of the race. Woman has advanced from chattel to person, to equality of personality. Co-education, equal education, is a part of this advance. My belief in

[52]

co-education at the University is a part of my belief in the University."

One constant friend the coeds had on campus was Mrs. Stacy. It was she who searched the town over for rooms for them. Year after year her reports entreated the trustees for better facilities, and all the while she was making every effort to work with what meager facilities were offered.

At the time that a decision was to be made about building a woman's dormitory, a little group of trustees and administrative officials met in President Chase's office, and Mrs. Stacy was called into the meeting. With her was May Belle Penn.

In the course of the meeting Mrs. Stacy said that the girls in Archer House had only one bathroom for every twenty-one girls. One trustee retorted, "Well, when I was in the University we didn't have any bathroom."

To which Miss Penn replied: "Maybe you didn't, but you men could go to the creek!" This remark provoked much laughter and eased the tension.

The appropriation was finally granted and a woman's building became a reality.

The original plans for Spencer Hall were not completely carried out, however. Two proposed wings of the H-shaped dormitory were eliminated. Several years later Mrs. Stacy, in the course of a conversation with Mr. Woollen, the business manager of the University, inquired, "When do you think I'll get my two wings, Mr. Woollen?" To which Mr. Woollen replied, "I think you'll get your wings when you get to heaven!" And I am sure she has.

Mrs. Stacy served the University as Adviser and later as Dean of Women from 1919 until her retirement in 1946.

Other Breakthroughs

The entrance of women into campus activities and organizations is an interesting chapter. Their first recorded formal organization after their admission was the Woman's University Club, established in September, 1906, "for the purpose of establishing cordial relations between women students, . . .promoting their interests," and bringing active members into touch with alumnae. In 1917, the twenty-five women students of that year formed the Woman's Association. By 1921, an Honor Committee, corresponding to the Men's Student Council, had been elected, a self-help bureau established, and a house organization effected. In 1922, the Honor Committee, which had represented only Association members, was replaced by a Student Council of Women Students representing all women students. In 1923, the Woman's Association was renamed the Woman's Student Government Association, and all women students became members on registration. In 1941, this Association was reorganized into three elected governing groups—the Honor Council, the Interdormitory Council, and the Senate—and renamed the Woman's Government Association.

Woman's government was again reorganized in 1946, and in recent years there has been a movement toward unifying the governing groups of the campus under organizations including men and women.

Sororities were among the first organizations promoted by women on campus. Two national sororities recognized local groups and established chapters here in 1923. New and perplexing problems arose as adjustment to Pan-Hellenic regulations and fierce competition occupied members. The problem of creating wholesome rivalry with only two social groups was of great concern when women began to come to the University in larger numbers. More than two sororities were needed if there were to be sororities, but other nationals refused for some years to establish chapters because of the University's policy restricting the admission of women. It was not until 1939 that a third national sorority was established. Others followed in the 1940s, the 50s, and the 60s. Today there are nine sororities, each with its own house. Their memberships range from sixty-five to seventy and make up about eighteen percent of undergraduate women. Their houses, some of them recently built or remodelled, are very handsome, indeed, and help in the never-ending problem of housing women students. In 1968 the sororities organized the Society of Hellenas which recognizes outstanding work in sorority matters.

The Woman's Athletic Association was organized in the 1930s, and in the 1940s a woman's gymnasium was built adjoining the Woollen gymnasium. During 1949–50, forty-four percent of undergraduate women were participating in a variety of intramural sports. By the 1970s there were 900 participants in fourteen intramural sports. In 1972–73, around 100 women were competing in intercollegiate sports, including basketball, volleyball, field hockey, gymnastics, swimming, tennis, fencing, and golf. In the same year, for the first time, the

University Athletic Association recognized women's intercollegiate sports by presenting awards for excellence.

Time will not permit the listing of all the activities of women and their gradual recognition on campus, but here are some highlights:

The first woman to receive the A.B. degree from the University was Sallie Walker Stockard in 1898, and she received the Master of Arts degree in 1900.

The first women to receive master's degrees were Katherine Ahern and Mary Kendrick in 1899.

The first women to receive Ph.D. degrees were Irene Dillard and Anna Forbes Liddell in 1924; and Guion Griffis Johnson and Lillie Fielding Cutler in 1927.

The first honorary doctorate granted a woman by the University was the L.L.D. degree to Cornelia Phillips Spencer in 1895.

At the commencement of 1922 women celebrated their 25th anniversary. It was a year of high scholastic achievement, for in that year the average grade of women students was found to be the highest of any group or class in the University, and they were the winners of several academic honors. Adeline Denham (Mrs. F. B. McCall) won a fellowship in philosophy; another woman, a fellowship in chemistry; and three others carried off prizes in pharmacy.

The following year stands out as the year in which women won a dormitory for themselves.

In the 1930s, they continued to come to the front in a variety of activities. Some were voted in as members of the University Club and the Di and Phi Societies. Others became cheerleaders, dance leaders, commencement marshals, and still others won campus political offices—the senior class secretaryship and the presidency of a literary society.

In the 1940s, the women's honor society, which had been in existence as a leadership sorority since 1935, was reorganized and named the Valkyries. Founded with the purpose of recognizing and honoring scholarship, leadership, service, and character among women, the Valkyries brought a quality and depth in the life of women on campus that had been wanting before. In this decade women were so well accepted on campus that they became charter members of the Order of the Old Well, an organization recognizing and honoring both men and women who achieve a certain number of points in several areas, such as scholarship, student government, athletics, publications, etc.

In the 1950s, a woman was for the first time editor of the *Daily Tar Heel*. Glenn Harden was elected to that office in 1950.

In the 1960s, women were voted in as members of the Society of Janus, an organization founded ten years before to honor students who make outstanding contributions to residence life.

In 1965, a woman for the first time became editor-in-chief of the *North Carolina Law Review*—Doris Bray, who entered the Law School with a Master of Arts degree from Yale. Other women have served through the years as associate editors.

The quadrangle of Alderman, Kenan, and McIver is a far cry from the "Battle of Spencer Hall," as are the other dormitories which have since been occupied by women students. Today, women occupy thirteen dormitories. Of these, nine are occupied exclusively by women, and four by men and women—Craige by graduate students and Hinton James, Morrison, and Ehringhaus by undergraduates. In addition to these, Granville Towers East houses women, and Granville Towers South houses both men and women.

The number of women students today is a far cry, too, from that early band of five in 1897. From 25 in 1917 the number has steadily grown to 120 by 1925; 247 by 1932; 827 by 1941; 1100 in 1946 (the first time there were as many as 1000); 1800 by 1960; 2,532 by 1964; 3,315 by 1966; and 4,478 by 1967.

The total number of women registered for the fall term of 1972 was 7,278; of these, 5,055 were undergraduates, 2,069 graduates, and 154 post-graduates (law, medicine, dentistry, etc.). The total number of men registered for the same term was 11,946.

Women began to enter in larger numbers after the University at Greensboro became co-educational in 1964, and the University at Chapel Hill began at the same time a more liberal policy in the admission of undergraduate women. In 1970, for the first time more freshmen were admitted here than junior transfers.

I doubt if we can realize the many problems that have to be dealt with as a consequence not only of such rapid growth but also of the changing manners and mores of recent years. Katherine Kennedy Carmichael, Dean of Women 1946–73 and now Associate Dean of Supportive Services, has witnessed much of the growth and changes here and has worked unceasingly through the years to help solve the inevitable problems arising. She succeeded Mrs. Stacy on her retirement in 1946, the first year the number of women students reached one thousand, and she has seen that number multiply seven-fold.

Dean Carmichael was recently honored by the Woman's Association of the University with a citation and plaque recalling her unselfish service, and marking the 75th anniversary of the first woman to be graduated from the University.

Women have gradually enrolled in most, if not all, of the departments and schools of the University, though their way has at times been far from comfortable. Dr. Cora Z. Corpening (1914–16) tells of her experience as the University's first woman medical student. When the all-male student body voted against admitting her she simply started going to class until she became "one of the boys" and was formally enrolled.

From the first organization of the Carolina Playmakers in 1918, women have taken an active part in that group and have been some of its most outstanding members. Some wit in the early years dubbed the Playmakers the Ladies' Aid Society because of the many women who registered in the department. Thomas Wolfe was the only man in the first class but soon several others, including Paul Green, became members; and so I think we may say that the men made up in quality for what they may have lacked in quantity.

The Schools of Public Health, Social Work, Library Science, and Nursing all have many women to register each year. Women still register in large numbers in the School of Education and the College of Arts and Sciences, and they register in substantial numbers in other schools and departments—law, medicine and allied sciences, pharmacy, dentistry, journalism, business administration, etc.

The first woman to teach under University of North Carolina auspices was Emily M. Coe of New York who was a member of the summer school staff of 1878 and taught kindergarten work. She was joined by other women in subsequent summers.

Women were not admitted to the regular faculty until 1927. The appointment of Sallie B. Marks as assistant professor of elementary education in that year paved the way for an accepted practice of the University today. Katharine Jocher, Guion Griffis Johnson, and Harriet Herring came to the University early in the 1920s on foundation grants, and worked as research assistants in the Institute for Research in Social Science, later becoming members of the faculty with the title of associate professor.

There are at present 259 women on the faculty at Chapel Hill out of a total of 1,617. They range from instructors to full professors, and their numbers are growing from year to year.

Recent Breakthroughs

Women are continuing to chart new courses and reach new heights in the University. They are being given larger representation on the General Alumni Association Board in keeping with their increasing numbers.

In 1970, a woman again served as editor-in-chief of the North Carolina Law Review—Joan Goren Brannon, a graduate of Smith.

In 1971, the first woman was granted a Morehead Fellowship. Norma Smithwick Harrell of Greenville, a Wellesley graduate, was granted a graduate fellowship in law. The following year two women, Blenda Woodard from Smith and Pamela Oliver from Stanford, were granted Morehead graduate fellowships in business and sociology, respectively. Women have now been granted undergraduate fellowships in the Morehead Fellowship Program.

The president of the University's chapter of Phi Beta Kappa in 1971 was a woman, Judith Ann Hippler of Atlanta, Georgia. Her activities covered a wide spectrum for she had also served as a cheerleader.

In the spring of 1972, for the first time, women were tapped for membership in the Order of the Golden Fleece. According to the Order, when it was founded in 1903 "there were few women on campus and...they were not involved in campus activities. Over the years, however, [they] have come to play a more prominent role at Chapel Hill and now with a greater number of women enrolled...there is a need for the Order to recognize their contributions. The Active Order agreed that if the Fleece was to justify its position as the highest campus Honorary, it must include women in its ranks. The final decision was a difficult one and not hastily arrived at." Great consideration was given to opinions of Argonauts on campus and elsewhere. The Valkyries were also consulted, and though they decided to remain separate and induct women only, they "favored the Golden Fleece's citation of women...," a consensus that strengthened the Fleece to proceed with its plans. Accordingly, four women—Mary Norris Preyer, Deborah Ann Potter, Katherine Vaden Carlton, and Anne Ellen Green—were inducted into the Golden Fleece on April 14, 1972.

In 1973, a woman was again elected editor of the Daily Tar Heel—

Susan Miller; a woman was for the first time elected speaker of the Campus Governing Council (successor to the Student Legislature)— Julie Tenney, a Chapel Hill junior coed; and Joyce Davis was the first woman to be elected president of the Law School Student Bar Association.

It is not without significance that the principal speaker at the University's commencement in 1972 was a woman—Elizabeth Koonce, former President of the National Education Association and then Director of the Women's Bureau, U.S. Department of Labor; and that the principal speaker at commencement exercises in 1973 was also a woman—Juanita Kreps, James B. Duke Professor of Economics at Duke University and a public member of the Board of Directors of the New York Stock Exchange, the first woman to serve on that Board.

And so the honors and achievements mount. Perhaps it is worth noting in conclusion that a woman was president of the student body at North Carolina State University in 1970; that a man was president of the student body at the University of North Carolina at Greensboro (the former Woman's College) in 1971; so perhaps we may look for changes still to come in the old University of North Carolina at Chapel Hill as time marches on. Since, in 1971, the North Carolina General Assembly, after fifty-one years—finally ratified the 19th Amendment, anything is possible!

Women have indeed a great heritage and tradition here at the University of North Carolina. As they were among the first to come to the aid of the infant University and help breathe into it the breath of life, so it was a woman who was largely responsible for its rebirth in 1875. During all those years, though never admitted as students, women loved the University and helped in its building. Today they are participants in the rich life of this campus.

The year 1973 marked the seventy–fifth anniversary of the first woman to be graduated here. I hope, and I believe, that it will mark the beginning of even greater things for the University, and that women will continue to justify the hope expressed by the trustees on their admission in 1897—that they will honor the University as the University has honored them, and that hand in hand they will march on to still greater achievements in the future.

V.
The Woman's Fight for Community Betterment

This material is excerpted from another book, *Citizens In Action:*

Background

The National American Woman's Suffrage Association

In the year 1840, Lucretia Mott went to London as an American delegate to the World Anti-Slavery Convention, and Elizabeth Cady Stanton went as the wife of a delegate. They were not allowed to attend the convention for the single reason that they were women; they got mad and made an agreement to return to America to start a woman's rights movement.

The first Woman's Rights Convention was held in Seneca Falls, New York, in 1848, and the delegates there joined in a declaration, saying: "It is the duty of the women of this country to secure to themselves their sacred right to the elective franchise."

In the years that followed, the women organized the National American Woman's Suffrage Association, followed by state associations, to carry on the fight for the ballot state by state.

In 1875, Susan B. Anthony proposed an amendment to the Constitution of the United States, saying: "The right of citizens of the United States to vote shall not be denied or abridged by the United States or by any state on account of sex." It was introduced in Congress the following year and every year thereafter until it was submitted by Congress to the several states in June, 1919, ratified by three-fourths of the States by August 26, 1920, and became the 19th Amendment to the United States Constitution.

The General Federation of Women's Clubs

In 1868, Charles Dickens came from England to the United States to speak at a dinner meeting of the New York Press Club. Interested women spent all day setting the tables for the dinner, decorating the hall, and doing all the odds, and ends to prepare for the great occasion. Then, they asked permission—not to sit at the table with the men, not even to sit as a group in some inconspicuous part of the hall—but to sit concealed behind a curtain in the gallery in order to hear the famous speaker. The men of the New York Press Club were outraged at this "impertinent" request and indignantly refused them permission for the simple reason that they were women.

The women were equally indignant and within forty-eight hours banded themselves together in the Sorosis Club of New York City, "to hold their own meetings and to do their own speaking." The first meeting of this club was held on April 20, 1868.

In the years that followed, women throughout the country organized in other clubs, and in 1889 the Sorosis Club celebrated its twentieth anniversary by inviting all these clubs to a convention and uniting them in one body. Invitations were sent to ninety-seven clubs; sixty-one of them sent representatives from seventeen states, and in this convention the General Federation of Women's Clubs was born, with the motto "Unity in Diversity."

State federations of women's clubs followed—first in Maine, then in Utah and Iowa, and so on—until federations of women's clubs in thirty states were organized within six years and joined in the General Federation of Women's Clubs. The movement continued until it included federations of women's clubs in every one of the United States.

The National Congress of Parents and Teachers

In February, 1897, two thousand mothers in the United States came together in Washington, D.C., and organized the National Congress of Mothers. In 1908 the name was changed

[61]

to the National Congress of Mothers and Parent-Teachers Association, and in 1924, to the National Congress of Parents and Teachers.

It has expanded its membership through the years to include parents of all school children and to all citizens interested in the welfare of children; today it has statewide organizations in fifty states and between forty-five and fifty thousand local units, with eleven to twelve million members.

They are working:

> To promote the welfare of children and youth in home, school, church, and community;
> To raise the standards of home life;
> To secure adequate laws for the care and protection of children and youth;
> To bring into closer relation the home and the school, that parents and teachers may cooperate intelligently in the training of the child;
> To develop between educators and the general public such united efforts as will secure for every child the highest advantages in physical, mental, social, and spiritual education.

The American Association of Junior Leagues

Around the turn of the century Mary Harriman and Nathalie Henderson brought together eighty-five of their New York debutante friends who had "a growing feeling of social responsibility for conditions around us," and organized the Junior League of New York. They went to work on problems at hand and helped form "clubs for boys and societies for wayward girls, transformed settlement houses in the slums into a combination day nursery, men's club, school, gymnasium, and employment bureau, and campaigned resolutely for improved sanitary regulations, better housing, and penal reform."

In the years that followed, members of the New York group moved to other sections of the country and planted the Junior League idea in new surroundings. In 1921, delegates of twenty-four Junior Leagues came together in New York City and organized the Association of Junior Leagues of America.

In 1971 the name was changed to the Association of Junior Leagues, and there are currently eight Leagues in Canada and in Mexico.

Their interests and activities expanded with the depression years of the 1930s, as they saw existing public agencies needed help in handling problems they were facing; they moved in to help them. They expanded again with the coming of World War II, as they joined women's branches of the armed services, took jobs in war industries, manned USO centers for service men and women, and set up nurseries for children of war plant employees. And further expansions of interests and activities have come with the problems of the 1960s and 1970s.

Two hundred twenty-eight Junior Leagues are operating throughout the United States, Canada, and Mexico, with 112,000 individual members, between the ages of 18 and 42, who are ready, willing, and anxious for voluntary participation in community affairs, demonstrating the effectiveness of trained volunteers in starting clinics, hospitals, low cost housing centers, halfway houses, drug abuse prevention centers and environmental councils.

At the end of a predetermined time period, on-going programs which are successful are turned over to other community organizations and local or state government.

The National League of Women Voters is Born

Coming events were casting their shadows before, and victory was in the offing when the National American Woman's Suffrage Association called its Golden Jubilee Convention in March, 1919, saying: "As a fitting memorial to a half century of progress, the National American Woman's Suffrage Association invites the women voters of the 15 full suffrage states to attend this anniversary convention and there to join forces in a League of Women Voters, one of whose objects shall be to speed the suffrage campaign in our own and other countries."

President Carrie Chapman Catt in her convention address proposed "A League of Women Voters to 'finish the fight' and to aid in the reconstruction of the nation." Over a year later, after Tennessee had ratified the 19th amendment and it had become "the law of the land," she issued a call to the women saying: "The vote is won. Seventy-two years the battle for this privilege has been waged, but human affairs with their eternal change move on without pause. Progress is calling to you to make no pause. Act!" The League of Women Voters, she went on to say, should have the "vision to see what is coming and what ought to come, and be five years ahead of the political parties."

The National American Woman Suffrage Association disbanded and the League of Women Voters was born with an expressed purpose to foster education in citizenship, to promote forums and public discussion of civic reforms, and to support needed legislation, . . . to organize citizenship schools to study the principles of government, . . . to conduct correspondence courses on government, . . . to hold "know your Town" study courses, . . . to get out candidate questionnaires, and to hold meetings. When only 50 percent of the eligible citizens voted in the presidential election of 1924, "the League of Women Voters found itself committed to no lesser purpose than to help make the democratic government in the United States a success."

Women's Clubs in North Carolina

Sallie Southall Cotten (1846–1929) was the leading spirit in bringing together at Salem College in Winston-Salem in May, 1902, the Sorosis and Round Table and Embroidery Clubs of Winston-Salem, the Sorosis Club of Wilmington, the Woman's Club of Goldsboro, the Circulating Book Club of Salisbury, and the Alphen Club of Statesville, and in organizing the North Carolina Federation of Women's Clubs.

North Carolina Federation of Women's Clubs

The number of federated clubs grew from seven to 17 by the first regular convention held in Winston-Salem in October, with 29 delegates attending; to 20 by the second convention in Concord, with 440 members; to 29 by the third convention in Goldsboro, with 550 members. It continued to with a membership of 13,000 in 1975.

In 1911, Sallie Southall Cotten summarized the activities of women's organizations in North Carolina in these words:

> The activities of the clubs were almost innumerable and clubs were being organized over the whole State. Clean-up Day, screening foods from flies and dust, getting garbage ordinances passed, the installation of trash cans on the streets, the writing of county histories, the securing and awarding of scholarships, improving conditions in railroad stations, medical inspection in schools, drinking fountains, and other health measures carried to success, play grounds equipped, and so many things done that the retrospect is wonderful and inspiring. Clean-up Day has become now an official function of every self-respecting town. The dust of bygone ages has been removed, sanitation has succeeded where carelessness with food once prospered. Man who thought housekeeping belonged solely to a woman's sphere is becoming himself a good public housekeeper and generally admits he learned it from the women.

The interests and activities of these Women's Clubs expanded and deepened through the years until the North Carolina Federation of Women's Clubs could make this summary report of its activities in 1975:

> ".... There is nothing under the shining sun the Federated Clubwomen of North Carolina cannot achieve if given the task."
> Senator Clyde R. Hoey

In back of Senator Hoey's faith in the clubwomen of North Carolina is over one-half century's work for social betterment at community, county, and state levels. Here are glimpses of the achievements of the North Carolina Federation of Women's Clubs since its establishment at Salem College on May 26, 1902.

The NCFWC joined the General Federation of Women's Clubs in 1902 and was incorporated in 1913. Its motto is "The Union of All for the Good of All." In June, 1957, the NCFWC was hostess to GFWC for its annual convention in Asheville.

In the field of education, the NCFWC inaugurated Traveling Libraries, forerunner of Bookmobiles, and established County Libraries, which led to the North Carolina Library

Commission. It pioneered the movement which grew into the Extension Division of the University of North Carolina. It helped to frame and secure passage of the bill for a state-supported, eight month school term. It has worked since 1914 for better pay for teachers and has supported every effort to expand education from lowest grade to highest institution of learning.

As early as 1908, the Federation started asking for a compulsory school attendance law; in 1923, it began calling for twelve grades in every school. In 1945, with other groups, it formed the United Forces of Education, through which it continues its efforts for better schools. Starting with a nucleus of $250 in 1913, NCFWC raised $60,000 for the Sallie Southall Cotten Loan Fund from which more than 300 young women borrowed for college educations. Interest from invested surplus SSC Loan Funds made it possible to establish in 1956 the NCFWC Scholarship Fund. These two funds were combined in 1965, and loans were discontinued. In 1968, the SSC Scholarship Fund amounted to approximately $80,000, interest from which provided four annual scholarships of $750 each. During the 1968–70 administration the scholarship fund was increased to an invested sum of $100,000 and scholarships were raised to $800 each for four students. In 1971 these were again raised, to $1,000 each for four students. During 1973–75 six girls received $1,250 each for study under SSCS programs.

The work of North Carolina Women's Clubs for Cultural Arts is definitely beyond the scope of this summary. As brief highlights: The Federation publishes books, circulates exhibits, helps perpetuate our state historic sites, in 1926 found the supposedly lost score of the state song, and provides music and art scholarships, trophies, and awards for creative writing.

Since 1967, all districts have sponsored District Arts Festivals, with the first festivals held at UNC-G. In recent years, the festivals have been held at Meredith College and Salem College with contests in Art, Music, Literature, Crafts, Drama and Public Speaking, Sewing, and Scholarship with cash awards of approximately $1,750 from the Art Fund.

NCFWC helped launch the North Carolina Symphony in 1933 and the State Ballet in 1961. It also helped start the North Carolina Art Society in 1924 (the Arts Chairman is an ex-officio member of the Art Society's board), provided a scholarship to the School of Performing Arts, endowed two seats in the John F. Kennedy Cultural Arts Center in honor of two former presidents, and has worked for years to secure better art education programs for public schools.

In efforts for conservation, the NCFWC had an early Department of Forestry, fostered the idea of a state school of forestry, and started use of living Christmas trees, the observance of Arbor Day, and Forestry Week. It served on the North Carolina Beautification Council, and named and fostered the "Model Mile Contest."

In citizenship and legislation, fifty years of ceaseless effort for purposeful participation of women in government are merely touched on by these highlights: with other state organizations NCFWC formed the legislative council (in 1971 the title was changed to Council for Social Legislation). With this council NCFWC helped secure the Australian Ballot for North Carolina, worked for extension of the ballot to Indians of North Carolina, and has had its own "Get Out and Vote" campaign for so long that clubwomen participate almost 100 per cent in all county, state, and national elections.

In the area of health, the NCFWC originated clean-up campaigns and pioneered the demand for medical inspection of drinking fountains, schools, dairies, restaurants. It began the fight against tuberculosis. It pioneered movements to lower infant and maternal mortality and to establish nurseries, inoculation, school lunches, and narcotics control. The NCFWC is continuing work for crippled children and cerebral palsy, mental, and polio patients. It raised the first funds for cancer control.

For welfare, the NCFWC contributed $1,000 and helped establish the Jackson Training School. It helped secure passage of a bill providing for a correctional school for girls and later a Farm Colony for older offenders. It worked twenty years to secure a training school for Negro girls and supported the training school for white boys at Rocky Mount and for Negro boys at Hoffman. NCFWC helped secure a Department of Public Welfare for North Carolina. It conducts programs of work in prisons, camps, county homes. It worked long years for a good child labor law, which was finally put through the Legislature by North Carolina's first woman senator, a State Federation president. Three able clubwomen have served as State Commissioner of Welfare.

In 1922, districts raised funds for furnishing the living room at Samarcand Manor. During 1958–60 approximately $18,000 was raised to beautify the grounds. In 1968, $500 was donated to purchase an altar set to honor the retiring president; and, through the former Helping Hand project, clubwomen continued to befriend the Samarcand students before and after their release. Over $5,000 was contributed toward building a chapel at Women's Prison. Through the Birthday Remembrance program, started in 1946, each child in state correctional schools receives a birthday gift; more than 45,000 have been aided with over 275,000 household articles, at an estimated valuation in excess of $355,000 through the Help-A-Home Project which began in 1954.

Community achievement has been expressed by way of the Community Achievement contest, sponsored since 1954 by the GFWC and the Sears Roebuck Foundation, and currently promoted as the Community Improvement Program. An amazing amount of community improvement along many lines, in cooperation with other civic groups, has been reported by clubs entering the contest. In 1962 Mooresville Women's Club and Junior Civic League were awarded fifth place, winning $1,500 in the National CIP contest. NCFWC has received two $500 awards and two $800 awards for having every club in state entering and reporting activity in CIP.

For peace and freedom, the NCFWC served on the National Council for Defense, maintained a furlough home for American soldiers abroad; turned clubs into Red Cross centers; raised $20,000,000 in stamps and bonds in recognition of which the ship "Sallie S. Cotten" was named for one of the Federation founders. With two other groups, it sold sufficient bonds to build the hospital ship "Larkspur" and aided in the recruiting of women in the Navy, Army and Nursing Corps; helped in rehabilitation of veterans; raised $14,000 for Korean war victims; set up the first international scholarships for students of Russia, France, Greece, Philippines, and Germany; sent the largest collection of any state for relief of Greek children. For many years, NCFWC has sponsored UNICEF Trick-or-Treat.

In the past twelve years, NCFWC contributed more than $14,000 to CARE; contributed funds for building a school in Bolivia, named as a memorial to the late beloved president, Marjorie Yates Yokley.

In 1968–70 the Public Affairs Department and the Citizenship Division have been emphasized. A Citizenship Day was held in Raleigh with more than 1,200 women attending. The purchase and use of U.S. flags are continually encouraged.

Sub-Juniors became per capita dues paying members in 1969.

In keeping with the national concern for environment, in

1970 clubwomen broadened conservation interests beyond beautification projects to pollution controls and land use planning. From the recycling of paper, glass, and metal to the development of parks and recreation and the protection of water, air, and land resources, clubs have rallied their energies. A special state project has been the establishment of a unique 1,371 acre N.C. Zoological Park, with the NCFWC pledge of $30,000.

A $5,000 permanent picnic shelter at the Huntersville campus of Boys' Home is another contribution of the Federation.

In 1971, the NCFWC headquarters was moved for the third time, into a spacious three-room suite in a modern office building. The new facilities have proved more suitable for the printing of Federation materials except the *Clubwoman* magazine. The headquarters staff was expanded to two full-time employees: an Executive Secretary-Editor and an Assistant Treasurer. A part-time Circulation Manager was also hired.

The Southeastern Council of the GFWC, with eleven member states, held its 1971 meeting in Asheville. At the General Federation Convention in 1974 the Southeastern Council was reorganized and North Carolina became a member of Southeastern Council #1, which includes the following states: Virginia, Tennessee, Kentucky, West Virginia, Maryland, and Washington, D.C.

There was much activity on the part of state leaders and club members on behalf of the Resolution on the Status of Women passed by the annual convention in support of ERA in 1971. The amendment was defeated in the 1974 North Carolina General Assembly.

NCFWC adopted in 1972 as a state project Girls' Haven, a home for neglected, underprivileged and homeless girls. The first units are to be built near Asheboro to serve the Piedmont North Carolina area, with other units being built throughout the state when funds are available.

The theme for the 1972–74 administration, "Education for Responsible Leadership," placed emphasis on the importance of leadership in all phases of Federation work. More opportunities were provided for club women to learn about what our Federation is, what it offers to women to enable them to make a more meaningful contribution to their families, their communities, and very specially to themselves. The availability of our NCFWC leadership as speakers and in training sessions to the local club membership is bound to bring increased membership to our organization.

Special emphasis is placed on working with young people through the "Justice for Juveniles" program of the GF, our own Sub-Junior clubs, Girls' Haven and Boys' Home, the state correctional schools, schools for the mentally retarded, and our support and promotion of the N.C. Zoological Gardens, rapidly becoming a reality.

Plans have been initiated for the Federation's part in the observance of the bicentennial celebration of our nation in 1976.

North Carolina Congress of Parents and Teachers

The first recorded forerunner of Parent-Teacher Associations in North Carolina is the Woman's Association for the Betterment of Public School Houses in North Carolina, organized around 1900 by Charles D. McIver, President of the State Normal and Industrial College in Greensboro. Its purpose then was "to unite the women citizens of North Carolina for the purpose of awakening their interest in the improvement of the public school houses of our communities."

In the summer of 1902, ten college girls in the junior and senior classes of that institution volunteered their time to organize local units of the Betterment Association and, during the summer vacation, enrolled 2,000 members in twenty-seven counties. Prizes for improvements were given in pictures, library books and cash. Parents came together to wash schoolhouse windows, beautify school grounds, purchase needed equipment, and assist with other improvements.

Mothers concerned with child welfare were meeting in local groups by the early 1900s in Rich Square, in Stoneville, Asheville, in Leicurter, in Randolph, in Rocky Mount, in Biltmore, in Burlington, in Charlotte. And in 1918 the Charlotte Federation of Parent-Teacher Associations called a meeting of these groups to organize the North Carolina Parent-Teacher Association; as their first act they passed a resolution asking that courses in child nurture be put into all public high schools and colleges in North Carolina and calling for a study of all state and national legislation affecting children.

By the end of the first year, 2,000 members were enrolled

and 40 delegates from 16 cities and towns attended the first convention. In this convention they discussed (1) expansion of housing for students in state schools and colleges, (2) the benefits of summer camps, (3) the benefits of physical culture, (4) increased pay for teachers, (5) the addition of kindergarten to the public school systems, (6) support of the Shepard-Towne bill for infant and maternal care, and (7) support for the Fess-Cooper bill to chart growth and to provide instruction in physical education.

In 1927 they extended their work to include black parents and teachers. Five hundred parents met at Shaw University on April 2, 1927, and organized a black Parent–Teachers Association. Eighteen months later this association included over 15,000 members in local units in 31 counties and 110 cities and towns. And they were on their way, providing black schools with pianos, stoves, maps, sewing machines, and furniture, equipping school auditoriums and offices, and providing kitchens and lunchrooms.

In 1928 they held their first summer institute, lasting ten days, with courses in program making, family problems, modern social problems, and local service programs.

The PTA pamphlet, "This, Too, is Our Heritage," carries the following statement on page 2:

> The National Congress of Colored Parents and Teachers was organized in Atlanta, Georgia, May 7, 1926, with Mrs. Selena Sloan Butler of Georgia as President.
>
> The North Carolina Congress of Colored Parents and Teachers was organized as a branch of the National Colored Congress in Raleigh, N.C., April 2, 1927, with Mrs. Annie W. Holland of Raleigh as President.
>
> On April 22, 1969, the two North Carolina branches [black and white] united as the North Carolina Congress of Parents and Teachers (in Charlotte, N.C.).
>
> On June 22, 1970, in Atlanta, Georgia, the two National Congresses unified and continue as the National Congress of Parents and Teachers.
>
> Both Congresses and all of their branches and member units have, from their beginning, embraced and supported the same objectives, policies and principles. It is a mark of true progress

that, though we have always travelled along the same path toward the same goal, we now travel under the same banner and name.

In the depression year 1933, the North Carolina Parent–Teacher Association, with Mrs. John Henderson as its president, was credited with keeping "the light burning through the darkest night known to public education in the history of North Carolina." A statewide movement was organized to study the emergency in education. It culminated in a statewide meeting which studied the problems facing the schools, including the school curriculum, indebtedness, budgets, teacher load, length of school terms, salaries, administration, transportation, textbooks, and so on.

In the years that followed they multiplied their efforts on all facets of their continuing program, looking toward the welfare of the child for local school supplements, adequate library services, teacher retirement and tenure provisions, effective child labor laws, hot lunches and clothing and medical care for needy children, and vaccination of children against contagious disease.

To these continuing programs they added war work in the 1940s, including Junior Commanders, block mothers, anti-inflation measures, health and safety measures, wartime care of children, volunteer services, blood donations, camp and field hospital services, recreation for service men, refugee garment collections, victory gardens, first-aid courses, cooperation with the Red Cross, the OCO, the OPA and USO, collection of twelve million pounds of scrap metal, and sales of staggering amounts of stamps and bonds.

In 1962 the state convention conducted a symposium on "Current Legislative Needs Affecting North Carolina Children," led by Dr. Ellen Winston, State Commissioner of Public Welfare, and Charles Harper of the N.C. State Board of Health.

An extensive PTA legislative program for 1963–66 was formulated with "action items" and "study items" in the areas of education, safety, and protection and care. The legislative program listed in the Proceedings for 1966–67 the following continuing concerns:

n the field of public education:
1. Active support of the UFE Legislation Program.
2. Public-supported kindergartens for all children.
3. Enrichment and expansion of the program of vocational education.
4. Means for insuring educational opportunities for migrant children while they are in our state.
5. Elimination of existing textbook fees.
6. Improved methods of selecting qualified local school board members.

n the field of public health:
1. Funds for an adequate program to educate the public to the need for dental health, including benefits of water fluoridation.
2. Comprehensive education programs on alcohol, drug addiction, tobacco, and venereal diseases.
3. Strict enforcement of air and stream pollution laws.
4. State programs for education on population (birth) control.

n the field of public safety:
1. Uniform system of bus transportation for all public school children.
2. The reduction and strict enforcement, by law, of the maximum number of children riding in public and private conveyances to and from schools, both private and public, to a number not exceeding the seating capacity of a given vehicle.
3. Elimination by law of the privilege of driving by persons mentally and emotionally unfit to drive.
4. More stringent laws covering the registration, carrying and concealment of firearms.
5. Proper safety equipment and adequate walkways provided by state law for children who walk to school.
6. Provide "No Smoking" signs on state-supported school

[73]

buses—to be painted on the inside.

In the Field of Protection and Care:

1. Enforcement of sanitary and health laws for migrant families.
2. Better state and local programs for the prevention, control, and treatment of juvenile delinquency.
3. Encourage adequate appropriations for the Aid to Dependent Children program.
4. Stricter laws dealing with sex offenders.

Its activities through the years have included pre-natal instruction for mothers, putting child hygiene clinics in every State Board of Health, reducing infant mortality, supporting physical education in the public schools, sponsoring local hot lunch projects as early as 1912 and starting a school lunch program on a national basis in 1941, starting the summer roundup of children in 1925 to examine the health of children and correct their defects, winning in 1957 the Award for "unprecedented participation in the historic development of measures against paralytic polio and for outstanding volunteer leadership in achieving record acceptance of the Salk vaccine," educating youth in the hazards of smoking, strengthening programs for the prevention of venereal disease, investigating conditions of child employment, working for the passage of a fireworks bill, urging schools for the deaf, sponsoring the Books for Appalachia project in 1965, sending books to teacher-training institutions overseas, urging that kindergarten programs be made part of the public school system as early as 1911, studying the needs of exceptional children, promoting reading groups and library facilities for parent education, supporting academic freedom and legislation for better schools and teachers, and so on.

In an effort to increase awareness of adolescents' need to be educated for parenthood and family living, the [North Carolina] PTA, in cooperation with the National Foundation-March of Dimes, is holding a series of parenting conferences in various parts of the state.

This series of conferences on "parenting" is designed to identify and promote family life education within school, family, and community settings as an effective means for strengthening the individual's quality of life in the kind of society now developing.

Broadly, the concept of "parenting" comprehends knowledge of the life processes and the skills of child development that adolescents should acquire in preparing for parenthood. Education in this most basic of human responsibilities can contribute measurably to the improved health of mother, fetus and newborn, thus advancing the prevention of birth defects.

Priority on development and expansion of the "parenting" concept will encourage true value judgments and critical decision making by young people about their own lives and the lives of their children, early enough to make a difference.

A public awareness program has been launched to inform the public, especially the Boards of Education, school personnel, and parents, through personal contact, the news media, civic groups, and cooperating agencies of the need for information about and preparation for family life education in grades K-12.

The North Carolina Junior Federation of Women's Clubs

The Junior Federation of Women's Clubs in North Carolina started as an outgrowth of the North Carolina Federation of Women's Clubs in 1927. By 1941, there were 66 Junior Women's Clubs in North Carolina, with 2,100 members, and in 1975 they were paralleling their parent sponsors in most, if not all, communities in the state.

For years NCJFWC worked hand in glove with its parent organization. By the 1940s it was looking for projects of its own—"Our state project this year," said the President's Report in the 1940s, "has been to sponsor a bicycle campaign to teach bicycle rules and help to prevent accidents." Sixty Junior Clubs took an active part in the campaign, organizing bicycle clubs, writing safety editorials and sponsoring safety contests.

"Sixty-five per cent of our club work," says the Junior Federation President, "has been in child welfare, such as sponsoring clinics of all kinds, furnishing lunches and teachers for underprivileged children, equipping playgrounds, aiding illiterate youths, and starting libraries. Outstanding work has been done in Indian welfare, American citizenship and aiding the Red Cross."

Here are illustrative activities of the North Carolina Junior Federation of Women's Clubs since its beginning:

They threw their weight behind the Children's Home in Greensboro, assisted fund drives and gave donations to support it, gave it clerical assistance, contributed clothing and met other needs, distributed literature, transported hundreds of children from the places of their birth to the central Greensboro Home, and provided a scholarship for a Children's Home caseworker to attend the UNC School of Social Studies. In one year, Junior Club Women gave 108,274 garments, worked 6,191 hours, donated $1,318.96 for clothes and shoes, and assisted 18,662 persons; many clubs gave bridge benefits, barn dances, pancake suppers, and sold candy and nuts to raise more money to expand these activities.

They adopted Caswell Training School in Kinston as a statewide project. They saw a child dragging a string across the floor, for lack of toys to play with, and Junior Clubwomen responded to this need in one year by sending 116 packages of used toys and games and donating $1,840 in cash—using the money to buy two dozen large pieces of outdoor equipment and materials for arts and crafts.

Through the years, these clubs have met many needs, such as furnishing a chapel and providing beauty parlor equipment for older girls. They financed the production of "The Caswell Story," a movie about Caswell that is still in use, showing the work and needs of Caswell so as to further understanding of its problems.

In one year Junior Clubwomen spent 1,411 hours on Caswell projects, gave 37 parties and dances at Caswell, served 1,976 residents, sent gifts and favors valued at $514.56, sent material donations valued at $18,522, donated $817 in money, and adopted 104 children to remember on birthdays and holidays with gifts, cards, and parties.

The Junior Federation of Woman's Clubs has added Murdoch and Western Carolina Centers—state-supported training schools for the mentally-retarded—to their special project list. With the children of the state divided among the various schools, it has become the policy of each club to aid the school to which the children in its area are sent. In 1964, cash donations of clothing, toys, books, games, favors, and radios with a total value of $2,232 were sent to Murdoch. Ten Junior Clubs gave $970.50 to Western Carolina Center to be used for playground equipment and play mats. Material donations, valued at $2,105, included clothes, toys, books, a record player, Christmas tree decorations, Christmas gifts, school supplies and items for the school "canteen," the Gold Door.

For many years the North Carolina Junior Federation of Women's Clubs has saved stamps for wounded veterans; this was started as a General Federation project to assist in the rehabilitation of wounded veterans. And always there is the reminder, "Leave the postmark, as it may mean home to the patient who receives it." In one year North Carolina Junior Clubwomen, with the assistance of nine Woman's Clubs, contributed 123,157 stamps and $62.46.

Reports show that 103 clubs participated in the School Drop-Out Program. Many clubs set up committees to study the situation and work on solutions. Investigations of the causes of "drop-outs" have shown that proper clothing and a hot meal may keep a child in school. Many clubs have helped in this way. Remedial reading classes, kindergartens for underprivileged children, free lunches and milk, shoe closets, summer school tuitions, and "little-sister" programs are some of the ways Juniors have attempted to help solve the "dropout" problem.

Junior Clubwomen report paying special teachers to support summer reading programs and kindergartens. Forty NCJFWC clubs worked with special education classes, and the state mental institutions received 346 contributions from clubs.

Local scholarships were given by clubs to 158 individuals, ranging from $1,585 for four scholarships to $25 for one.

Junior clubs alone gave over $11,000 in scholarships for teachers and children.

Thirteen Junior Clubs have held school art, music, or crafts classes regularly. One club cooperated with other groups to hire a public school music teacher. Charlotte Juniors helped the Charlotte Symphony ticket drive so successfully they had a sold-out house for the first time. Two clubs dressed 500 dolls for needy children and 14 clubs conducted crafts workshops for children.

HOPE was an outstanding project for the Juniors, who reported sending $346 and many toys, gowns, and other articles.

Junior Clubwomen have worked with the Children's Home Society, scouts, various teen-age groups, Federated Sub-Juniors, Candy Stripers, the Summer Fitness Program for girls age 10 to 14, well-baby clinics, day-care centers, Boys' Home, local orphanages and homes for children, crippled children's clinics, children's heart clinics, and physically and mentally handicapped children through Caswell, Murdoch, Western Carolina, the special education classes in local schools, and summer camp projects. Summer reading programs and story hours were conducted. To aid underprivileged children, they maintained Clothing Closets, participated in Birthday Remembrance and Helping Hand, dressed dolls, developed a toyshop project, "adopted" children in local foster homes, had parties for needy children and orphans at Christmas, and encouraged the creative talents of children through arts and crafts exhibits and classes, concerts by the N.C. Symphony, "cherub" choirs, and theater groups.

Recognizing the home as the most important element of our society, Juniors improved their homemaking abilities through programs and workshops on family living (in America and other countries), cooking, home decorating, consumer trends, home management, and finances. Family togetherness was stressed through worship. Clubs had religious programs and club members are active in their own religions. Juniors worked to improve the homes of their community through participation in Help-a-Home, community health clinics and fund drives, and work with senior citizens.

To prepare teen-age girls for later club work and to give them a part in meeting their communities' needs, the Federation organized a Sub-Junior division. In 1964 there were 13 Sub-Junior clubs in North Carolina with a total membership of 386. The girls have their own State Jamboree with workshops on programs, projects, publicity, and ways and means. Their report indicates the valuable contribution they are making: baby sitting with handicapped children, volunteer work for a mentally retarded children's day camp, making pocket books for Caswell and Murdoch, assisting in rest homes, dressing dolls for needy children, helping needy families, visiting orphanages and carrying the children skating, making tray cards for hospital patients, and assisting with blood banks. Many of their projects show their appreciation for education, as several clubs gave scholarships and others contributed to school furnishings and beautification. To support their projects, they made money by selling candy, Christmas wrapping paper, cakes, and fire extinguishers, and by holding dances, benefit bridge parties, teen-age carnivals, and fashion shows.

The North Carolina Association of Junior Leagues

The chairman of Area Council III of the Association of Junior Leagues has written this "brief overview of the Junior Leagues in North Carolina and their recent projects":

The 228 [national total] Junior Leagues are geographically divided into six Areas, each with an elected Area Council whose function it is to assist the Leagues in the facilitation of their programs by identifying and developing resources, improving communications, and offering training workshops and seminars. Area III, of which I am chairman, includes North and South Carolina, Tennessee, Georgia and Florida. Each of these Leagues is autonomous but all seek to plan and implement outstanding projects to serve their communities and, most importantly, to *train* their members.

There are Junior Leagues in Asheville, Charlotte,

Greensboro, Winston-Salem, High Point, Wilmington, Durham, and Raleigh.

The Asheville League's big accomplishments have been establishing Camp Loquastee for children with learning disabilities, and a Children's Zoo and Nature Center. It also worked with the United Fund to expand the Volunteer Service Bureau into a 24-hour Information and Referral Service.

The Charlotte League served as a catalyst to initiate the local Voluntary Action Center; it also began the Drug Education Center and the Speech and Hearing Center. Their professionals (those members gainfully employed) work with juveniles in the Youth Services Bureau.

The Greensboro League sponsored *Gateways,* an on-going project of community study and goals, for citizen participation in effecting future courses of action. Its members are also involved in Youth Care, Inc., providing temporary, emergency shelter for troubled children. Its Public Affairs Committee concentrated this year on improving North Carolina services and educational opportunities for children with special needs.

The Winston–Salem League hosted a Grantsmanship Center Workshop and subsequently published a guide to local funding information. It helped establish a home for severely retarded children, Horizons, Inc. Another recent project involves teacher training and testing and tutoring learning disabled children.

The Junior League of High Point was involved in establishing a local Environmental Center, and in a restoration and docent program at Haley House, a local historic structure. Their "Volunteers to Court" program provides a one-to-one relationship between Junior League volunteers and misdemeanants.

The Wilmington Junior League compiled and published a *Study of Female Juvenile Delinquency in New Hanover County* and established a group care home as a result of its findings. It is also developing a historical and architectural guide to the city.

Activities of the Junior League of Durham include a Volunteer Services Bureau, Community Planning Services, and Community Arts.

The Raleigh League pays the salary of a full-time legal aid attorney. It also began Haven House—a unique concept of small group homes for temporary care of troubled youth—last spring; it sponsored speakers at the North Carolina Association of Children with Learning Disabilities.

The only kind of statewide organization which the North

Carolina Leagues have is the State Public Affairs Committee. This committee is organized to provide communication and education between Leagues in the state, to evaluate studies of individual Leagues, and to initiate studies of its own.

The Chairman of the North Carolina State Public Affairs Committee of the Junior Leagues of North Carolina writes:

The North Carolina SPAC was organized on January 13, 1972. It was the result of the eight Leagues' growing awareness and interest in Public Affairs and their need to communicate and learn from each other in the Public Affairs area.

The first SPAC meetings became mainly arenas for an exchange of ideas on projects rather than strictly Public Affairs forums. However the delegates felt that SPAC should be more than an organization of communication and education.

Under Association Policy any League acting in its own name had to get permission to take a public stand from the other Leagues in the state. The 1973 SPAC wrote and all eight Leagues passed a waiver which granted permission for any of the Leagues in North Carolina to act in its own name without receiving prior release from the other Leagues.

It was also in 1973 that the eight Leagues joined together for the first and thus far only time to take a united stand on an issue. Spearheaded by the Junior League of Charlotte's research and activity the eight Leagues endorsed Legislation which would establish a Public Kindergarten System in the state. Each League lobbied for passage of the Legislation. Local legislators were written to, talked with and wined and dined. The culmination of the effort was the passage of the legislation.

In 1974 the Purpose, Policies and Procedures were developed by the Committee in an effort to continue to define the activities of SPAC.

The committee chose legislation pertaining to children as its study item and masses of research reports were generated. Greensboro was joined by Winston-Salem and Charlotte in supporting the funding of positions in Early Childhood screening and special education teachers in the schools. The Asheville League supported bills in the area of Juvenile Justice.

This year SPAC has chosen Child Advocacy as its study item. On October 1st there will be an all day seminar at the Institute of Government. The morning will be spent on legislative process and the afternoon will stress legislation pertaining to areas of Child Advocacy, Daycare, Child Abuse and Neglect, and Early Childhood Screening.

It is the hope of this year's committee to zero in on one or two areas of child advocacy so that we can research them well and be prepared to take action where necessary when the legislature is in session again.

On the Association level, Public Affairs as an integral part of League program has come of age. The Association has chosen Child Advocacy as its area of concern. We are voted to become advocates—to take a stand.

The Association has turned Public Affairs back to the Leagues. No longer will the Director-at-Large have to oversee a League's Public Affairs activities. The waiver is no longer necessary since association policy now provides that each League may take a stand on state and local issues in its own name without the permission of other Leagues in the state.

Public Affairs has come a long way from the days when Leagues shunned publicity and wanted to keep a very low profile in the public arena. Leagues still go through the long and thorough process of study and research, education and finally action. Leagues still are bound by the tenet that Public Affairs activities be germane to total League program, but they move into the area of Public Affairs with more confidence and assurance because of the growth in knowledge of the area through SPAC.

The Garden Club of North Carolina

Garden Clubs were organizing in localities throughout North Carolina before the 1900s. Individual women were trying to beautify the surroundings of their own homes, and this led to the efforts to beautify their neighborhoods, and then to beautify their communities.

On November 6, 1925, representatives from garden clubs in Asheville, High Point, Raleigh, Reidsville, and Winston-Salem met in Winston-Salem and organized the Garden Club of North Carolina. This state-wide organization now includes 800 local garden clubs with 18,000 members.

Mrs. Roy McMillan, a former President of the Garden Club of North Carolina, had this to say about its aims and purposes:

Perhaps a careful study of the plan and program of the Garden Club of North Carolina from its organization will reveal one characteristic that belongs both to the Club and to the state it represents—a silent but strong determination, little by little, to have this North Carolina that we love so much become the marvel that labor and love might make it. In our hearts we set no limits to what we think North Carolina might be. Formally and publicly we subscribe to our motto *Esse Quam Videri;* but what I should like to write upon the portals of our state is the inscription from *The Faerie Queen:* 'All that in this delightful gardin growes, Should happie be, and have mortal bliss.'

In the foreword to a brochure on the history of 34 years of club activity, issued in 1959, W. C. Coker, then chairman of the botany department of the University of North Carolina at Chapel Hill, wrote these words:

The pleasure I take in writing a few words for this publication is found in the opportunity it gives me to express to the garden lovers of the state my conviction that they are the prophets of a distinct improvement in the appearance and well-being of our state. It is humiliating to admit that in the past man has done little to preserve and much to destroy the wonderful dignity and beauty of the earth. Your work is a sign that we are beginning now to see that man and nature are one—that man is a part of nature. We cannot sit among ugly and sordid things and grow in either grace or power. From slow incubations through the infinite past man has been molded and lifted and guided by the forces that operate in this world to make it what it is. Every worthy impulse, every higher inspiration, has been instilled into man from something without that touched his spirit through unseen sources.

I have known some mean and selfish people, but among them I never knew one who could enjoy deeply any part of the manifold pageantry of nature—not one who must make a garden and enter into communion with it. But the relation is reciprocal. "We are a part of all we have met," and I must believe that if every child could see around it something of real beauty every day, there would be fewer cramped and sordid souls.

You remember Hawthorne's story of "The Great Stone Face": When only a boy, Ernest saw it there on the mountain, the wonderful lineaments of a divine face, carved from the living rock by the hand of God. It was with him day by day. His mind took it in; his soul absorbed it; his tentacles of love and faith went forth and touched it. He rose to meet it—until at last

[83]

he stood transfigured, grown into the likeness of that majestic face.

The Garden Club of North Carolina can and will develop a consistent policy; a more and more scientific and therefore intelligent attitude toward living things; the encouragement of experiment and plant breeding; the exchange of ideas and materials among members; the *habit of recording and preserving observations and experiences;* the p.omotion far beyond their own circles of an interest in and preservation of all natural beauty. They will become a great factor in the improvement of the farms and the roadsides.

The Garden Club of North Carolina provides a clearing house for the inter-change of local clubs and stimulates their activities by working through committees on: Awards, Beautification, Birds, Botanical Garden (Daniel Boone), Blue Star Memorial Highway, Club Programs, Club Sales, Club Yearbooks, Conservation, Conventions, Crocus Planting, Dogwood and Crape Myrtle Planting, Elizabethan Garden, Engagement Calendar, Finance, Flower Show Consultant, Flower Show for State, Flower Show Schools, Fragrance Garden, Garden Centers, Garden Councils, Garden Therapy, Gardening for the Blind, Headquarters, High School Gardeners, Historian, Home and Garden Tours, Horticulture, Junior Gardening, Landscape Design, Landscape Design School, Legislative, Life Membership, Litterbug, Membership, Memorial Gardens, Memorials, Model Mile, National Council Books, National Council Projects, National Gardener, Nominating, Organization Study, Personnel, Projects, *The N.C. Gardener,* Radio and Television, Restoration, Roadside Development, State Judges' Council, Tryon Palace Commission, Visiting Gardens, and World Gardening.

One of the early projects of the state club was the publication of a book on wild flowers of North Carolina. The group commissioned Dr. B. W. Welles, Botanist, to write the book, and arranged for sales. Tree schools were inaugurated and the bi-monthly magazine, *The North Carolina Gardener,* went to press as successor to the Yearbook.

In 1933 the Garden Club of North Carolina began its concentration on highway beautification, a concern that has developed into a life-long concern of the Garden Club. The president from 1933–35 reported on the progress being made at that time:

> The beautification and improvement of roadsides has been accomplished through conferences and co-operation with the State Highway Commissioner. All groups confer with the Division Engineer in planning their work, following a booklet issued by them last year. Federal funds allotted for the purpose employed a landscape architect to assist the engineering forces in planting for beauty and better maintenance of roadsides.

Wayside tables and parks have been part of the Garden Club's beautification program, and in 1949 the Garden Club prepared a set of resolutions which the president took to the Board of Conservation. Garden Club members joined the Board in seeking from the General Assembly the ordinances and funds that would enable the Highway Commission to secure and develop the land for this purpose.

The Garden Club realized early in its efforts that roadside improvement could be achieved only if those who lived and worked along the road were enthusiastic too. In a report made in 1942, it was stated, "A real program for roadside development cannot succeed until more people than Garden Club members enter actively into it. It needs, particularly, the people who live along the highways. We should ask Home Demonstration Clubs and men's clubs to join with us in such undertakings."

Another outstanding Garden Club project for the beautification of highways is the Blue Star Memorial Highway program, which the Garden Club began in 1945. Getting the legislature to designate highways 301 and 64 was the first step, followed by the erection of markers and then planting and beautifying the area around each marker. This program was carried out in memory of those who served in World War II, and was a national project, designed to link the country through a living memorial of inter-state highways.

Memorial gardens represent the Garden Club's efforts through many years to adorn North Carolina with a special crowning glory. The first of these, the Maude Moore Latham

Memorial Garden at Tryon Palace, is the result of the vision of one woman and the enthusiasm of another.

In 1937, the Garden Club of North Carolina expanded its work to include the restoration of old homes and gardens, and appointed a Restoration Committee. This committee published two books, *Old Houses and Gardens in North Carolina,* and *Cradle of North Carolina,* a brochure on New Bern. After the publication of this book, Mrs. Maude Moore Latham announced a gift of $100,000 toward the restoration of Tryon Palace.

In 1945 Garden Club members used all their influence to get the General Assembly to appropriate $150,000 for the purchase of land on the original site of the Palace. In 1949 Mrs. Latham set up a second trust fund of $150,000 for the restoration, and in 1950 she presented to the state antiques valued at $125,000. Upon her death in 1951 she bequeathed to the restoration the residue of her estate, then valued at more than one and a quarter million dollars.

The Garden Club of North Carolina worked with the Tryon Palace Commission, appointed in 1945 by Governor Cherry. In 1958 it gave to the Commission the money it had been collecting, $9,022, to build a memorial garden to Mrs. Latham.

The Elizabethan Garden

In 1949–50, Mrs. Charles Cannon of Concord, Mrs. Inglis Fletcher of Edenton, Sir Evelyn Wrench, head of the English Speaking Union, and Lady Wrench were visiting Fort Raleigh and *The Lost Colony* drama on Roanoke Island. The idea came to them to ask the Garden Club of North Carolina to sponsor a two-acre garden on a ten-acre tract adjoining Fort Raleigh National Park. It was their thinking that the creation of a cultural attraction such as a garden would enhance the value of this area as a permanent memorial.

The matter was presented to the Garden Club at the annual meeting in Wrightsville Beach in 1951, at which time the state organization voted to build such a garden on property leased for ninety-nine years from the Roanoke Island Historical Association....

Daniel Boone Native Garden

In March, 1957, at a flower show school in Hickory, H. Stuart Ortloff, nationally known landscape architect, opined upon the difficulty of studying native plant material due to its inaccessibility and recommended that a small area near a school with a botany department, easily accessible to the traveling public, be set aside for such purpose. This was the suggestion that "caught on" and led to the creation of the Daniel Boone Native Garden in the Blue Ridge mountains at Boone near Appalachian State University. The Garden was adopted as a project of the Garden Club of North Carolina at the 1959 Convention in Greensboro and was to be a plant sanctuary containing a wide collection of North Carolina native plant material, landscaped and labeled for education and conservation purposes. . . .

The Martha Franck Fragrance Garden

In the 1950s, Martha Franck saw in front of the new Rehabilitation Center for the Blind in Butner one acre of ground which was filled with the debris of several large army barracks that had been razed at the end of World War II. In wet weather, it was a sea of red mud dotted with rows of three-foot white cement columns left from the foundation of the barracks. She visualized it as a Garden for the Blind—designed for the teaching and the pleasure of the blind as an "outdoor living room" with six brick flower planters three feet wide, sixteen to eighteen feet long, and raised to a height of three feet so that the plants were in easy reach of the blind students. These six planters were originally planted and maintained by six garden clubs in Durham. In the center a round planter was built with a flag pole located therein to fly the national and state flags. The planters were filled with flowers and herbs of interesting texture and delightful fragrance. Approximately five hundred trees and shrubs were interspersed throughout with the entire Garden enclosed with an abelia hedge.

In 1960, it was adopted as a project of the Garden Club of North Carolina and called The Martha Franck Fragrance Garden.

Brunswick Town Nature Trail

Three garden clubs in Southport—the Southport Garden Club, Woodbine and Live Oak Garden Clubs—visited the North Carolina historical site of Brunswick Town and saw in this natural, low terrain a spring-fed pond which was rich in indigenous flora and fauna. They realized the unique possibilities of building a rustic nature trail where plant life and wild life could be identified and displayed for education and enjoyment, but the undertaking of clearing the pond, developing the trail, erecting interpretative signs and maintenance proved to be more than the local clubs could handle physically and financially.

At the Annual Meeting in Charlotte in April, 1963, the Garden Club of North Carolina voted to establish and develop a winding Nature Trail at Brunswick Town on the banks of the Lower Cape Fear River in Brunswick County amid the ruins of a colonial settlement and a Civil War earthworks fort as a joint project with the State Department of Archives and History.

The North Carolina League of Women Voters

The North Carolina League of Women Voters was organized in Greensboro in 1920 to follow up the work of the North Carolina Woman Suffrage Association. It was affiliated with the National League of Women Voters from 1920 to 1937, when it disbanded. Interest was renewed in 1943 and an "Interim Organization" was formed.

By April, 1950, seven local North Carolina Leagues had been organized: Asheville, Chapel Hill, Charlotte, Durham, Greensboro, Raleigh, and Winston-Salem. These Leagues met in convention in April, 1951, and were recognized by the national board as the North Carolina League of Women Voters.

1951–52: The first agenda of the reorganized League called for a consideration of the administrative organization of state government in North Carolina—with a view toward attaining improved efficiency and economy.

This continued a study already begun by local Leagues and built on a handbook of state government prepared by a small committee to guide the local Leagues in their study.

1952–54: The second agenda said: The League of Women Voters of North Carolina will work for increased efficiency and economy of state administrative agencies with emphasis on the penal system.

In 1953 the League testified in the General Assembly in favor of a bill to separate the prisons from the Highway Department.

1954–56: The League (1) called for meetings of governing bodies during the consideration of public business, (2) called for detailed study of the Constitution of North Carolina, and

(3) testified before the Commission on Legislative Representation on the inequities arising from the failure of the General Assembly to comply with the reapportionment mandate.

1956–58: The League worked toward a revision of the Constitution of North Carolina so as to provide (1) equitable representation in the General Assembly, (2) a more effective judicial system.
It testified in the General Assembly in support of a bill calling for compliance with constitutional provisions on reapportionment, and testified again in support of a bill separating the prisons from the State Highway and Public Works Commission—which passed in 1957.

1958–60: The League testified in favor of (1) the State Bar Association bill proposing a uniform and unified court system and a compromise bill evolved in General Assembly discussions, (2) a proposal to create a State Department of Water Resources which would combine and reorganize existing agencies, and (3) a bill to create watershed improvement districts.
It called for a study of sources of revenues in the tax structure of North Carolina, continued its support of reapportionment of seats in the General Assembly after each census, and kept its eye on changes in the prison system.

1960–62: The League (1) continued its study and evaluation of specific taxes and the need for new tax sources, (2) supported a bill to create a statewide system of lower courts and provide North Carolina with a unified court structure—the bill was passed and a constitutional amendment affirmed by the people in 1962, (3) supported a bill reapportioning House of Representatives seats according to the 1960 census—which was passed, (4) supported a bill calling for automatic reapportionment by the Speaker if the House failed to reapportion, (5) supported a bill calling for redistricting the Senate.

1962–64: The League (1) called for a study of state election laws and procedures, (2) supported a bill requiring a sworn application for an absentee ballot either in person or by mail—it passed, (3) called for a uniform statewide system of continuous permanent registration and loose-leaf record keeping, signature comparison at the polls for voter identification, adequate purgation methods, improved methods of soliciting and training election officials, and enforcement of absentee ballot laws which preserve and extend absentee voting and eliminate irregular practices.

It continued its support of measures to establish a unified and uniform court system, and testified before the Court Commission in support of an Administrative Office of the Courts with a director responsible to the Chief Justice of the Supreme Court.

It continued its support of measures to promote equitable representation in the General Assembly, took a position against the "little Federal" plan of redistricting and cooperated with other citizen committees in organizing a statewide campaign to defeat it in 1964.

1964–65: The League (1) called for a study of election laws, including voter qualifications (age, literacy, and residence requirements), and a follow-up on the new absentee voting law as it is locally administered, (2) supported the lowering of residence requirements for presidential elections from one year to between thirty days and six months, (3) undertook a study and evaluation of the "Speaker Ban" Law, and took a position opposing "legislation which regulates visiting speakers at state-supported colleges and universities," and supporting "academic freedom as essential to a firm foundation for our educational system."

It continued its support of a "unified and uniform court system" and "equitable representation in the General Assembly."

1965–67: The League (1) called for a continued study of state election laws with emphasis on administration and support of those measures which would promote, extend, and encourage use of the elective franchise, and actively supported laws in the General Assembly to that end—several were passed in the 1967 session, (2) continued to support in the General Assembly measures to establish a unified and uniform court system, including an intermediate Court of Appeals, (3) continued to oppose "legislation which regulates visiting speakers at state supported colleges and universities," and testified in the General Assembly against it.

1967–69: The League (1) called for a study of the North Carolina education system through the secondary level, including historical background, administrative structure, sources of revenue and their allocation, and present and future needs, (2) continued its support for election law changes and for a "unified and uniform court system," (3) continued to oppose speaker-ban laws, and (4) testified in the General Assembly in support of eight bills which would give the North Carolina Board of Water Resources the power to accomplish its purposes.

1975–77: The state program for 1975–77 calls for a study of:

I. Criminal Justice
  A. Courts
    1. Support of measures to provide for adequately trained and paid judiciary.
    2. Reassessment of the merit selection system.
  B. Juvenile Justice
    1. Support of mandatory procedural guidelines pertaining to juveniles
    2. Support of mandatory special training for all law enforcement, court, and corrections personnel handling juveniles
    3. Support of community alternatives to incarceration in state training schools and local jails
    4. Opposition to agency fragmentation of services for juveniles
    5. Support of juvenile services free of political consideration.
  C. A continued study of criminal justice with emphasis on the adult.
II. Education
  Support of measures to provide sufficient financing for broadened instructional programs with adequately trained and paid personnel, improved administrative procedures

and fuller use of school facilities and equipment in N.C. education system throughout the secondary level.

III. Election Laws
Support of those measures which safeguard the rights of the voter and encourage clear and democratic election procedures.

IV. Land Use
Support of land use policies of statewide and regional application which would effectively guide development to meet human needs and which would effectively conserve resources and protect the natural environment.

V. Property Tax—Continued support of measures which will provide a current and equitable basis for tax assessments including land value vs. improvement taxation; allow limited use of special tax measures for human needs.

VI. Taxes
A study of the tax system of North Carolina.

Current activities of the North Carolina League of Women Voters included the following year-round citizen information services: providing information on government structure and services; a telephone service; manning "walk-in" offices; publishing information booklets ("Know Your" town, city, county, area, *et al.*); flyers or TV shows that help citizens find out how to get food stamps, where to apply for a driver's license, how to get trash collected—the gamut of citizen needs.

Conducting courses and seminars for citizens: how to run for political office; learning about government structure; practical politics; how to testify; whatever aspects of citizenship are of interest to your League and your community.

Working to improve election administration by monitoring registration and elections.

Seeing—and providing—improved training of election workers.

Working with selected groups to inform them about the workings of government; designing government and politics courses for young students, naturalized citizens; publishing or

[92]

broadcasting information in other languages for non-English speaking citizens.

Offering unbiased pro and con presentation on various subjects: this can be part of the services of a speakers bureau. In most cases, issues on which the League has positions are not appropriate for this type of pro/con presentation because once the League takes a stand on an issue it should work to advocate that stand and gain acceptance of its position.

Acting as a catalyst to bring "opposing forces" together in the community to discuss issues (e.g., holding town meetings).

Having an active observer corps that keeps abreast of developments at various commissions, boards, etc., and gets this information to members and the public.

Current activities also include the following services to voters during elections: sponsoring candidates meetings and interviews. Besides encouraging members and the public to participate in these meetings, many Leagues get radio and TV coverage for these events to reach a wider audience.

Publishing voters guides/candidates questionnaires. In addition to publishing in English, many Leagues publish foreign language editions to meet the needs of non-English speaking citizens. Several Leagues have been successful in having local newspapers print their guide or questionnaire in pre-election editions of the paper as well as getting the newspaper to run extra copies for members to distribute throughout the community.

Making available registration and voting information. In many communities the League of Woman Voters is often the best source for up-to-date information on registration and voting procedures. Some Leagues publish information in easy-to-read brochures distributed to citizens through libraries, community centers, Welcome Wagon, Newcomers Clubs, citizens associations and business outlets—wherever people can be reached. In addition, many Leagues maintain a pre-election telephone service to give this information to callers. TV and radio spots have also been produced by Leagues for this purpose.

Having members serve as deputy registrars and poll watchers.

Organizing community efforts to provide transportation for citizens to and from registration and polling places.

Designing "get out the vote" campaigns—slogans, buttons, banners, balloons, bumper stickers—all manner of eye-catching and attention-getting techniques are used by Leagues.

Voters guides/candidate questionnaires and meetings: In all voters' service, the board will want to keep in mind that all candidates for an office (whether of major or minor parties or independent) should be treated alike. When putting together a guide or questionnaire or getting ready for a candidates meeting, the League should invite all candidates certified to appear on the ballot to participate.

Women's Clubs in Raleigh

Background

In the aftermath of Civil War, an incident occurred in the city of Raleigh which is inspiring to me as I read about it now—over one hundred years later.

In 1866, women in Raleigh came together and organized the Ladies Memorial Association to locate and collect the bodies of their soldier fathers, brothers, sons, and kinsmen who "lay on a hundred battlefields, or who were scattered in cemeteries ruddy laid out near hospitals or on the site of former camps, in many cases exposed to desecration.....," and to bring them home.

They persuaded owners to give them land for a cemetery to which their loved ones could be brought. They raised money "in every way, by gifts, by work of members who had organized a sewing society, and finally by a bazaar held just before Christmas in 1866, where nearly $1200 was realized."

They gathered their dead, made new graves, catalogued the

identity of each burial, got new caskets, and held the first Memorial Day for their Confederate dead. Federal officers stood guard, warned against having any procession, and threatened to shoot on sight if one were formed. But they proceeded despite the warning, and this description was written: "On this day there were no exercises of any kind, not even a prayer, and it demanded some courage and some independence from those who walked under the dripping skies through the ankle deep mud of the country."

The Ladies Memorial Association did not stop their efforts with graveside services—through their efforts the Soldier's Home was erected to care for disabled veterans, a confederate monument was erected on the Capital Square in their honor, and they worked in and out of the legislature in the interest of the old soldiers until their efforts were merged in later years with the United Daughters of the Confederacy. They had demonstrated the capacity of women to organize, plan, and carry through a great and difficult undertaking.

In the early 1900s Rudyard Kipling described the American man as one who "turns a keen, untroubled face home to the instant need of things." On the record I submit that the activities of the Ladies Memorial Association of the city of Raleigh, and the women's organizations of Raleigh from the early 1900s to this day, establish with all the stinging freshness of demonstrated truth the fact that Kipling's description of the American man is just as true of the American woman. For in the latter 1800s coming events were casting their shadows before. Let me illustrate my meaning with five of the clubs in the city of Raleigh, and there are many, many, more.

The Woman's Club of Raleigh

Woman's organizations were sprouting in Raleigh in the later 1800s. There was the Johnsonian Book Club in 1895, the Olla Podrida Club in 1899, the Tuesday Afternoon Book Club of Women "with a yen to study Shakespeare"—flavored, according to the minutes of an early meeting, with a "second helping of Mrs. McNeil's famous tipsy cake served from her wonderful old cut glass compote."

The Woman's Club of Raleigh was organized in 1904, with 106 charter members, and with interests going beyond the normal "literary" and "cultural" activities of other clubs to include community service activities, growing with the years. To illustrate:

—It started the first free milk fund in Raleigh and Wake County,
—The first baby clinic,
—Gave free school lunches for needy children,
—Began tuberculin seal sales and established a clinic to detect the illness in its beginning stages,
—Promoted establishment of county health departments and secured the first public health nurse,
—Instigated a system of milk inspection,
—Sponsored the organization of the Raleigh Garden Club, the Junior Woman's Club and the Cerebral Palsy Center,
—Helped establish Samarcand and a Juvenile Court,
—Established and maintained the Carolina Art Sales Gallery where artists can display and sell their paintings and organized the North Carolina Literary Forum where artists can discuss their writings,
—Organized the Women's Wake County Civil Defense Council,
—Helped start a city craft center and establish craft centers at the Salvation Army Hospital at Lowes Grove,
—Held weekly Bible studies at Woman's Prison and gave $1,000 to help build a chapel on the grounds,
—Helped organize the Dorothea Dix Hospital Guild,
—Helped furnish Wake County Juvenile Detention Home and gave $1,000 for a new kitchen,
—Sponsored a bill banning crime comic books,
—Supported legislation providing for a driver training program in schools,
—Gave financial support to the YWCA, Salvation Army Center, Girl Scout Camp, YMCA, and helped finance a school psychologist,
—Supported the NCFWC project "Dollars for Scholars" and

the Ann Kiser Bost Scholarship,
—Gave two scholarships annually,
—Prompted adult education by seeking out illiterates and funding classes for them,
—Informed its own club members through departmental club programs,
—Sponsored the Consumer Institute,
—Held a sidewalk art show,
—Contributed to the Raleigh Arts Council,
—Supported and participated in the Children's Theater,
—Contributed to the starting of the North Carolina Symphony,
—Organized a choral group,
—Assisted foreign students,
—Developed a directory of local residents who speak foreign languages,
—Contributed furnishings to the International Students Center,
—Promoted CARE and UNICEF,
—Helped sponsor a Community Ambassador,
—Sent stamps to Norway to help provide T.B. threatened children,
—Participated in the NCFWC project, Help-a-Home,
—Assisted with the establishment of Head-Start in Raleigh schools,
—Sponsored youth groups,
—Maintained a conservation booth at the State Fair,
—Assisted in the beautification of the old city cemetery,
—Assisted with the building program for YWCAs in Raleigh on Jones Street and Bloodworth Street.

Here are examples illustrating the involvement of the Woman's Club of Raleigh in one particular year:
—Involved in the food booth at the State Fair,
—Worked in the State Fair booth to promote conservation, safety, and beautification of North Carolina trees,
—Entertained foreign visitors in their homes in 1965,
—Corresponded with foreign pen-pals,
—Participated with their husbands in Open House programs

for foreign students,

—Prepared cookies, transported foreign students upon arrival, and acted as hostesses during two days of orientation for foreign students,

—Participated in English Language School at State College, providing transportation and nursery,

—Participated in the stamps for Norway program; 18,000 stamps were collected,

—Participated in the magazines for friendship program,

—Participated in the Study of Areas and Nationalities Division's planning and executing a workshop and program,

—Assisted the Raleigh Chapter of the American Association of United Nations in holding a public meeting—preparing decorations and food,

—Attended United Nations Week celebrations,

—Attended a fashion show which raised $190.00 to be used in a Welfare Project,

—Participated in Federation Heritage Week tours planned and scheduled by club women,

—Sold 600 boxes of UNICEF cards for the International Department,

—Executed the second Antique Show held at Memorial Auditorium,

—Participated in the policy making, buying, and publicity for the continuing operation of the Carolina Art Sales Gallery,

—Participated in creative writers' group meetings once each month to criticize the writing of each,

—Participated in Pioneers—a group from the Mature Years Division met twice each month for bridge and lunch,

—Worked on nine exhibits and teas honoring artists and authors held at Carolina Art Sales Gallery (hours given: 500),

—Planned and executed Crafts Day,

—Participated in Youth Recognition Night, which required the services of club women in charge of the various youth groups represented,

—Participated in Side Walk Art Exhibit, requiring 700 man-hours in securing, hanging, and returning paintings and art work which filled all Cameron Village show windows,

—Sold North Carolina note cards to finance the General Federation Convention's Diamond Jubilee trip to Chicago,
—Gave to Ten Penny Art Fund (10 centers per member),
—Participated in planning and executing the Consumer Institute,
—Participated in the planning and execution of the policies and programs of the Education Department in general,
—Participated in two six-week sessions of Bible classes at Woman's Prison,
—Participated in literacy classes made possible by the Board of Directors (teaching courses for 60 hours),
—Worked as Junior Civic Council Advisers,
—Were involved in the selection of the club scholarships made by the scholarship committee,
—Were involved in the planning of and participated in leadership training courses,
—Composed the handbook for officers, spending 60 hours.

Activities of the Woman's Club of Raleigh in the 1970s have included the following:

The Conservation Department has assisted Crabtree Watershed plans and programs to "Bring Back the Bluebirds"; educated club members on their responsibility to the environment; promoted recycling of reusable materials; sought solutions for the energy crisis; supported the Raleigh Scenery Commission in its project to establish "areas" along the streams and in selected areas in the city of Raleigh, and in the reforestation program of their "areas"; continued beautification of clubhouse grounds and Glenwood Avenue entrance; beautified grounds of the cottage for the blind multihandicapped.

The Education Department has sponsored study programs on investments and securities; supported continuing education programs and the Public Library system; provided information on school priorities; promoted Bible study at the Correctional Center for Women; organized informal groups to study the language and culture of at least one foreign country; and participated in study of "Great Decisions" in world affairs.

The Home Life Department has provided information on legislation concerning consumer protection laws; helped with Haven House in Raleigh and Girls' Home in Asheboro; sponsored programs on mental health in North Carolina; provided drivers for Meds on Wheels; provided interior design lectures for making a home more functional and esthetically pleasing place in which to live; cooperated with other civic groups in promoting the betterment of the city; stressed the importance of physical fitness for all members of the family; sponsored activities of the Pioneer Group; cooperated with the Consumers' Council; and sponsored a Christmas card party for club members and their children.

The Arts Department has conducted art classes for beginners; promoted Arts Festivals, Sidewalk Art and Craft Shows, Raleigh Children's Theater, women's club chorus, and creative writers' groups; conducted a Literary Forum; and carried a Traveling Art Show to homes for the aged and hospitalized.

The International Department has sponsored a World Affairs study program in Great Decisions; responded to International Disaster Appeals; provided welcome packets of geographical and historical brochures for new foreign students at North Carolina State University and a bus tour of the area for foreign students; participated in tours of the United Nations; and given time, money, clothing, and so on to Care, Project Concern, Community Ambassador, etc.

The Public Affairs Department has worked to improve environmental health; assisted the Veterans program; studied legislation pertaining to the status of women; worked in the volunteer program on citizenship; worked for rehabilitation in the prison system; helped in the areas of social service; and participated in a variety of public activities having an impact on the daily lives of all.

The Special Projects Department has sponsored the Boys Choir; helped in volunteer work at Rex Hospital; promoted fashion shows; assisted in a program for the Home for Wayward Girls; worked in the division of Vocational Rehabilitation; conducted Antique Shows, Food Bazaars, and a cafeteria at the North Carolina State Fair; supported Carolina Arts programs; the "Table Extraordinaire;" the Flea Market; conducted tours of Raleigh and Research Triangle Area; sponsored Special Auctions; and provided scholarships.

Here is a summary of activities for the year 1974-1975:

Unity of purpose amid diversity in membership characterized the club during its 70th year of organization. Membership as of May 31 was 593. Fifty members were added to the roll during the year, and a one-day orientation class was held for each of the three groups of new members voted into the club.

As a part of the club's Bicentennial emphasis, a new project, Custom Tours, was initiated. It is under the auspices of the Ways and Means Committee and promises to develop into one of the club's oustanding efforts, both financially and community-service-wise. The Spring Antique Show was moved from Memorial Auditorium to the Governor Scott Building on the N.C. State Fair Grounds. It was the most successful antique show to date in number of dealers, advance ticket sales, attendance, and profit. Approximately $12,000 was made. For the first time, the club's catering department provided the food service for the show.

Curbing and guttering were laid on the driveway immediately in front of the clubhouse, and the parking lot was paved. It became necessary to cut a large number of pines from the rear and side of the clubhouse because of infestation by southern pine beetles.

Authorization was given to the Conservation Department, and funds appropriated, to begin a Japanese Garden.

Through the efforts of club members and other friends, and as a result of certain legislation enacted by the 1974 General Assembly, property tax on the clubhouse and grounds was adjusted to apply to rental space only.

The catering department had its most successful year on record, with a profit of approximately $11,000. Included were final payments on the $10,000 note for kitchen equipment, which obligation the Catering Department had assumed in November, 1971.

In January a section of the Area Mental Health Association took occupancy of the lower level office space vacated by the Easter Seal Society the previous November.

A contribution of $200 was made through the Conservation Department to the N.C. Zoological Gardens, a project of NCFWC. That department was responsible for beautifying the median on the Glenwood Avenue entrance to Woman's Club Drive. The Home Life Department made possible a gift of

$400 to Girls' Haven in Asheboro, a NCFWC project, and was responsible for approximately $800 in labor and equipment for the kitchen of Haven House. The Special Projects Department donated a TV to Haven House. The Home Life Department sponsored a series of five one-hour classes on interior design and culminated this highly successful program with a bus trip to High Point to visit the Furniture Mart.

The Arts Department sponsored a Spring Crafts Show, in addition to the Fall Show which had been the most successful on record, and joined the Special Projects Department in supporting the Raleigh Boys Choir. The Education Department held a two-day seminar under the direction of its Investments and Security Division. This event was open to the public, and a special invitation was mailed to the clubs in District 8, NCFWC, as well as to a number of civic clubs in Raleigh. Attendance and interest exceeded that in a similar seminar sponsored by the department the previous year. A third scholarship of $500 was awarded to a local high school senior.

The club building on Hillsboro Street had "Open House" each weekend and many times during the week for servicemen during the war years, as well as being used for civic and social functions; it has always been utilized in this manner.

In 1915 ground was broken for this building and it was occupied in 1916. It was utilized for civic and public functions for more than fifty years. In 1967 as the city expanded in population, so grew The Woman's Club of Raleigh. The Club accepted the opportunities to render greater service to the community, and in so doing they recognized the need for greater facilities that would be more accessible to the public. In 1968 the clubhouse was sold and the property at 3300 Woman's Club Drive was purchased. In 1971 this edifice was occupied and at the present time it serves the members and community as a place for socials and many cultural activities. It is a lovely building and beautifully furnished with many antiques that have been given to the club, many of them in memory of loved ones.

The Junior Woman's Club of Raleigh

With twenty members, the Junior Woman's Club of Raleigh had its beginning in 1928 as one of the two major projects of the Raleigh Woman's Club. It was later incorporated as a member organization in the North Carolina Federation of Women's Clubs. The club now has around 75 members beween the ages of 21 and 36. It is interesting to note that over one-third of the members are employed outside of the home and over half have children under the age of six.

Because all Junior Woman's Clubs are members of the Federation of Woman's Clubs, some of the projects that the Raleigh Juniors have supported over the years have been chosen on a statewide or even national level; a few such projects are the North Carolina Children's Home Society, Volunteers in Public Schools, National Association for Retarded Citizens, National Kidney Foundation, and Association for Children with Learning Disabilities.

Some of the important local projects that the Junior Club has spearheaded since its founding have included these: fulfilling a $5000 YMCA pledge; initiating a city-wide drive for the fluoridation of water; sponsoring a county-wide vaccination campaign to inoculate children against rubella and rubeola; donating over $8000 to the Tammy Lynn Memorial Foundation which, partly through the sustained efforts of the club, has recently been able to complete our area's first residential care center for severely retarded children.   The purpose of the Junior Woman's Club of Raleigh as set forth in its handbook is "to maintain an organized center for study, recreation, training for citizenship, and sound development among the young women of Raleigh, and to equip them for service in the community. The Juniors have always felt that the best way to pursue this goal is to work to provide quality support to the Raleigh community in any and all areas in which their talents and energies can be of service. A list of the major activities of the club for the year 1974-75 will provide an idea of the broad area of concerns which is covered by the Junior Club. An asterisk appears next to those projects which carry over from year to year. The projects are listed under the six department headings that are used by all women's clubs in the general federation.

Arts

—Sponsorship of city-wide art contest for area high school students.

—Craft workshop for girls living at a local home (Nicky Cruz

Home) for runaways.

—Bus trips to Jug Town and Williamsburg for members.

—Design and completion of a needlepoint tapestry commemorating the bicentennial.

—Monetary support of the North Carolina Symphony.

—Formation of a club chorus and book discussion group.

Conservation

—Collection of paper and glass for recycling.

—Support (monetary and publicity) for N.C. Zoo and Raleigh's Greenway project.

—Workshops for members on landscaping and houseplants.

—Providing information and incentives for energy-saving among members.

Education

—Interviewing applicants and awarding a $600 scholarship award to a local high school senior.

—Providing educational materials for Raleigh's Cerebral Palsy Center and for Project Enlightenment, a kindergarten for children with learning disabilities.

Home Life

—Teaching a babysitting course for 90 area teenagers.

—Providing luncheon, birthday cakes, and taxi fare for local Golden Ager Club.

—Testing for hearing difficulties at pre-schools and day-care centers.

—Manning a telephone referral service (Birthchoice) for girls with problem pregnancies.

—Helping at local and state Special Olympics for retarded children.

—Driving for Meals on Wheels (hot noon meals to shut-ins).

—Sponsoring a tea for 200 members of the Retired Senior Volunteer Program.

International Affairs

—Supporting foreign student wives by making them guest members and including them in club activities.

—Raising $120 each year to support an adopted child living at an orphanage in India.

—Preparing and donating school and hygiene kits for use of

Project Concern.

—Supporting and encouraging the work of UNICEF.

—Participating in "Great Decisions" study groups.

Public Affairs

—Providing a docent service to give spring tours through the Governor's Mansion.

—Sponsoring a public debate on ERA between a state senator and president of ERA United.

—Sponsoring an Art Contest for inmates at Polk Youth Center.

In addition to these department projects, the club has sponsored one large fund-raising Special Project this year. $2500 was raised for the North Carolina Kidney Foundation through the organizing and conducting of a vacation auction.

A detailed report reveals that during the year 1974 the women in the Junior Woman's Club of Raleigh gave tens of thousands of hours of themselves and their time in the following activities:

The Arts Committee worked with students and teachers in the elementary grades and in the junior and senior high schools and with other organizations in carrying out the Student Art Contest, the Annual Arts and Crafts Contest, and the District and State Art Contests. It put on macramé workshops, Christmas workshops, and workshops with schools, churches, and senior citizens groups.

The Conservation Committee collected newspapers for the Raleigh Rescue Mission and the Halifax Day Care Center; distributed pamphlets on the correct use of pesticides; distributed soil testing boxes to members to find out what their lawns were lacking; re-cycled calendars for the use of children; planted flowers at the Governor Morehead School; helped with the Flea Market; put on a terrarium workshop; planted a tree at Haven House; gave money to the Zoo for the purchase of animals; and carried out a project at an area center for underprivileged and retarded children.

The Education Committee awarded the Sallie Southall Cotten Scholarship; studied a typical public school kindergarten program; held a "going off to College Shower"; worked with the

Raleigh Recreation Department on courses involving continuing education; worked with the Project Enlightenment program; investigated continuing education ideas; distributed pamphlets on Investment and Securities; collected books and magazines for Haven House Library; and made cookies for American Education Week.

The Home Life Committee worked out a program of meals on wheels providing hot meals for shut-ins; transported babies to Children's Homes; worked with the YWCA in preparing food, fixing meats, vegetables, salads, rolls and dessert for a Golden Agers' Luncheon and cooked cakes for Golden Agers' birthdays; studied pros and cons of abortion; conducted baby-sitting courses; gave clothing and money to the Children's Home Endowment Fund; prepared cookbook recipes; worked with Birthchoice—an organization assisting girls with problem pregnancies; sponsored a maternity clothes closet; organized information packets for area pediatricians on learning disabilities; raised money for Children's Home; and contributed funds to help needy families at Christmas time.

The Committee for Retarded Children helped collect for the March of Dimes at a local theater for two weeks; took children from Shelby School to a fire station, out to lunch, and to a hat store and music store many times; worked with the Raleigh Parks and Recreation Department on "Special Olympics," and with the Cerebral Palsy Chairman; helped with a bridge benefit for Shelby School by selling tickets and modelling fashions; helped with Tammy Lynn Outreach Program; and helped with the North Hills Halloween Carnival for retarded children.

The Public Affairs Committee supported the Polk Youth Center's Art Program; distributed brochures and showed slides on kidney diseases; made sixteen bedspreads for a dorm at Polk Youth Center; conducted an art contest at Polk Youth Center; prepared questions for political candidates on current issues and brought them in for discussions; helped with the special projects Bridge—Fashion Benefit Show; purchased gifts for Christmas Fund at O'teen Veterans' Hospital; distributed brochures and conducted programs on highway safety; and distributed brochures and conducted programs on drug abuse.

The *International Affairs Department* supported an adopted child from India; asked club members to save food labels and turn them in at each meeting, for these reasons: "Welch's Jelly labels will provide enough antibiotic to save a child from blindness due to trachoma; Dentyne or Trident gum labels will provide enough triple vaccine to protect a child against diphtheria, whooping cough, and tetanus; Kool-Aid labels will protect one child against small pox; Chocks vitamins labels will provide 100 servings of high protein supplement; Royal dessert labels will provide five glasses of milk for hungry children; Blue Bonnet Margarine labels will provide enough BCG vaccine to protect a child against TB." They made pictures in Rex Hospital of mothers and babies at the time of birth to send to fathers in the service; participated in the Great Decisions of 1974 study group; conducted discussions on India; sponsored a mini-bazaar for needy areas in rural sections and provided medical and dental supplies; contributed items for the Flea Market; contributed articles to go into hygiene kits for Project Concern; contributed to relief of areas devastated by hurricane; and held an auction of baked goods and plants for the Christian Children's Fund.

The *Sub-Juniors Committee* collected bottles, cans, and papers for recycling; wrote the script, made awards, and prepared the refreshments for a tea honoring mothers; collected money at a local theater for the March of Dimes; collected paperbacks for the Veterans Hospital; held an Easter party at Blind School; participated in Special Olympics programs for handicapped children; collected games, puzzles, and records for Polk Youth Center; assisted the Raleigh Community Relations Committee; made candy apples, candy pumpkins and cupcakes for 25 children at Methodist Children's Home; helped Hillcrest Home; gave a dinner for a convalescent home; and collected toys for a Christmas party.

The *Special Projects Committee* organized and conducted a Flea Market at State Fair grounds; organized and conducted a Fashion Show; held a Bridge Benefit; and gave profits from these ventures to a variety of causes. The work done on the Flea Market at the State Fair grounds gives an idea of the planning and performance that went into these undertakings. Here is a report from the chairman:

> In January it was decided that we would have a Flea Market at the State Fair grounds the first weekend in June.
> This was announced in April so the girls could begin getting things together. Each department was put in charge of two hours on Friday to bring their merchandise. Then from 8:00-6:00 on Saturday and 8:00-6:00 on Sunday the two booths were manned by Departments in shifts. There was full club participation in bringing the merchanidse and working. Each club member was asked to bring merchandise that she thought would bring at least $10 minimum. Each girl worked an average of four hours, with full club participation; this made 62 girls working 248 hours during the three days at the Flea Market. The Department Chairmen spent an extra ten hours telephoning and getting the girls' items together. With all department chairmen participating this was an additional 60 hours. As Special Projects Chairman, I spent 5 hours on Friday and 10 each on Saturday and Sunday at the Flea Market. On Monday morning I went back to clean up and spent four hours. Before the Flea Market, setting up committees, telephoning department chairmen, looking into the project, and general preparation for the Flea Market took 50 hours. In all I spent 79 hours on this project. Money made: $442.85, 63 girls, 387 hours.

This summary does not include the less spectacular but no less metriculous and exciting work of the other club officers and committees, including the Ways and Means Committee, Publicity Committee, Membership Committee, Newsletter and Ditto Committee, Social Committee, and other committees suporting and guiding club activities.

The Junior League of Raleigh

Twenty-five young women in Raleigh came together in 1927 and organized the Raleigh Junior Guild. It joined the American Association of Junior Leagues in 1929, and became the Junior League of Raleigh.

Here are illustrative activities of the Junior League of Raleigh since its organization:

In 1929, it established a prenatal clinic in connection with the baby clinic, employed a nurse for clinic duty and to serve as a visiting nurse, and established a milk station. By 1932, this clinic had 840 patients, and in 1935 the League spent $1,000 on milk for clinic patients. In 1937, they moved their clinics to Rex Hospital and turned over the financial responsibility to the hospital and the Wake County Health Department. League volunteers continued to be responsible for the operation of the clinics, which continued to grow—in 1938-39, 1,233 patients were treated at the two clinics. In 1939-40, they expanded the white prenatal clinic to include a postnatal clinic. The Raleigh Junior League also financed, established, and operated black well-baby and prenatal clinics which treated, during their first two years, 3,024 patients. In 1943, the administration of these clinics was turned over to the Wake County Health Department for the duration of the war, League volunteers continuing to serve at all four clinics and on the medical clinic at Rex Hospital, but on a reduced scale. The milk fund was turned over to the county welfare department as a permanent public program.

In 1937, the League financed a survey of the Community Chest and its agencies which resulted in the reorganization of the welfare set-up in Raleigh and Wake County; and in 1939, they provided the salary for a case worker for the Family Service Society and continued to pay a portion of the salary for several years.

In the 1940s, volunteer service of Junior League Members expanded to include participation in local defense work, Traveler's Aid, war services, hospitality to service men, hostesses to the Convalescent Service Clubs at Butner General Hospital, and, at the request of the Raleigh Chamber of Commerce, the League accepted a project to house veterans and succeeded in placing 275 veterans.

After the war, Junior League volunteers assisted with draft board registration, conducted a block survey for the Red Cross, and adopted the project of building and financing a premature baby ward on the pediatric floor of Rex Hospital.

The first legislation actively supported by the Junior

League of Raleigh was a bill before the 1951 General Assembly providing for the enforcement of the Compulsory School Attendance Law. In 1956-57 it worked for fluoridation of water, and supported the City Hall Bond election and legislation to provide training in the public schools for trainable retarded children.

Throughout its history the Junior League of Raleigh has contributed to the cultural enrichment of the city's children through its participation in Children's Theater and through puppet shows, story hours at the library, and its "Appreciation in Music" project, instigated by the League with Dr. Benjamin Swalin to broadcast recordings to public schools in the city and county. League volunteers have served as assistants at the Museum of Natural History and the North Carolina Art Museum. Audubon screen tours were League sponsored in 1956-57.

Other League projects have included dressing Christmas dolls for needy children, helping with the Lion Club's Toy Shop, and supporting the Community Ambassador project, Student Exchange, UN Week, the Newcomers' Party, and a Health Affairs Roundtable.

The League has pioneered in its use of radio to entertain, instruct, and inform—its radio series for children, "Books Bring Adventures," won the Peabody Award in 1947. Its weekly teen-age program, "Under 21", produced by the Radio Committee, ran for 13 weeks in 1953 and again for eight months in 1954. In 1960-61, it sponsored "Meet Mr. Wizard", a science series, coordinated with science classes in the Raleigh Public Schools.

The League began a series of documentaries aimed at educating the public to the dangers of contemporary society: it conceived the idea for a television film on narcotics and sponsored "The Walking Death," produced by WRAL-TV as a public service. Ministers, the State Bureau of Investigation, addicts, and professionals were enlisted to explain the extent of drug addiction in North Carolina and its dangers.

Its Project Finding Committee developed a panel discussion of teenage problems today, using professional citizens of the community; they taped it and circulated it to women's clubs across the state for program material. The committee compiled Fun Books for hospitalized children. With eight girls on the committee, 1400 copies were delivered in a single year to hospitals and health and welfare agencies.

In cooperation with the Raleigh Housing Authority and the Raleigh Recreation Department, the League initiated, administered, and operated a kindergarten in the Halifax Court low-cost housing development, providing six volunteer teachers and one paid director. It voted to help compile and finance a handbook, *North Carolina's Capital, Raleigh,* in cooperation with the Historic Sites Commission. Members assisted with the research necessary to the preparation of the book.

It discovered the need for a central clearing-house for arts organizations and brought an Arts Council Director to Raleigh to explain the workings of Arts Councils to 40 local arts groups; it formed a steering committee and the Raleigh Arts Council evolved. A paid director administers the Council with the guidance of a Board of Directors consisting of three League members, four members from the Community, and eight members from participating organizations. The Junior League donated $21,000 over a three-year period to the project, interested citizens have given money, and a Charity Ball has helped finance the Council.

The story of League service at the North Carolina Museum of Art is the story of an awakening to art for over 40,000 school children visiting the museum annually. Volunteers trained to augment the small museum staff have guided visitors through the four floors of paintings and assisted the museum education department in establishing communication with teachers to encourage them to use the museum and to prepare their classes for it.

These volunteers led the League to adopt a new Museum project: a syllabus called "Masterpieces in the North Carolina Museum of Art" which contains 40 slides and an accompanying text, representing the museum's permanent collection, ranging from the thirteenth century to the twentieth century.

"Preparation for the museum visit has paid dividends in

every respect, from telling the story of the museum and its collection to having a more responsive group for docents to tell it to," said Beth Paschal, League docent, in the *Junior League Magazine* (May-June, 1966). The syllabus, she explained,

> will be not only a pleasant introduction to the museum, but also of use to schools, libraries, or study groups as a high-quality reference work. It will be sold to visitors at the museum bookshop. Additional plans call for Junior League museum-trained volunteers to take the unit into local classrooms for what might become a pilot program for the entire state.
>
> Slides can never, of course, take the place of actual works of art. But they can stir imagination and whet appetites. Used properly, they can bring alive an idea, an epoch, a poem, a whole era. They can enlarge a child's world and make it easy for him to approach a museum or a work of art with an open mind and a warm heart.

The League gave $8,000 to the cost of the first addition of the *Guide,* consisting of 1,000 complete packages and 4,000 additional textbooks. Future editions are expected to be self-sustaining.

Although the Junior League of Raleigh has used varied means of financing its projects, most of the $160,000 it contributed to the community through 1967 has come from its Bargain Box, Follies, its snack bar for the legislature, and the Inaugural Ball which the League has co-sponsored with the American Legion. Major financial contributions are as follows through 1972:

Major Junior League Contributions to the Community
(and the agency which assumed sponsorship of the program when League support was terminated)

Welfare projects (1927-1941) ·	$24,092.00
Baby Clinics—were taken over by Rex Hospital	
Caseworker Salary for Family Service Society— Family Service Society now funded by United Fund and fees	
Out-Patient Dept. Rex Hospital (1941-45)	750.00
Now a part of Rex Hospital budget	
Premature Baby Ward (Rex Hospital) and Pediatric Surgical Ward (1948-49)	12,500.00

(these were capital improvements)

Wake County Cerebral Palsy Center (1952-64)	12,500.00
Now funded by United Fund	
YWCA Teenage Room (1952-55)	12,900.00
(capital improvement)	
Special Education in Public Schools (1955-57)	6,600.00
Teachers' salaries now provided by state and local funds	
Hilltop Home (1958-63)	38,000.00
Now a United Fund agency	
WUNC-TV Science Series (1960-61)	600.00
WUNC-TV is state-supported; this particular program was discontinued	
Raleigh Cultural Center	2,625.00
Now supported through contributions, projects, and fees	
Audiometer (Health Department)	309.00
Now operated through county funds	
Arts Council of Raleigh, Inc. (1965-69)	21,000.00
Member agencies assumed partial support. Council was later discontinued because of lack of necessary support	
N.C. Museum of Art (1965-66)	8,000.00
Art slide portfolio and booklet, costs of preparation and printing contributed to museum which is state-supported. Served as a pilot project; museum has followed it with several similar portfolios and booklets	
Raleigh Book (1966-67)	12,500.00
"North Carolina's Capital, Raleigh", a joint project with the Raleigh Historic Sites Commission, a city agency. Copyright for this book now owned by The University of North Carolina Press.	
Halifax Court Kindergarten (1966-69)	8,950.00
Director's salary and other expenses; kindergarten building provided by Raleigh Housing Authority. Program now supported by Presbyterian Urban Council	
Boy's Club (1967-69)	30,000.00

Now a United Fund agency

Mordecai House (1967-70)   26,000.00
League funds provided matching for a federal
HUD grant for restoration; house is maintained
by Raleigh Historic Sites Commission, a city
agency

Forum, Emotionally Disturbed Child, TV spots,
brochure (1969)   4,230.00
Led to increased state appropriations for emo-
tionally disturbed children

New Bern Avenue Day Care Center (1970-72)   6,000.00
Supported through state, local, and federal
funds, tuition, contributions

Mental Health Center of Wake County (1970-72)   6,300.00
Recreational therapist, now supported by the
Center budget, which receives local, state and
federal funds

Sound-on-Slide Humanities Course (1971)   1,175.00
Now maintained by the Raleigh City Schools

Drug Action of Wake County (1971-73)   28,000.00
Supported by local, state, and federal funds, and
contributions

Raleigh School Athletic Department   500.00
Special contribution for support of a local athletic
event

Tuttle Community Center   2,400.00
Supported by United Fund, tuition, contributions

Tammy Lynn Home   14,400.00
Supported by local civic and church organiza-
tions, tuition

In-Service Teacher Training Couse in field of
Learning Disabilities   4,000.00
Paid for by the Junior League

Learning Disabilities Study Committee   1,500.00
Paid for by the Junior League

Developmental Evaluation Clinic
In the process of being opened. Funded by the
N.C. Legislature through the Department of Hu-
man Resources.

Other projects for 1974-75 included
Haven House	$10,000.00
DEC Educational Consultant, Supplies and Materials	25,620
Association of Children with Learning Disabilities—State Conference	2,000
Legal Aid	18,000

Movements Which Have Been Written into the Laws of the Land

1959—Endorsed legislative bill to establish Western Carolina Center for the Retarded.

1969—Sponsored *Forum on the Emotionally Disturbed Child in North Carolina* which led to a legislative bill establishing the Study Commission on North Carolina's Emotionally Disturbed Children.

1970—Endorsed and actively promoted passage of a bill establishing the Governor's Advocacy Commission on Children and Youth. This was the major recommendation of the above-named study commission, on which two League members served and many more League members from all N.C. Leagues worked as research volunteers.

1973—Extension of existing DEC program to include Wake County.

A Closer Look at Several Junior League Projects
Drug Action of Wake County, Inc.

This project has been one of the largest in terms of financial aid, volunteer hours, and numbers of people reached that has ever been undertaken by the Junior League of Raleigh. Because of the growing realization of the scope and effect of illegal drugs on our community, the Junior League began intensive research into the area through the Community Research Committee in 1970. By 1971 there was a real concern within the community that there be a central group to examine and deal with the county's drug problem. The Junior League was involved in all planning sessions that resulted in the formation of Drug Action of Wake County, Inc., and there was a Junior League member on the original board.

In April, 1971, the Junior League of Raleigh made available to Drug Action the sum of $25,000, to be used over a period of two years. The first year $17,000 was allocated to be spent in the following areas: salary of the Executive Secretary, educational material, travel expenses, and part-time clerical help. The sum of $8,000 was made available in the second year for the same areas mentioned above.

The purpose of this project was to better co-ordinate efforts within the drug abuse prevention field, to educate the citizens of Wake County, to identify the needs of the drug culture and provide solutions and alternatives and treatment that would be effective.

An estimate of the number of people the programs of Drug Action reaches is bound to be only an estimate. At present there are 24 Board members, 15 volunteer staff members and 8 paid staff members. Community education programs and Task Force programs have reached well over 800 people. There are drug therapy programs at Women's Prison and the Harp Program at Dix. The statistics from The House (a short term crisis intervention center established by Drug Action in 1970) are

4,127 telephone calls
  420 walk-ins
   50 parents involved in a seminar
   13 heroin addicts
  150 on Speakers Bureau
  150 in state-wide workshop
   40 in programs at Woman's Prison
   83 clients in medical clinics.

In February of 1973, the Junior League of Raleigh gave an additional sum of $3,000 to Drug Action for community education programs. This money was used in part to put on a continuing Arts Festival for all ages and races. Crafts such as photography, macramé, candle making, leather work, and pottery have been demonstrated and taught in four different workshop locations around Raleigh. The purpose of the Arts Festival is to give young and old a creative alternative to drug use, to give a sense of accomplishment and at the same time to teach a worthwhile skill. Sponsored by the Churches and Education Task Forces it is estimated that upon completion of the ten week long workshop sessions 200 people will have been reached in each of the weekly workshops.

The total amount of money given by the League to Drug Action is $28,000. The money raised for all Junior League Projects comes from our on-going moneyraising activity, the Bargain Box; from royalties on the Raleigh Book—*North Carolina's Capital, Raleigh*—and from other special activities such as the

1967 Follies, and the 1969 and 1973 Inaugural Balls. A conservative total of the hours spent by members of the Junior League in work with Drug Action is 2,762 in two years with about 500 being spent between April, 1971 and December, 1971.

In-Service Teacher Training Course in the Field of Learning Disabilities

This project was undertaken to help the regular classroom teacher diagnose, treat, and prescribe for the learning disabled child who was still within the normal classroom. It involved initially 20 teachers from Wake County (15 in the city elementary school system, 4 in the county school system, and 1 private school teacher). It is impossible to estimate the number of people who have benefited from this course because each teacher was to be the resource person for her own school; numbers of children have been helped. Because of the new awareness of the problems of the learning disabled child, many schools have requested similiar courses to be taught for their whole faculty. The interest in this field within the Junior League is tremendous, so much so that there are ten girls tutoring learning disabled children on a one-to-one basis in the public schools. These girls have had a training course put on by the Wake county Mental Health Department.

Because of the success of this first training course for the regular classroom teacher, the public school system requested that there be a second course, taught in the summer of 1973.

The cost of each course has been approximately $2,000, making a total of $4,000. All Junior League projects are financed from monies in the Community Trust Account which is funded by the Bargain Box, Raleigh book, Follies, and Inaugural Balls. The course was one of the recommendations which came out of a two-year study by the Learning Disabilities Study Committee. A conservative estimate of hours, is 1,365.

Developmental Evaluation Clinic

After two years of study by the Learning Disabilities Study Committee, their recommendation to the Junior League of Raleigh was that we seriously concentrate efforts on influencing legislation to obtain state money to establish a Developmental Evaluation Clinic in the Wake County Area. There are eleven such facilities in the state at the present but the two nearest to Raleigh are located in Durham and Chapel Hill and are training clinics more than diagnostic clinics. State funding for such a facility is imperative to insure continuity. This money had to be written into the state budget under the Department of Human Resources, Office of Public Health. Intensive con-

[117]

tact was made with this department and their cooperation secured. Efforts of League volunteers were then placed upon educating the state legislators as to the need for such a facility for Wake County. Two dinners were held–one for the Wake County delegation and one for the Appropriations Committee. An educational program was presented at each dinner. Many League girls attended legislative committee meetings to talk with legislators and to answer questions.

Estimated cost of Learning Disabilities Committee on the above effort is $1,500. The number of hours spent is estimated to be 1,143.

Salary for the Nursing Supervisor at Tammy Lynn Home

At the request of the Board of Directors of the Tammy Lynn Home for two years' firm funding for services, the Junior League of Raleigh considered and granted their request for the nursing supervisor's salary. At present there are nine severely retarded children in residence and nine more in the day care program. Nursing care is essential for these children. Training of these children to do simple everyday tasks is one of the primary goals of the staff. The Tammy Lynn Home also provides relief to parents and a child in a stress situation and will care for a child on a short term basis to free parents for a vacation.

Money appropriated for this salary is $7,200 per year for two years—totaling $14,400. The money comes from the Community Trust Account of the Junior League.

The Raleigh Junior League has two members doing placement there for a total of 97 hours and also 2 members on the Board of Directors who have just begun to serve their terms.

Camp Friendly for Mentally Retarded Children

This was not considered a project but rather a donation which is not the usual Junior League procedure. Because of past associations with the City Recreation Department and the Cerebral Palsy Center, the Board of Directors of the Junior League felt that this exception could be made.

In its forty-eight years of service to the community, the Junior League of Raleigh has raised and contributed into the hundreds of thousands of dollars towards community services, and Junior League members have given three-quarters of a million hours of their time.

The Raleigh Garden Club

The Raleigh Garden Club is an outgrowth of the Civic Department of the Woman's Club of Raleigh, and was organized in 1925 with 21 charter members. It has 278 members in 1975. Its purpose was, and is, "to encourage the beautification of parks, streets, and gardens of the community, and to aid in the protection of trees, shrubs, wildflowers, and wildlife." Any person living in Raleigh or its vicinity who is interested in the object for which this club is organized is eligible for membership.

The Raleigh Garden Club has provided Raleigh's leadership in striving toward the goals of beautification, conservation, and civic improvement. The club held two flower show schools in 1934, the first of such schools in the South Atlantic Region.

In 1925, the Raleigh Garden Club was one of the five clubs that met in Winston-Salem, N.C., to help form the Garden Club of North Carolina.

Mrs. R.L. McMillan was the chairman of the club's first nature map which came out in 1937. Mrs. McMillan also helped organize the North Carolina Camellia Society.

In the 50 years as a Garden Club, the Raleigh Garden Club has carried out many projects that have benefitted the city and state. To list a few of the outstanding ones, they are
—the Chapel Garden at Dorothea Dix Hospital
—the Model-Mile Highway 64 East
—Paul Scarlet Roses around the beltline at Raleigh
—beautification of the grounds at the Commission for the Blind
—landscaping the grounds at the building for the multi-handicapped children at Camp Butner
—aid with school gardens and nature trails.

The Raleigh Garden Club was the first to have a flower show consultant. It supports:
—The Mary Lee McMillan Garden on the grounds of the Woman's Club of Raleigh.
—Hymettus Woods Nature Park
—Conservation of wildflowers, rescuing them from the bulldozer and planting them in city parks
—Funds for the planting of trees, shrubs, bulbs and other

plants
–The Raleigh Rose Garden.

The Raleigh Garden Club helps support four state gardens with financial aid:
– the Elizabethan Garden at Manteo, N.C.
– the Martha Franck Fragrance Garden at Butner, N.C.
– the wildflower garden at Boone, N.C.
– the Nature Trails at Brunswick, N.C.
It also supports the national project of world gardening in Central America, as well as helping with scholarships for deserving students in horticulture at N.C. State University.

Over 3000 bulbs were given to the city of Raleigh in 1975; they were planted in six areas around Raleigh.

Among the Raleigh club's many outstanding projects are the State Hospital Chapel Garden—planted and maintained by the Raleigh Garden Club—the Blue Star Memorial Highway, and the "Model Mile", Highway 64 East, along with an anti-litter and clean-up campaign, tree planting, and flower shows. The Club traditionally decorates the Governor's Mansion the first Christmas a new governor is in residence there. Also traditional is the Garden Club's Christmas show, which for many years has transformed the Woman's Club with its exquisite expression of the beauty of the Christmas season.

As Raleigh grew, small neighborhood garden clubs began to crop up, giving neighbors a chance to know each other and work together for causes of mutual interest. Many of these neighborhood garden clubs have become the nucleus of fellowship as well as the agency through which women help each other in illness and bereavement.

In recent years Sears-Roebuck, which has maintained garden centers and an active interest in garden clubs, began its HANDS (Home and Neighborhood Development Sponsors) program. Any neighborhood group is eligible to report civic improvement projects in competition for a cash award given by Sears and by local businesses that add to the prize money. The response of small garden clubs to this stimulus has been truly marvelous.

The HANDS report of Raleigh's Grow Together Community Club is an example both of what the small club is doing for the community and what HANDS is doing, bit by bit and community by community, for the nation: "This is our third year to enter the HANDS contest. Being in the contest is a real privilege and a great financial help to our low economic neighborhood. However, the most important thing is that we have become better neighbors and have learned to work together to make our community one of which the City of Raleigh can be proud."

Many of the 49 Raleigh clubs competing for HANDS awards reported the use of all or part of previous HANDS award money for the beltline beautification project and for azaleas for Moore Square. Other projects reported included cleaning up and painting; and planting and beautifying entrances to the State Hospital, Hilltop Home, Mayview Rest Home, the County Home, the library, the Raleigh Rescue Mission, and the Cerebral Palsy Center.

One older neighborhood club, with twelve widows in the membership of 25, works to keep the neighborhood clean and attractive. Their efforts resulted in the clearance of an unsightly railroad bank and the restoration of a sub-standard house.

Members contact owners of rental property and encourage their cooperation in maintaining well-kept houses and surroundings; they also welcome all newcomers as an aid to keeping the area beautiful. Not confining their talents to their immediate community, these ladies started an herb garden at the Governor Morehead School for the Blind. They assisted third grade students in planting the herbs and at Christmas they made for these children large sachets, each one trimmed differently with ribbon, lace, and flowers so that each student could identify her own by feeling.

It is interesting that the clubs from older neighborhoods report projects to remove unused barns and garages, to restore old homes, and to clean yards and prune shrubbery for older, retired citizens, while the clubs in new sub-divisions report overcoming traffic hazards at school crossings, sponsoring Scout troops, assisting new schools with planting, and establishing nature trails. As former Mayor Travis Tomlinson stated, "The effectiveness of the HANDS Program lies in the individual and neighborhood actions among the forty-nine groups now working through this community. To me, the fact that while each of the Clubs has its own program as each neighborhood has its individual need, all of the Clubs have on occasions joined together to participate in broad community projects such as the planting of roses along the beltline, the beautification of Moore Square, and the City Cemetery.

"We are also grateful," Mayor Tomlinson continues, "that in the past 10 to 15 years this organization has grown and flourished along with the growth of the community such that I would not like to think how our city would be now without this program. As has been said many times, government cannot and should not be expected to care for all community needs. Many things in our neighborhoods and communities can best be done by direct action of our citizens."

Raleigh Garden Club Projects

Joel Lane House Garden: "Wakefield", circa 1760, the oldest house in Raleigh, was the home of Joel Lane, patriot and leading citizen who sold Raleigh's original site to the state for its capital. Wakefield is now owned and has been restored by the National Society of Colonial Dames of America in the State of North Carolina. The Raleigh Garden Club plans to help the Colonial Dames achieve a period garden by giving money, providing supervision, and assisting with maintenance. (Wakefield is on the National Register of Historic Places.)

Hymettus Woods: An individual donated this property to the city. The Raleigh Garden Club has assisted in developing this area into a park for nature study by "staying one jump ahead of the bulldozer" and transplanting to this park wildflowers that would otherwise be destroyed. Meredith College uses the park for botanical study. Each tree is to be identified. The Raleigh Garden Club has saved and put native plants in the garden at Mordecai House, another National Historic Register site.

Edna M. Wells Park: This site is maintained by the city; Raleigh Garden Club makes cash contributions for its beautification.

Glenwood Towers: This is an apartment complex for low-income senior citizens. The Raleigh Garden Club instigated the addition of a greenhouse which was purchased by Saint Michael's Episcopal Church. Garden Club members give horticultural assistance along with lectures on how to arrange flowers. Approximately 20 members have participated. The Raleigh Garden Club has also given talks and demonstrations at Capital Towers, another apartment complex for senior citizens.

E.C. Brooks School: Elementary grades plant, care for, harvest, and prepare several vegetables, thereby learning about nature's cycles. This had the cooperation of approximately 18 members and one very active grade mother. Raleigh Garden Club provided for plowing and furnished seeds and plants. The Garden Club would like to extend this project to other schools, but its success depends on having a really gung-ho teacher or grade mother.

The Raleigh Garden Club gave bulbs to students at another school to plant on the school grounds and gave each child at Sherwood Bates School a bulb to plant on the school's nature trail. The Raleigh Garden Club also taught school children how to build terrariums and provided the materials.

Tucker House Landscaping: The Raleigh Garden Club plans to landscape the grounds of Tucker House, an early twentieth-century mansion which was recently moved to Oakwood (Raleigh's earliest continuous community, now on the National Register of Historic Places) where it will be used as a community center.

Greenway: The Raleigh Garden Club will further investigate the idea of a Greenway around Raleigh, encouraging Garden Club members to go along with it. (Property owners have not been entirely cooperative.) Garden Club hopes to promote walks and bridle paths and to leave a buffer zone to save vegetation from builders.

In addition to the talks and demonstrations mentioned above, the Raleigh Garden Club has given talks and demonstrations at the Wake County Mental Health Clinic and the Women's Division of Central Prison, where crafts were taught also. The Raleigh Garden Club gave over 3000 bulbs to the City of Raleigh to plant in 6 areas around Raleigh. The Raleigh Garden Club contributed financial help to four gardens ($10 to each garden), projects of the North Carolina Garden Club. It also contributed $225 to the N.C. Garden Club's horticultural scholarship fund. This money was obtained from the sale of engagement calendars, a state project.

The Raleigh Garden Club contributed $10 to the project of the National Garden Club, World Gardening in Central

America. This money helps provide implements, fertilizer, seeds, and plants, Peace Corps workers and other individuals give assistance.

Ways and Means: The Raleigh Garden Club had three money-making projects: it sold bulbs; held a plant exchange (people bring plants from their own gardens to exchange or to sell); and hosted an antique show at Crabtree Valley Shopping Mall.

The Raleigh Fine Arts Society

In 1965, a small group of women in Raleigh met and organized the Raleigh Fine Arts Society in order:

— to operate exclusively for educational and literary purposes,
— to further art in the community by sponsoring and encouraging art exhibits and in providing for the proper display of art in its varied forms,
— to promote, stage, operate and sponsor public exhibitions, concerts, and recitals calculated and intended to advance, foster and encourage public appreciation, enthusiasm, support, and understanding of art, music and literature,
— to provide for the proper expenditure, use and conservation of any legacies or bequests which may be used in the furtherance of an appreciation of art, music and literature,
— to do any and all things which, in the opinion of the Board of Directors, may be necessary or advisable in order to carry out the objects and purposes set forth in preceding paragraphs.

A letter from Ann B. Turner, President, in May, 1975, says:

We calculate that our seven community projects have reached a total of 57,119 people in the past year. These projects are:

Color and Light Machine Demonstrations. In 1970 RFAS gave $950.00 to the Raleigh City Schools for the design and construction of a Color and Light Machine by Joe Cox of NCSU for the purpose of teaching color in light. This year RFAS volunteers with the assistance of St. Mary's students have demonstrated the machine to more than 2500 people. In addition to the sixth grade centers, demonstrations have been given at Meredith College, St. Mary's, NCSU, North Carolina Central School for the Deaf, PTA's and bookclubs.

[124]

Governor Morehead School Dance Program. A professional dance instructor is paid by RFAS to teach tap dancing to blind students. RFAS volunteers assist the instructor.

Governor's Mansion Docents. In May of 1966, we voted to undertake this project after receiving a request from Mrs. Dan K. Moore, then First Lady of North Carolina. We share this involvement with other city women's groups and we serve in the spring, summer and fall. This year 50 of our members gave tours to some 22,300 children and adults.

North Carolina Museum of Art Docents. Twenty-five of our members served as docents and guided approximately 24,000 students through the Museum this year. We participate in the fifth grade slide program which RFAS initiated and which was incorporated into the Education Department of the Museum last year. Seventeen of our members contribute time to the Art Rental/Sales Gallery of the Museum.

North Carolina Museum of History. RFAS volunteers conduct tours, demonstrate the arts of spinning, weaving and throwing pottery and are involved with research on special projects.

Wake County Artists' Exhibitions. RFAS adopted the Wake County Artists' Exhibition as its first project on our first meeting on September 15, 1965. With the Wake County Public Libraries we co-sponsored a preview show called "The Jury's Choice" last year, followed by four exhibitions of paintings by Wake County artists.

Last year a special project was conceived, that of publishing a guidebook of hallmark quality which presents Raleigh artistically, culturally and historically. This has been officially designated a Bicentennial Project by the North Carolina Bicentennial Commission and has received a grant of $2900.00 from the North Carolina Arts Council. RFAS has voted the sum of $5000.00 to further finance this project. Many of our members are involved in research for the Guidebook which is tentatively scheduled to be published in the Fall of 1975.

The Raleigh Fine Arts Society has supported the North Carolina Symphony with contributions and has donated Symphony tickets to the elderly residents of Glenwood Towers. We went on record in a letter to the Site Selection Committee for the North Carolina Symphony supporting Raleigh as the permanent home of the Symphony. A contribution was made to the Broughton High School Choral Ensemble to aid its fundraising efforts for a trip to Vienna, Austria, to participate in an international competition. A purchase award was given to the Mordecai Square Historical Society in support of its Need-

[125]

lework Exhibition.

Our purpose is two-fold, after all—we wish to educate as well as to serve. Our two seminars have been educational ones having as their main subjects art, porcelain, pottery of N.C., Oriental rugs, and Irish decorative accessories, the last given by the Honorable Desmond Guinness, Founder of the Irish Georgian Society. This year we have a British lecturer coming to talk on "The English Country House" in November. In October we will travel to Richmond to visit the Museum, Wilton, Virginia House, St. John's Church, and the private art collection of Sydney Lewis. We have planned ahead as far as May when a trip to the Wilmington, Delaware, area is scheduled which includes Winterthur, the Hagley, Delaware Art and Brandywine Museums and Longwood Gardens.

The guidebook progresses well. Many members have been involved in the research and the writing is going well. Of the monies given by the North Carolina Arts Council, $1900.00 is marked for photographers, artists, and writers and $1000.00 for design and graphic arts. Members are acting as business manager, publicity director, art/photograph selection committee, and exhibition committee. I think I should reevaluate our contribution in hours upward to 10,000.

1975-76 Raleigh Fine Arts Society Projects include:

Color and Light Machine Demonstration—A gift of $950 from the Society in 1970 enabled the Raleigh school system to commission Professor Joe Cox of the School of Design at N.C.S.U. to design and construct a Color and Light Machine for the purpose of teaching color in light. Members of RFAS have demonstrated this machine, as well as two others that were subsequently acquired, to students in the city's sixth grade centers, Meredith College, North Carolina State University, North Carolina Central School for the Deaf, St. Mary's Junior College, and to adult groups upon request.
Governor Morehead School Dance Program—The Society will again underwrite a program which will allow a professional instructor, Mr. James Leocarta, to teach tap dancing to blind students with a small but dedicated group of our volunteers as assistants.
Governor's Mansion Docents—At the invitation of Mrs. James E. Holshouser, Jr., the First Lady of North Carolina, the Society will continue to provide docents when the renovation of the Mansion is completed in 1976. This has been a popular program of RFAS since 1966 when the project was undertaken at

the request of Mrs. Dan K. Moore, then First Lady.

Mordecai House Docents—Society docents have conducted tours through this historic house since it was opened to the public. Several members serve on the Board of Directors of the Mordecai Square Historical Society and others chair committees. In addition to volunteer hours, RFAS contributed the first Founder's Gift of $1000 which was used for draperies.

North Carolina Museum of Art Museum Docents—Many of our members first became interested in the visual arts through the influence of the Museum of Art and its docent training program. There will be a strong and active delegation from RFAS again serving at each docent level.

School Slide Program—In 1967, RFAS initiated a fifth-grade slide-lecture program in the Raleigh Public Schools. Members continue to support this program which enters its third year under the guidance of the Education Department of the Museum.

Art Rental/Sales Gallery—Volunteers are among those who staff this gallery, a service of the Art Society in cooperation with the Museum of Art. The gallery is devoted to contemporary North Carolina art, and encourages collection of these works through a rental/purchase arrangement.

North Carolina Museum of History—Members conduct tours, demonstrate crafts, participate in slide programs which acquaint school children with historical artifacts, help prepare museum exhibits, research special projects and staff the gift shop and information desk.

Wake County Artists' Exhibitions—The Society adopted the Wake County Artists' Exhibition as its initial project at the first meeting on September 15, 1965. With the Wake County Public Libraries, the Society co-sponsors juried exhibitions each year, carrying out an admonition found in the Articles of Incorporation to " . . . further art in the community by sponsoring and encouraging art exhibits . . ."

Guidebook to the City of Raleigh—This special project, involving efforts over a two-year period, will culminate in the publication in the late fall of a guidebook to the city which will focus on artistic, cultural and historical areas of Raleigh. Funded by the Society, with the addition of a grant from the North Carolina Arts Council, this project was given official Bicentennial status by the North Carolina Bicentennial Commission.

The League of Women Voters of Raleigh-Wake County

The Raleigh League of Women Voters was organized in

1920, as "a non-partisan organization established to promote political responsibility through informed and active participation of citizens in government." In 1975 the name was changed to the League of Women Voters of Raleigh–Wake County to show the scope of interest and the change in the makeup of the membership. The office moved to Cary.

In the fifty-five years from then to now, the League of Women Voters has suited actions to its words. To illustrate: it has conducted workshops on land use planning, solid waste recycling, housing, juvenile justice, the structure of local government, and the property tax.

It has distributed handbooks of information on local government in Raleigh and Wake County and nonpartisan material on procedures of the government, tax structure, the Federal poverty program, water resources, foreign economic policy, the United Nations, library facilities and needs; it has given local public school financing to schools, libraries, interested groups, and citizens generally.

It has distributed pro and con flyers concerning local issues and provided information on registration, information on candidates for office, and demonstrations of voting machines. It has provided Voter Information Booths and Speakers' Bureaus, and sponsored general meetings open to the public on the Headstart Program and the United Nations.

Study and observation have provided the backbone for the Wake County League's approach to local problems and issues. It has studied means of improving the county library system, the feasibility of public kindergartens, the local use of the federal poverty programs, State Election laws, the apportionment of the State Legislatures, and water resources, among other items. It has observed local government in action through sending regular representatives to the City Council, the City School Board, the County Commissioners, the Wake County School Board, and Wake County Opportunities, Inc. These observers report back to the membership on items of League interest.

It has members outside of Raleigh in Cary, Wake Forest, and Wendell. In all, some sixteen boards and commissions have a League member either as a member or an observer. As a service to the North Carolina League, Raleigh-Wake County League members monitor the workings of the General Assembly.

A church-sponsored meeting provided the stimulus for the Raleigh-Wake County League's 1955-56 study of housing with emphasis on slum clearance and a minimum standards housing code. Facts on public housing and housing conditions in Raleigh were presented at unit meetings. It held a workshop on the city's housing problems and a panel discussion on a Minimum Standards Housing Ordinance, and passed two resolutions, one supporting the Board of Commissioners of the Raleigh Housing Authority in their efforts to improve housing conditions and the other supporting the Minimum Standards Housing Ordinance.

In 1953-54, the Raleigh League made a study of its city and county school boards and went on record as favoring the election of school board members. In 1956-57, it studied the Pearsall Plan coming out of the special session of the legislature. Although no consensus came out of the study, it did help to open lines of communication between the League and the school board. After several attempts, two League members were allowed to observe school board meetings for the first time. Continuation of the school item the following year included the organization of a series of public meetings which was concluded with the first public appearance of the school board to answer questions about school problems. This series earned special commendation from the North Carolina Council on Human Relations in its bulletin.

It has issued and distributed for new voters a bulletin on the *ABC's of Voting and Registration*, giving information on: (1) Who May Register To Vote, (2) When and Where Do I Register, (3) Do I Need To Register For Every Election, (4) Where Do I Vote, (5) Polling Hours, (6) When Do I Vote: in Party Primaries, General Elections, Municipal Elections, Special Elections, (7) Voting Procedures, (8) How To Use A Voting Machine, (9) Absentee Ballot For General Election—For Primary Election.

It has issued and distributed *A Citizen's Guide To Raleigh and Wake County* with short descriptions of the history and geography of these local units of government, the activities and responsibilities of city and county agencies and officials, boards, commissions, and committees, and a calendar of the meeting times and places of these official agencies.

A companion publication "A Citizen's Guide to Officials of Raleigh and Wake County" is updated regularly.

It issues and distributes from year to year a *Candidates Questionnaire on Issues and Answers,* and holds public meetings where voters can meet the candidates, hear their discussions, ask them questions, and get their answers.

In 1970 *Facts About Raleigh City Schools* and in 1971 *Wake County School Facts* were published by the Raleigh-Wake County League. These two publications described in detail both school systems. The League is presently updating the information on schools for a new publication for the fall of 1975.

The Cary members of the Raleigh-Wake County League after five years of observation and study of their local government came to consensus about their form of government. Their recommendation was that the present 5 at-large council members be increased in size to 6 and that 4 of those 6 be elected from districts, with 2 council members being elected at-large. Also, they recommended that there be an election of mayor (he was presently chosen by the council members from among themselves) bringing the total number on the council to 7. The Cary members felt that this would lead to better representation, responsiveness, and accountability from the town's leadership.

They first proposed their idea to the Cary Town Council in March, 1974, and met with opposition from the council and later from the Jaycees, Rotary Club, and one homeowner's association. Despite much lobbying for their beliefs, the council refused to place the issue on the ballot. The Cary members then organized a week-end petition drive to collect enough signatures to place the issue on the November, 1974, ballot. They needed 600 names and got 1200.

Through a legal technicality the council then declared the

petitions illegal. After a series of meetings between the Cary League members and the council, the council agreed to hold a special election in February, 1975, on the issue.

Although the turnout was poor for the special election, the League's issues were passed by the voters.

The council is now drawing district lines with input from the Cary League members and other interested citizens. In November, 1975, the Cary voters will begin implementing their new form of government: 4 council members from districts, 2 council members at-large and an elected mayor.

The Raleigh-Wake County League has studied, analyzed, taken positions on, and commended and worked for "measures to provide a more accountable, effective, and decisive municipal government:"

> The League of Women Voters of Raleigh-Wake County is in support of measures to ensure a representative and responsive form of local government and to encourage active citizen participation in the political structure and decisions of that government. To provide a more accountable, effective and decisive municipal government, we recommend these measures:
> **Mayor**—the direct election of a mayor with the same voting power as a council member.
> **Council Members**—an increase in the number of council members from the current seven with an equal number of council members from districts and council members elected at large.
> **Term of Office**—four-year terms for both council members and the mayor and staggered terms for the council members in order to provide continuity of effort and information.
> **Type of Election**—non-partisan elections for city government.

The League encouraged actions taken by governments which would provide for cooperation on a regional basis to develop methods of solid waste management that promote the reuse, recycling, and reclamation of solid waste.

It supported measures to assure adequate and sound financing of local schools, and supported local school board policies which will continually improve educational standards in the areas of personnel, program and facilities; which assure equal educational opportunity and interracial teaching and learning experience for all children; which seek for new and different approaches to achieve racially integrated schools; and which seek the active enlistment of parents and other organizations in school activities (position since 1966); supported the establishment of public kindergartens (1964 position); supported the proposed merger of the Raleigh and Wake County schools systems (1969 position).

Position on Local Government

The League continued study of the city council, county commissioners, and Triangle J Council of Governments, in order to determine how local government should be structured in order to provide necessary services to the citizens of Wake County; and to determine the budgetary process and how citizens can influence it. It supported measures to improve governmental operations which include land use, housing, parks and recreation, transportation, public protection, health, and schools.

A leaflet lists the following highlights for 1973-74:
In 1973-74 the League of Women Voters of Raleigh-Wake County has:
- updated a "Citizen's Guide to Raleigh-Wake County" and published a companion peice, "A Ctizien's Guide to Officials of Raleigh-Wake County".
- held a series of Candidates' Meetings in various parts of Wake County.
- distributed voter information and furnished transportation to polls.
- held voter registration drives in four different locations.
- had League Observers reporting on 19 different boards and commissions including the City Council, County Commissioners, School Boards and the General Assembly.
- sponsored, with other organizations, a city-wide forum on landlord-tenant relations.
- on the state level, came to consensus on juvenile justice and taxation as it affects land use.
- started a League discussion group in Eastern Wake County.
- Cary members came to consensus on the manner of election of their Town Council and circulated petitions to have this matter placed on the ballot.
- worked with the Planning Department in developing Goals and Policies for a new Comprehensive Plan.

[132]

In 1973-74 the League has also:
- admitted men as full members.
- continued work with Goals for Raleigh, which included publication of "Low Cost Transportation"
- worked with the Task Forces of the Citizens' Advisory Council.
- established priorities for the coming year which include:
  Consolidation of Raleigh and Wake County School systems.
  Establishing coalitions to work toward reforming the juvenile justice system in North Carolina.
  Reaching more citizens through an expanded Voter Service program.
  Establishing more League groups in Wake County in addition to Cary and Eastern Wake.
  Seeking a comprehensive planning process for all of Wake County.
  Passage of Equal Rights Amendment.
League members served on:
ACTION Advisory Board, Bicentennial Comm., City Charter Comm., Civic Center Auth., Comm. on Exceptional Children, Greater Raleigh Area Comm., Green Survival City, Legislative Tax Study, Raleigh Community Relations Comm., Raleigh Planning Comm., Wake Opportunities Board, Wake Health Services Board.

Following are the 1974-75 *Annual Report* of the League of Women Voters of Raleigh-Wake County and its program for 1975-76:

Raleigh-Wake County League of Women Voters
Annual Report

Raleigh-Wake is seeing a change in our membership with more young mothers becoming active in leadership roles. It is our policy to provide babysitting at all daytime meetings; the service is free, if the activity benefits the League as a whole, and the charge is $1.00 if it is just a self-enriching activity. Members can earn their dues by babysitting at $2.00/hour. With so many new active members we have spent a great deal of time in training programs, sometimes using our own expertise and occasionally bringing in consultants for workshops. The Board had a weekend retreat which was most helpful. As part of our planning for next year each board member completed a job analysis and made recommendations for ways to improve our operation. As a result of this we have a proposal to change the bylaws to allow for three vice presidents who will have responsibility for Program, Service to Members and Service to Community.

On the national level our main concentration this year has been in Great Decisions. We were instrumental in establishing four groups with ninety people participating. Approximately fifty League members were involved and the remainder were husbands and people from the community. The *Raleigh Times* agreed to run the UPI Great Decisions series. We secured the services of the N.C. State University's Urban Affairs and Community Services Center to process all of the ballots.

We are fortunate in having the General Assembly here; on the state level we have focused on the Juvenile Justice item. All during the summer, members of the C.J. Committee monitored the legislative study committee's work, so as soon as the session began we were primed for action. Our C.J. group has held several community meetings inviting representatives of every organization and agency dealing with children in trouble. At these meetings we have exchanged information, brought people up to date on the Legislature's activities, and done a bit of consoling with one another. The Juvenile Justice Forum we held on behalf of the State League is still paying dividends in community involvement.

Our greatest emphasis has been on the local level this year. The Cary group has fought and won a trying campaign to change the town charter and the way the town council and mayor are elected. Formerly there were five councilmen elected at-large and the mayor was selected from that number. Now the mayor will be elected at-large, two councilmen at-large and four councilmen from districts. To accomplish this, members had to get petitions signed, force the issue on the ballot, and turn out the vote at a special election.

Again this year we were able to get a grant from the N.C Humanities Committee and appropriations from the Raleigh City Council and the Wake County Board of Commissioners in the total amount of $28,000 to continue with our Goals for Raleigh/Wake project. The emphasis in the county this year has been to get the local municipalities to begin a goals-setting process of their own. We have recently been visited by members of the Washington-based Citizens Involvement Network which is funded by the Rockefeller, Lilly, and Kettering Foundations. CIN is interested in a network of twenty cities of various sizes and locations being joined to share information about citizen participation. They came to see us because of our Goals program. The League submitted an application to the All-American City contest along with some 500 other cities to make a presentation before the jury headed by George Gallup; the featured speaker was our own Ruth Clusen. On April 14, the formal announcement was made that Raleigh was one of twelve cities selected in 1974 for an All-American Award. Truly the League had a big hand in making Raleigh an All-American City.

Betty Ann Knudsen, President

Proposed Local Program for 1975-76

I. LOCAL GOVERNMENT: A Continued Study of the City Council, County Commissioners, and Triangle J Council of Governments

Scope: Determine how local government should be structured in order to provide necessary services to the citizens of Wake County. Determine the budgetary process and how citizens can influence it. Determine whether it is possible to assure selection of a qualified sheriff. The League of Women Voters of Raleigh—Wake County is in support of measures to improve governmental operations which include:

County—County manager system of government for Wake County with a full-time professionally trained executive officer.

Land Use

1. Support of a Wake County Planning Department with a professional planner and staff to coordinate and direct an adequate long-range plan for the orderly growth of our county; enlarging Planning Board responsibilities, powers and duties to go beyond zoning to include planning, basing zoning on accurate data of physical conditions (soil types, floodplain, ecologically fragile areas).

2. For both city and county—a coordinated planning process that takes into consideration human problems and encourages citizen participation in the decision-making process; the establishment of a Joint City-County Planning Commission and Department; support of the Joint City-County Land Use Code and the Model Land Use Code.

Housing

1. Urban Renewal programs which emphasize human needs.

2. Support of the Goals for Raleigh/Wake Housing Plan of Action with emphasis on increase of housing stock and rehabilitation of dilapidated housing in order to preserve existing neighborhoods.

3. Support the establishment and enforcement of building and inspection codes in the county.

4. Support an active County Housing Authority.
5. Support of Triangle J Council of Government program to rehabilitate sub-standard housing and construction of new housing.
6. Support means to define obligations and improve landlord/tenant relationships.

Parks and Recreation
1. Provisions for parks and recreation which include neighborhood parks, especially in high density areas; local cooperation with state and federal agencies in acquiring and maintaining parkland; subdivision regulations which require large land developers to set aside parkland; preservation and advance acquisition of land for parks and recreation and open spaces; Raleigh Parks and Recreation Department's "Greenway" proposal.

A mechanism must be found to determine the needs for all of Wake County. In Raleigh the neighborhood CACs and the Parks and Recreation Advisory Board do this. In the County there is no established mechanism. Therefore we recommend that:

2. A Master Plan for Parks and Recreation be established for the entire County.
3. Both the funding and administration of the Parks and Recreation programs be extended throughout Wake County.
4. Great care be taken to insure that each community be free to set its own priorities to meet the basic standards for recreational facilities.
5. Encourage year-round use of schools, including media centers and physical education facilities as an integral part of the total Parks and Recreation Program.

Transportation
We recommend that:
1. A strong Transit Authority with power to enter into contracts be established whose membership would have broad-based citizen representation.
2. Mass transportation services be extended into the County and to the Research Triangle.

Public Protection
We recommend that:
1. A mechanism be found to *assure* the selection of a qualified sheriff.
2. The screening program for the police include psychological profiles with periodic evaluations.

[136]

3. The Police Review Board in Raleigh be expanded to include citizen representation.

Health

Support for the Information and Referral System for the delivery of human services as proposed by Goals for Raleigh/ Wake, with adequate safeguards to protect citizens' privacy.
Support for a comprehensive plan for the delivery of health services for Wake County.
Decentralization of health services into smaller municipalities.
  1. Mobile units operating in rural areas to provide preventive medicine, family planning, etc.
  2. Establishment of outpatient clinics with designated hours.

The Instant Need of Things

Rudyard Kipling described the American man in these words: "He turns a keen untroubled face home to the instant need of things." I do not know of a better description of the American woman. Illustrations of "the instant need of things" are to be found in plenty—heaped up, packed down, and overflowing in every community in the land:

The instant need of things shines out of the faces of men, women, and children—caught up in the slings and arrows of outrageous fortune: old age, sickness, accidents, loss or lack of jobs, physical handicaps, mental troubles, and all the ills that flesh is heir to—ills which will not wait on meetings of the federal congress, state legislatures, county commissioners, or city councilmen.

The instant need of things stares out of all the interstices of our society—in city, county, state, or nation —in hardship cases where the free enterprise system is failing to find and clothe and educate and provide even a primitive, minimum level of subsistence for those unable to keep up with basic needs in a competitive market, where economic forces do not strike a balance and the countenance of justice is sometimes hard to see.

It is into this instant need of things that women are at work in their woman's clubs and on their own, plugging their electric energy into the social sockets of their communities, bringing the saving graces of pity, mercy, and compassion, and the plain common sense of business into play in their efforts to help people get going to the point that they can keep on going on their own; supplementing official agencies of local government and their budgets for health and welfare and parks and playgrounds, adding beauty to their homes, streets, highways, and public places.

Here in North Carolina, when I see them doing all these things, while keeping house, raising children, and getting them off to school and college, and meeting the unending demands of home and family life, I leave them with the ancient ritual blessing spelled out in the Book of Numbers in the Old Testament: "The Lord bless thee and keep thee; the Lord make his face to shine upon thee, and be gracious unto thee; the Lord lift up his Countenance upon thee."

VI.
The Woman's Fight for Political Equality

IN THE UNITED STATES

Abigail Adams

In the spring of 1776, John Adams was representing the Colony of Massachusetts in the assembly of delegates meeting in Philadelphia to decide whether thirteen colonies strung along the Atlantic Seaboard "are and of right ought to be free and independent states."

On March 31, 1776, his wife, Abigail, wrote to him from their home in Braintree, Massachusetts, saying:

> I long to hear that you have declared an independancy—and by the way in the new Code of Laws which I suppose it will be necessary for you to make I desire you would Remember the Ladies, and be more generous and favourable to them than your ancestors. Do not put such unlimited power into the hands of the Husbands. Remember all Men would be tyrants if they could. If perticuliar care and attention is not paid to the Ladies we are determined to foment a Rebelion, and will not hold ourselves bound by any Laws in which we have no voice, or Representation.

On April 14, John Adams replied:

> As to Declarations of Independency, be patient . . .As to your extraordinary Code of Laws, I cannot but laugh. We have been told that our Struggle has loosened the bands of government every where. That Children and Apprentices were disobedient—that Schools and Colledges were grown turbulent—that Indians slighted their Guardians and Negroes grew insolent to their Masters. But your Letter was the first Intimation that another Tribe more numerous and powerful than all the rest were grown

discontented—This is rather too coarse a Compliment but you are so saucy, I wont blot it out.

On May 7, Abigail responded:

I can not say that I think you very generous to the Ladies, for whilst you are proclaiming peace and good will to Men, Emancipating all Nations, you insist upon retaining an absolute power over Wives. But you must remember that Arbitrary power is like most other things which are very hard, very liable to be broken—and notwithstanding all your wise Laws and Maxims we have it in our power not only to free ourselves but to subdue our Masters, and without violence throw both your natural and Legal authority at our feet. . . .

If I had to put my finger on one point in time and space when the woman's fight for political equality in the United States began, it would be Abigail Adams' letter to John Adams on the thirty-first day of March, 1776. It was the first joint in the backbone of that fight.

Lucretia Mott and Elizabeth Cady Stanton: 1840–1848

If I had to put my finger on the second joint in the backbone of woman's fight for political equality in the United States, it would be an incident occurring in England in the year 1840.

The world Anti-Slavery Convention was being held in London. Two American women were there: Lucretia Mott was an American delegate to the convention, and Elizabeth Cady Stanton was the wife of an American delegate. Both of these women were denied the privilege of attending and participating in the convention proceedings—for no other or better reason than that they were women. It made them mad, and they entered into a solemn compact that they would return to the United States and start a movement to do something about winning the rights of women.

They did just that.

Out of their efforts came the first Woman's Rights Convention, held in Seneca Falls, New York, in the year 1848. There the women of the conference drew up this Declaration of Sentiments:

The history of mankind is a history of repeated injuries and usurpations on the part of men toward women, having in direct object the establishment of an absolute tyranny over her. To prove this, let facts be submitted to a candid world:

He has never permitted her to exercise her inalienable right to the elective franchise.

He has compelled her to submit to laws in the formation of

which she had no voice.

He has withheld from her rights which are given to the most ignorant and degraded men—both natives and foreigners.

Having deprived her of this first right of a citizen, the elective franchise, thereby leaving her without representation in the halls of legislation, he has oppressed her on all sides.

He has made her, if married, in the eye of the law civilly dead.

He has taken from her all right in property, even to the wages she earns.

He has monopolized nearly all the profitable employments, and from those she is permitted to follow she receives but a scanty remuneration.

He has denied her the facilities for obtaining a thorough education, all colleges being closed to her.

He has created a false public sentiment by giving to the world a different code of morals for men and women, by which moral delinquencies which exclude women from society are not only tolerated but deemed of little account in man.

He has usurped the prerogatives of Jehovah Himself, claiming it as his right to assign for her a sphere of action, when that belongs to her conscience and her God.

They wound up the convention by proclaiming that "it is the duty of the women of this country to secure to themselves their sacred right to the election franchise," and calling for "the immediate access to all the rights and privileges which belong to them as citizens of the United States." The fight for women's rights had begun, and on a national scale.

The National American Woman's Suffrage Association–1869

If I had to put my finger on the third joint in the backbone of woman's fight for political equality in the United States, it would be the organization of the National American Woman's Suffrage Association in 1869.

The 1848 Woman's Rights Convention was followed by similar conventions in many other parts of the country. In 1850 a National Woman's Rights Convention was held in Worcester, Massachusetts; it drew delegates from all parts of the country, and this convention was repeated throughout the 1860s. These conventions attracted derision, ridicule, and descriptions of the delegates as "Amazons," "unsexed," "disappointed of getting a husband," "a hybrid belonging to neither sex," "dull and uninteresting and, aside from their novelty, hardly worthy of notice."

But out of their continuing efforts came the National American Woman's Suffrage Association (NAWSA) organized in 1869 to stimulate women to work, state by state, for the right to vote and hold office. And that is what it did.

By 1875, Susan B. Anthony had drawn up an amendment to the Constitution of the United States, saying: "The right of citizens of the United States to vote shall not be denied or abridged on account of sex." It was introduced in Congress the following year, and every year thereafter for forty-five years, until Congress finally submitted it to a vote, state by state. It was ratified by three-fourths of the states in 1920 and became the Nineteenth Amendment ot the Constitution of the United States.

IN NORTH CAROLINA

The struggle of women for the right to vote and hold office in North Carolina has been prolonged and thorny.

The 1776 constitution of North Carolina did not mention women, nor did the constitutional amendments of 1835. The limited mention in the 1868 constitution was more honored in the breach than in the observance for fifty years. In a speech to the Equal Suffrage League in Greenville in 1916, Chief Justice Walter Clark of our Supreme Court gave this description of the political status of women in North Carolina: "The Constitution and the laws of this state grant the right of suffrage to every adult excepting only four classes: 1. Idiots and lunatics—because they are mental defectives. 2. Convicts—because they are moral defectives. 3. Illiterates—unless their ancestors were white. 4. Women—the mothers, wives, and daughters of the . . .men of North Carolina."

From the 1850s to 1913

Some newspapers in North Carolina tried to head off the movement for women's rights which was gaining ground in the north, and to keep it from spreading to North Carolina.

In 1850, the *Raleigh Register* wrote: "Woman's sphere is about the domestic altar and within the tranquil precincts of the social circle. When she transgresses that sphere and mingles in the miserable brawlings and insane agitations of the day, she descends from her lofty elevation and becomes an object of disgust and contempt."

In 1858, the *Oxford Leisure Hour* wrote: "The most ridiculous escape in this century is the unwise, foolish, and incomprehensible position assumed by certain trous-a-loon women of the north. All this originates in a false state of Society that in the south would not be countenanced for one day."

But countenanced it was, though sparingly, grudgingly, and with recognitions few and far between. In the year 1894, according to Nell Battle Lewis, writing in the *News and Observer*, Helen Morris Lewis called a meeting in the Buncombe County Courthouse in Asheville where she, Florence Cunningham, and Thomas W. Patton, Mayor of Asheville, spoke out for woman suffrage. The next day, forty-five men and women met in Mayor Patton's home and organized the first Women's Suffrage Association in North Carolina, with Helen Morris Lewis as President. She ran for the position of "water superintendent" in the city of Asheville in 1899 and was defeated, but it gave her the distinction of being the first woman in North Carolina to run for public office.

The first bill to allow women to vote in North Carolina was introduced in the General Assembly in 1897 by J. L. Hyatt, a Republican senator from Burnsville, Yancey County. In an article on the woman suffrage movement in North Carolina, Elizabeth Taylor tells what happened to the bill: "The bill . . . was referred to the committee on insane asylums, of which Hyatt was chairman. Hyatt appealed to his fellow senators to refer the bill to another committee, but in vain. He said that he 'tried Republicans and Democrats . . . but they would do nothing. It was plain that they thought the right committee had the bill.' "

Other efforts facing in the same direction died aborning in the early 1900s. There was a statute providing for a vote of "freeholders" before added taxes on property could be levied. A woman owning land sought to vote in the election. The Supreme Court of North Carolina held that a "freeholder" was a term of "ancient legal usage" and meant a free man and not a free woman.

A statute enacted in 1915 provided: "That the Governor is hereby authorized to appoint women as well as men to be notaries, and this

position shall be deemed a place of trust and profit, and not an office."
The Governor promptly appointed a woman as notary public. The
Supreme Court held this statute to be invalid, that a person could not
hold "a public office" unless he was a voter, that a notary was a "public
office," and that a woman, not being a voter, could not be appointed to
it, and that the General Assembly could not turn a "public office" into
"a place of trust and profit" to which women could be appointed
merely by calling it such. The Court quoted Portia in *The Merchant of
Venice* in support:

> 'Twill be recorded as a precedent;
> And many an error by the same example
> Will rush into the state. It cannot be.

The Supreme Court divided three to two on the question.

A year later, the Court denied a woman the right to serve as deputy
clerk of court on the same theory, the Court saying: "The propriety
and wisdom of female suffrage, and of eligibility of women to hold
office, are questions which must be settled by the people, and which
we cannot discuss or consider in the determination of legal questions."

The woman suffrage movement in North Carolina was revived in
1913 as women gathered in Charlotte and organized the North
Carolina Equal Suffrage League. The first year's report showed local
Equal Suffrage Leagues organized in fourteen cities and towns, including Morganton, Reidsville, Charlotte, Salisbury, Asheville, High
Point, Kinston, New Bern, Raleigh, Chapel Hill, Henderson,
Goldsboro, Washington, Greenville, and Hickory, and the movement
spread to other localities throughout the state. Pamphlets were published and distributed, giving the arguments for woman suffrage;
local, state, and national speakers addressed meetings throughout the
state.

The High School Debates

The Dialectic and Philanthropic Literary Societies of the University
of North Carolina at Chapel Hill organized a High School Debating
Committee and issued a widely distributed pamphlet giving the pros
and cons of the woman suffrage issue:

Affirmative Arguments
    I. Granting that the suffrage is not a natural right nor a right

given by the Constitution of the United States, it is a right to which they are entitled.

A. It should be provided for on the ground that mental equipment rather than physical ability is the correct basis for granting the privilege of voting.

    1. Women are the equals of men in mentality.

B. It is in keeping with the prevailing ideas of American democracy of today.

    1. All people, barring certain restrictions, who are governed have a voice in determining the character of their government.

II. The suffrage would be beneficial to women.

    A. It would broaden them mentally and socially.

        1. By reason of the right to vote they would be led to study civil and political questions.

        2. By being placed on an equality with men, women would receive greater respect for their opinions.

    B. It would result in laws more favorable to woman's economic and legal rights.

        1. New occupations would be open to women.

        2. They would receive better wages.

        3. They would legislate against inequalities to which they are subjected under present laws.

            a. They would do this in regard to the division of property.

            b. They would do this in regard to the division of taxation.

III. Woman suffrage would be beneficial to the State.

    A. By reason of their character women are well qualified to vote.

        1. They have a keener sense of right and wrong than men.

        2. They are qualified mentally to vote.

        a. They are better students than men.

    B. Equal suffrage would result in less corruption in politics.

        1. Women would demand that candidates be of high moral character.

        2. They would carry the wholesome conversation of the home into politics.

    C. Equal suffrage would result in laws more favorable to homes, schools, public health, etc.

    D. Women would be better trained, as a result of their activity in politics, to instill correct ideas of citizenship in their children.

IV. The reasons and considerations that make woman suffrage advisable and efficient in other States hold good in North Carolina.

A. Equal suffrage has proved successful where it has been tried.
  1. Better men have been nominated for office.
  2. Elections have been more orderly.
  3. The dignity of woman has not been lowered and the welfare of the home has not been endangered.

B. There is no fundamental difference between the people of North Carolina and the people of the States which have woman suffrage.

C. The absence of large towns in this State makes impossible the corruption at the polls which exists in large cities.

D. North Carolina's progress, especially in education, warrants this progressive step.

Negative Arguments

I. The suffrage should not be granted to women.

A. Women are not the equal of men mentally.
  1. They have not shown their mental equality.
    a. In constructive policies.

B. They could not carry into effect the measures they migh enact.
  1. They do not have the physical power.

C. The granting of the suffrage to women is not demande by the principles of present day democracy.
  1. Women have representation in government throug men.
    a. Even Congress works through representative committees.
  2. Many men pay taxes and are not allowed to vote.

II. The suffrage would be detrimental to women.

A. It would burden women with new responsibilities.
  1. They would be placed in office.

B. It would lower them in the estimation of men.

C. It would take them out of their proper sphere of life.

D. Their suffrage would be used by bad, as well as goo women.

III. The suffrage would be detrimental to State interests.

A. Women would not fully understand the issues involved and would be a dangerous tool in the hands of scheming politicians.

B. More unscrupulous women would vote than conscientious ones.

    1. The corrupt element of a city usually gets control of the city's government.
    2. Men who do not vote are often the best of men.
    3. Bad ones are often used by scheming politicians.

C. Women would neglect the home.

    1. Political duties would take their attention away from the home.
    2. Women's organizations, religious, civil and moral, would lag.

D. It would result in dissensions in the home.

    1. The unity of the home would be broken.
    2. Quarrels over political matters would ensue between husband and wife.

IV. Results in States which have tried woman suffrage do not warrant its adoption in North Carolina.

A. Women, having obtained the right in other States, show little interest.

    1. Comparatively few have registered or voted.
    2. Almost none have attended the primaries.
    3. Enthusiasm in Colorado, Utah, and Oklahoma is short-lived; a fad.

B. There is no demand for it in this State.

    1. No organized movement has shown itself.

C. Conditions in North Carolina are not similar to those prevailing in other States.

    1. North Carolina is a conservative state.
    2. Southern women and particularly North Carolina women have always been noted for their ideal home life, and not for a political or business-like temperament.

D. North Carolina's progress, especially in education, is no argument for woman suffrage.

    1. Woman suffrage does not necessarily follow the education of women.

In the early months of 1913, 360 debaters in 90 high schools discussed this question before local audiences in their communities. In the spring of the year, 64 high school debaters from 16 high schools came to Chapel Hill as winners of local contests for the final round of contests and the Aycock Memorial Cup was presented to the winner.

These debates focused state-wide attention on the woman suffrage issue. The *Charlotte Observer* got out a special suffrage edition in 1914, the *News and Observer* in 1915. The *Greensboro Daily News* ran a series of editorials and feature stories. Suffrage bills in the General Assembly were still debated with regularity, but the margins of defeat were growing smaller with every legislative session.

The General Assembly in 1919

Three bills were introduced in January of the 1919 session of the North Carolina General Assembly: (1) to permit women to vote in the primaries; (2) to permit women to vote in municipal elections; (3) to permit women to vote in all elections. All of them were defeated.

Thereafter, in June, 1919, the Congress of the United States finally voted to submit to the states for ratification the nineteenth amendment stating: "The right of citizens of the United States to vote shall not be denied or abridged by the United States or by any state on account of sex."

The tempo of discussion in North Carolina picked up as one state after another ratified this amendment. North Carolina newspapers were all unanimous in supporting it. The Republican Party endorsed it in state convention in 1918 and put the endorsement on the line by nominating a woman, Mary Settle Sharpe, as a candidate for State Superintendent of Public Instruction on the state ticket. When the Democratic Party Convention met in Raleigh in April, 1920, thirty-five states had ratified it, and the role of North Carolina became crucial as only one more state would be needed to meet the three-fourths request for adoption. The convention ratified it by a roll call vote of 585 to 428. President Woodrow Wilson wired Governor Bickett: "I am sure I need not point out to you the critical importance of the action of your state in the matter of the Suffrage Amendment." Governor Bickett replied that he honestly hoped that the state of Tennessee would relieve North Carolina of that responsibility, called a special session of the General Assembly to consider the question, and in his opening address recommended ratification as a gesture of yielding to the inevitable. The fight was on.

[148]

The General Assembly in 1920

The North Carolina General Assembly met August 20, 1920, with the opportunity to become the thirty-sixth ratifying state, thus giving the three-fourths majority required by the United States Constitution. The Tennessee legislature was in session, faced with the same opportunity. A "round robin" of 63 of 120 members of the General Assembly of North Carolina sent a delegate to Tennessee saying: "North Carolina is not going to ratify the proposed amendment and we hope you won't ratify it either."

Tennessee Ratifies and the Fight is Won

Tennessee ignored the plea, ratified the amendment, and North Carolina lost the opportunity to turn the proposed amendment into the "law of the land."

The House of Representatives of the North Carolina General Assembly found votes for women a bitter dose that was too hard to swallow. It even refused to support a resolution ratifying a *fait accompli*, by a vote of 71 to 41. It then voted to table a resolution rejecting the amendment which was already "the law of the land"! Not until its 1971 session did the General Assembly of North Carolina ratify the amendment giving women the right to vote.

Here is what happened when Tennessee became the thirty-sixth state to ratify the woman suffrage amendment. The ratification certificate was signed by Governor Roberts, with an injunction hanging over his head, and was sent by registered mail to the Secretary of State in Washington. It was received at the State Department at four o'clock in the morning on Thursday, August 26, 1920, referred at once to the Solicitor General, who had been waiting all night to certify its correctness, returned to the State Department, and at eight o'clock Secretary of State Bainbridge Colby signed the proclamation of the woman suffrage amendment to the federal Constitution.

There was a mass meeting in Washington that night. Next day, Mrs. Carrie Chapman Catt, Charl Williams, and Harriet Taylor Upton went to New York. At every stop they were met by victory delegations. When they rolled into Pennsylvania station in New York, they were welcomed by Governor Al Smith, Senator Calder, and a great crowd with the 71st Regiment band. Then, escorted by a guard of honor, they were placed at the head of a marching column, and so with music playing and flags flying the last suffrage parade passed through New York into history.

THE NATIONAL LEAGUE OF WOMEN VOTERS IS BORN

The current *In-League Guidebook* of the League of Women Voters gives these historical highlights on the founding of the League:

The 19th Amendment to the Constitution was on the way to final ratification by the 66th Congress of the United States when Carrie Chapman Catt sent out the call to the 50th Anniversary Convention of the National American Woman Suffrage Association to be held in St. Louis, Missouri, March 24–29, 1919.

As a fitting memorial to a half-century of progress, the association invited the women voters of the fifteen full suffrage states to attend this anniversary and there to join their forces in a League of Women Voters, one of whose objects was to speed the suffrage campaign in our own and other countries.

A League of Women Voters was accordingly set up, composed of the organizations in states where woman suffrage had already been attained. It was to act as a section of the suffrage association until the 19th Amendment was actually ratified.

The League was formally organized in Chicago on February 14, 1920; the official name was the National League of Women Voters. In describing the function of the new organization, Carrie Chapman Catt said:

> In the League of Women Voters we have an anomaly; we are going to be a semi-political body. We want political things; we want legislation; we are going to educate for citizenship. In that body we have got to be nonpartisan and all-partisan. Democrats from Alabama and Republicans from New Hampshire must work for the same things.

At the same time, she made it clear that she expected women voters to take part in partisan politics: "The only way to get things done is to get them done on the inside of a political party . . . ."

The National League of Women Voters was incorporated in the District of Columbia in 1923. The Certificate of Incorporation said the objectives were:

> . . . to foster education in citizenship and to support needed

legislation; to encourage interest in government and in the Nation's problems; to promote participation by the newly franchised women in the civil life of our country; to stimulate activity in public affairs, particularly registering and voting at every election; to develop intelligent use of votes by the women of the United States; to render such other services in the interest of education in citizenship as may be possible, and for the mutual improvement of the members and to do every act appropriate or necessary to carry out any of the foregone objects.

League Purpose and Policy

The League purpose and policy (as distinguished from its structure and procedures) have changed little since the founding days. The purpose, as it appeared in the national bylaws in 1920 was "...to foster education in citizenship and to support improved legislation." The beginnings of the non-partisan political policy also appear in the 1920 bylaws: "The National League of Women Voters urges every woman to become an enrolled voter, but as an organization it shall be allied with and support no party."

In 1923 the purpose was enlarged to include efficiency in government and international cooperation to prevent war. The year 1938 saw the League's objective as promoting "political education through active participation of citizens in government." In 1946 the purpose was further clarified as being to "promote political responsibility through informed and active participation of citizens in government," and the policy stated: "The League may take action on governmental measures and policies in the public interest. It shall not support or oppose any political party or any candidate." The purpose and policy of the League today remain the same.

Citizen Information/Voters Service

Citizen Information/Voters Service has been an integral part of the League from its earliest days. Demonstration classes were organized in the League's first year to explain to newly enfranchised women the proper way to mark a ballot and other technicalities of registration and voting. Citizen schools for the study of principles of government at all levels were also started in 1920 and were a popular League activity. Many of the schools were conducted in cooperation with universities or colleges. The first year also saw the establishment of a correspondence course on government.

[151]

Later in the 1920s, the League set up institutes on "defects in our system of government," started "Know Your Town" surveys, initiated candidate questionnaires and meetings, and held classes to train volunteer teachers for citizenship schools. Such citizen-directed activities laid the foundation for the many diverse and creative Citizen Information/Voters Service efforts undertaken by the League from its earliest years to the present day.

BY WAY OF TRIBUTE

In the 1950s a member of the Illinois state senate criticized the League of Women Voters for its activities in pushing through permanent registration measures for voters in Illinois, and Senator T. V. Smith replied on the floor of the state senate:

The League of Women Voters is not run by those who shirk other duties to do this one. The Senator is wrong in suggesting that they neglect the art of reproduction in their zeal for legislation. They represent not the sophisticated but the dedicated crowd of women. I am not commissioned to speak for the League; but I do bear them the honor of believing that there is no organization in America which makes less noise and sheds more light on public questions than the League of Women Voters. When I meet its representatives they are better informed than I as to measures upon which they speak and that is the basis for wholesome deference—a deference which I am willing to yield any man—or woman either. They choose their subjects; they study them as I have never seen legislators study measures; and then they push them as rapidly as courtesy permits and as long as patience is required to put them over. We may lose this battle today for honest elections and, alas, we may ourselves forget it, as Senator Monroe suggests; but there is one group, if I know my women, who will not forget this matter until it is settled right— and that is the League of Women Voters. They have only begun to fight when legislators elect to call it a day. You may differ with people like that, Senators; but you've got to respect them— though they be women. And no innuendoes will faze them or mar the gratitude we owe them for persistence in a good cause, while others forget or fall away. This is preeminently the organization, Senator Monroe, which carries on the general work for better citizenship upon which you yourself think we must rely to get slowly ahead. They do not have to be either mothers or citizens; they are both mothers and citizens.

People acquainted with the work of the North Carolina League of Women Voters could come to a similar conclusion about its work.

VII.
The Woman's Fight for Equality of Rights under the Law

WHERE I CAME IN AND WHY

Let me tell you where I came into this discussion and why:

For many years I taught the course in Family Law in the Law School of the University of North Carolina at Chapel Hill. In that course I followed the struggles of married women for the right to control the property they brought to the marriage altar, for the right to go into business and make a living on their own, for the freedom of their persons from the husband's physical power.

I followed the efforts of women, married and unmarried, to overcome the customs, traditions, and laws; which denied them the right to education beyond the high school, to assemble in voluntary associations and participate in activities beyond their household walls, and to vote and hold office.

In the late 1960s I wrote my studies into the first draft of a short book, *By Her Own Bootstraps—A Saga of Women in North Carolina*, ending with the chapter on Woman's Fight for Political Equality.

A year or two later, Congress submitted the Equal Rights Amendment to the states for ratification in 1972. Shortly thereafter bicentennial committees began discussing how best to celebrate two hundred years of freedom and independence since 1776. It suddenly dawned on me that I did not know of a more inspiring story in the history of liberty in that two hundred years than the long unbroken struggle of *married* women in North Carolina to free themselves from the shackles of the medieval common law and statutes of England coming to North Carolina with the early settlers in the 1660s, and from the customs and traditions restricting the activities of all women.

I saw all of these struggles culminating in the struggle for an amendment to the Constitution of the United States, saying: "Equality of rights under the law shall not be denied or abridged by the United States or by any state on account of sex." That is why I decided to add the chapter on Woman's Fight for Equality of Rights under the Law.

The woman's fight for "equality of rights under the law" in North Carolina did not begin with the submission of the Equal Rights Amendment to the states by the federal Congress in 1972. It did not begin with its first submission to the Congress of the United States in 1923. The records show that here in North Carolina it had been going on for a hundred and fifty years. Let me illustrate my meaning:

THE SHACKLES OF MEDIEVAL LAW

The early settlers coming to North Carolina in the 1660s and thereafter brought with them the common law and statutes of medieval England. Under those laws a woman might go to the marriage altar as the greatest heiress in England, but with the pronouncement of the magic words of the wedding ceremony, the sorcery of the common law transferred to her husband all of her personal property and the rents and profits of all her lands—everything except her wearing apparel. A bow, perhaps, to the laws forbidding indecent exposure.

Her property was not all the woman lost in the wedding ceremony:

She lost the power to make a binding contract, and to go into business and make a living on her own—man and wife were one, and the man was the one.

She lost the right to keep any earnings for her labors—her labors belonged to her husband.

She lost the right to sue and recover damages for slander and libel—her name belonged to her husband.

She lost the freedom of her person to her husband. He was allowed by the law of the land, and, I quote from a court decision, "to use towards his wife such a degree of force as is necessary to control an unruly temper and make her behave herself."

These were the shackles put upon the married woman by the law of the land in North Carolina for two hundred years—from the 1660s to the 1860s. Any further falling had to be uphill.

THE FIGHT TO REMOVE THESE SHACKLES

The married woman's uphill fight to remove these shackles, brought nibbling changes in the laws of the General Assembly in 1837 and 1848. The tide began to turn in the married woman's favor with an amendment to the Constitution in 1868, giving the wife *complete control* of her personal property, and *control of her real property—with one limitation:* she had to have the "written assent of her husband" before she could convey it.

By the latter 1800s, she had won a decision in the courts saying that "the old doctrine that a husband had a right to whip his wife with a switch no larger than his thumb is not law in North Carolina, and that the husband has no right to whip his wife under any circumstances."

By 1911, she had won removal of the limitation on the married woman's right to make contracts—permitting her to go into business for herself and make a living on her own, and later, the right to sue in her own name for her work and earnings and keep the money for herself.

By 1913, she had won the right to sue in her own name for injuries to her person, and keep the money for herself.

By 1920, she had won the right to sue her husband for injuries to her person, and keep the money for herself.

By 1964, the requirement of "the written assent of the husband" for the conveyance of her real property was taken out of the Constitution and put in the hands of the General Assembly.

At long last, the wedding ceremony is more of a celebration and less of a sacrifice. The woman can go to the altar to the strains of Lohengrin and come away to the strains of Mendelssohn with the satisfying assurance that she is no longer giving up control of her property or her person. She may still look upon her husband as her lord—but he is no longer her landlord. And, as far as the law is concerned, he has to talk to her with more of persuasion and less of command.

At long last, equality of rights to own and control property and to freedom of her person, under the laws of North Carolina, were no longer to be denied to married women on account of sex.

OVERCOMING CUSTOMS AND TRADITIONS

The next great chapter in the woman's struggle to free herself from the shackles of customs, traditions, and laws that cramped her style, is illustrated in three movements beginning around the turn of the century here in North Carolina.

First: Women began to realize they could not correct or control many of the problems they faced in their homes, without trying to correct and control conditions in communities surrounding their homes, and they began to come together in village betterment societies and in a multiplicity of women's clubs—despite all that custom and tradition could do to stop them.

Second: They began fighting for and winning the right to education beyond the high school, and then began enrolling in colleges and universities throughout the state in numbers equal, almost, to men—despite all that custom and tradition could do to stop them.

Third: They began fighting for, and winning, the right to vote and hold office, over the ridicule of men in and out of the General Assembly which sent the first bill introduced for woman suffrage to the Committee on Insane Asylums.

At long last, equality of these rights: (1) to assemble freely in voluntary associations outside the home, (2) to education beyond the high school, and (3) to vote and hold office, were no longer to be denied to any woman under the laws of North Carolina on account of sex.

BY WAY OF SUMMARY

By the grace of the wedding ceremony and the teeth of the common law, for centuries the husband kept all of his own property and took most of the wife's. Later he argued against its restoration on the ground that she had no experience in its management!

By the grace of the wedding ceremony and the teeth of the common law, for centuries the married woman lost her right to enter into binding contracts on which others could rely, and was kept from making a living on her own, and in later days husbands argued against the restoration of this right on the ground that she had no experience in business!

By the grace of the wedding ceremony and the teeth of the common law, for centuries the husband took control of his wife's person on the theory that man and wife are one and the man is the one; in later days he argued against the restoration of her liberty on the ground that she had no experience in its use!

For centuries the customs of our society confined the woman to the home as her operating base, and to the public school as her educational forum; in later days men argued against her joining a woman's club, or going to college, and entering the professions and other gainful employments on the ground that her sheltered existence had given her no acquaintance with the outside world!

For centuries the laws of the land denied women the right to vote and hold office, and in later days men argued against giving them these prohibited rights because they had no experience in political affairs!

The irony of these attitudes and contradictions continues to this day in Social Security laws and regulations looking on "housewives" as "non-working" women and giving them half the social security benefits given to the husband. And now that government researchers are belatedly trying to correct this condition of affairs and to determine the value of "woman's work" at home, they are listing the kinds of jobs women are doing in the homes and calculating what it would cost them to hire people to do those jobs; they are using the current hourly minimum wage standards as the basis for their computations. The cost of the mother raising a child is rated at the fee for a baby sitter. The wife's house cleaning is rated at the wage of a hired housemaid. Home management, home decorating, and social activity in the family and beyond are rated at the going hourly stipends. And this comes after man's argument through the centuries that the running of the home is so important that the woman could not take out time to manage her property, or join a woman's club, or go to the polls!

This procedure for determining the cash value of a woman reminds me of the old story of the scientists who reduced a human body to its basic chemical parts, found varying amounts of water, potash, carbon, hydrogen, oxygen, nitrogen, sulphur, calcium, *et cetera*; they gave to each part its market value and came out with a figure of less than five dollars as the value of a man—not more than ten dollars after allowing for inflation through the years.

These measures of man or woman are worthy of the comment of one nun to another after they came out of the performance in a circus tent and found that a cloudburst had flooded the street they had to cross. They were pulling up their long skirts to walk across when two circus clowns came by fresh from the performance with their faces painted in many colors and offered their backs to carry the nuns across. In transit one of the nuns, sensing the ludicrous sight, called out to the other: "This is virgin on the ridiculous."

WHO WAS PUTTING WHO ON A PEDESTAL?

Is it not fair to ask "who was putting who on a pedestal" when a woman met her prospective husband at the altar, gave up her name and took his name as her own, and added the gift of all of her personal property and the rents and profits of all her lands? Who was putting who on a pedestal when she gave to him the right to her services and earnings, and the right of going into business to make a living on her own, and threw the gift of her personal freedom into the bargain? May it not be fairly said that woman was putting man on a pedestal, and paying for the pedestal to boot?

Robert Frost said that education was the art of catching on. At long last women began catching on. At long last women began to ask men to "level" with them, in the belief that "leveling" would raise them far above the proverbial "pedestal," and to the infinite betterment of both men and women, and the cities, the counties, the state of North Carolina, in which they live and move and have their being?

THE NORTH CAROLINA GENERAL ASSEMBLY

It is this continued and unbroken struggle for full equality with their brothers on *many* fronts which provides the background and underpinning of the current struggle for equality with their brothers on *all* fronts—so far as this equality can be achieved by an amendment to the United States Constitution, saying: "Equality of rights under the law shall not be denied or abridged by the United States or by any state on account of sex."

In 1973, a bill to ratify this amendment was voted down in the North Carolina Senate by a vote of 27 to 23.

In 1975, it was voted down in the House of Representatives by a vote of 62 to 57.

In the 1977 General Assembly, the House of Representatives ratified the Equal Rights Amendment by a vote 61 to 55 and sent it to the Senate, where a tug of war began. Opponents feared supporters had the edge, and called for *less* speed and *more* deliberation. Supporters felt they had the edge, and called for *more* speed and *less* deliberation. Opponents feared they would lose in a Senate vote, and sought to take it out of the Senate and let the people decide, while supporters felt they had the edge and sought to keep it in the Senate and let the Senate decide.

MASS MEETING IN DORTON ARENA

One week before ERA was brought to the Senate floor for discussion, a group of ERA opponents called a mass meeting in Dorton Arena, as a prelude to the public hearing for opponents in the Legislative Building that afternoon. Fifteen hundred people came to hear the two most effective campaigning opponents of the Equal Rights Amendment in the nation. There was the national chairman of the movement to *Stop ERA*, who to my way of thinking has been, and still is, the most articulate and effective opponent of ERA who has surfaced in this country. I have often said, and I believe it to be true, that if she had surfaced on the side of ERA, it would have been ratified long ago as the 27th Amendment to the Constitution of the United States. And there was Senator Ervin, who had opposed ERA from the beginning to the end of the debate on the floor of the United States Senate in 1972. To my way of thinking, he has stated the best reasoned case against it on the national or state levels.

I will reproduce Senator Ervin's argument in detail later in this paper. It is the tenor and the tone of his companion speaker that I am looking at now. Here is a tape recording of some of her words:

> It is a great thrill to me to be here on the platform today with your Senator Ervin, whom we consider to be the greatest living American today... His speech back in 1972 is one of the greatest speeches of all times, in which he set out everything which is the matter with the Equal Rights Amendment.

She then went on to say: "There is absolutely nothing that the Equal Rights Amendment will do for women...

It will give women no rights, no opportunities, no advantages that they haven't got now...

Another thing I've learned is that there is no law that discriminates against women. There are, however, many laws that benefit them and those are the laws that ERA will get rid of . . .

ERA will legalize homosexual marriages and give them all the rights that homosexuals want—including the right to teach in the schools, and adopt children . . .

[Pass ERA,] and all the rest of a woman's life, she's lost the legal right to be a homemaker. . . .

The Equal Rights Amendment would have a destructive effect on moral values and the family."

She did not explain why, or how, ERA would do these things. She simply said: Take it from me. And they did—with rapturous applause.

Senator Ervin responded with becoming grace to the compliments of the *Stop ERA* chairman:

> Friends, I'd just like to say that the President of the National *Stop ERA* movement is the most charming and the most intelligent girl I've ever met, with the exception of my wife." He then went on to say:
> The ERA has two purposes . . . It is designed to nullify every existing law, federal or state, that makes any distinction between the legal responsibilities of men and women, no matter how wise that distinction is. The second objective of the Equal Rights Amendment is to rob Congress and the legislatures of fifty states of the power to enact at any time in the future any law which makes a distinction between men and women, no matter how wise that distinction is.
> It will do horrible things to our legal system. It will do horrible things to our governmental system. It will do horrible things to the men, women, and children who inhabit the earth. It will put the legal system in chaos. It will jeopardize, indeed it will destroy the constitutionality of every existing law—federal or state—which makes any distinction between the legal rights and responsibilities of men and women, no matter how sensible and just that distinction is. Wives, mothers, and widows will be robbed of their protection, and laws relating to rape and seduction and other sexual crimes will be annulled . . .
> If ERA is ratified by three fourths of the states, it will remain part of the Constitution until the last lingering echo of Gabriel's Horn trembles into silence. . . .
> ERA supporters, [said Ervin], even if they happen to be temporarily residing in the White House or the Governors Mansion, don't know any more about ERA than I do about the particles of the milky way—and that is precisely nothing. . . .

The news reporter wrote: "The crowd loved Ervin, who shouted and gesticulated broadly to make his points. He was interrupted repeatedly by applause. . . . The rally atmosphere was a cross between a political rally and a church revival. Spectators sported white balloons bearing an anti-ERA message, and carried elaborately decorated signs."

The *Stop ERA* chairman did not stop with her charges against ERA. She went on to ask her fifteen hundred listeners to stand up, hold up their right hands, and take a solemn pledge to defeat every legislator in the next election who voted to ratify ERA, and she promised to give them their names to pin up on their kitchen walls so that they would not forget them.

Here is what she said:

> I am going to ask each and everyone here today to take a pledge with me, and I'll read it first so you will know what you're taking. Then I hope you'll stand up and repeat it with me. It goes like this: Because the Equal Rights Amendment would have a destructive effect on moral values and the family, I promise to show my sincere appreciation to the Senators and Representatives who vote NO on ERA or to vote for a referendum by voting and working to re-elect them. Will you do that? Alright, stand up and repeat after me. I'll take it phrase by phrase. Because the Equal Rights Amendment . . . would have a destructive effect on moral values and the family . . . I promise to show . . . my sincere appreciation to the Senators and Representatives . . . who vote NO on ERA . . . to vote for a referendum by voting and working to re-elect them . . .
>
> You have enough people in this room to re-elect anyone you want. You transfer that message over to the Legislative Building and I know that you can defeat ERA. We will provide the lists to you after the vote so that you will know and you can paste it up in your kitchen and you can remember for the next year and a half how each and every one in the Legislature voted, so that you will know which ones are pro-family and which ones are anti-family. You'll know which ones you want to re-elect and which ones you want to replace.

She did not stop there. She told them to go up town to the Legislative Building and seek out legislators in the halls, in the corridors, in the offices, and at the lunch tables, and carry them this message. And that is what many of them did—with fire in their eyes and brimstone in their hearts. Old timers said they had never seen such a spectacle and many of them concluded that the question of ratifying the Equal Rights Amendment had transcended the limits of a legislative inquiry into the merits of the proposition and turned into a raw struggle to shift the balance of political power in state and local elections.

THE TENSION MOUNTS

Tension mounted in the week that followed and the day of the Senate vote approached. Eighty thousand letters villifying the Equal Rights Amendment were mailed from the post office in Falls Church, *via* Maryland, to constituents in North Carolina, including three postcards in each letter, written and addressed to appropriate legislators in the General Assembly of North Carolina, ready to be signed by the recipients and mailed to their respective representatives—two hundred forty thousand in all.

In the columns of newspapers, in letters from constituents to legislators, in bruising exchanges in the corridors of the Legislative Building, opponents of the Equal Rights Amendment were caressing supporters with such endearing names as: Atheists, Anti-Christ, Anti-home, Anti-family, and Anti-God. They were calling them heathens, radicals, socialists, communists, and homosexuals. An eye and ear witness told me that one woman backed a Senator up to the wall, saying, among other things: "If you vote for ERA you are publicly admitting that you are a homosexual." Another told me that a preacher with a bible in his hands went up and down the corridors of the Legislative Building saying to women supporters of ERA; "I understand you want to go into the bathroom with me." Another rabid ministerial opponent proclaimed that "ERA is an invisible acid eating away at the moral ankle-irons of North Carolina Society" and that ERA supporters were "rodents spreading vice and immorality wherever they go."

These extremist tactics may be highly effective in changing votes of legislators who verily believe that in a democracy "the voice of the people is the voice of God." If a man is in the legislature and wants to come back, and voting another way than the way he promised to vote will come nearer to bringing him back, or if he changes his mind on the merits of the issue at the last minute, I can understand why he would vote one way rather than the other. It is a calculated risk for anyone who feels free to take it. And in the sharp calculations which personal ambition makes, it is *not* surprising that an avalanche of letters and postcards, descending on a legislator on the day before a crucial vote, can persuade him that under such circumstances a man would be "a fool not to change his mind." Particularly when they threaten to defeat him in the next election if he does not vote as they tell him to and promise to re-elect him if he does. It *is* surprising when only two Senators under these pressures changed their promises to vote *for* ERA to promises to vote against it. But they were enough to turn the tally from 26 to 24 *for* ratifying ERA, to 26 to 24 *against* it.

It is not surprising that Senators coming out strong for referring it to the people as long as they did not have the votes to stop it, found they had lost all interest in a referendum as soon as they found they did, and wanted the Senators to come up to the lick-log and do their duty under the constitution in a forthright vote on the Senate floor.

It is not surprising that ERA opponents applauded the two Senators who saw the light in time to come over to their side and turn defeat into victory—echoing the sentiment of the old gospel hymn: "while the light holds out to burn, the vilest sinner may return." And it is not surprising that ERA supporters echoed the sentiments of the Old Testament Prophet: "The Lord loveth a man who sweareth to his own hurt and changeth not."

It is not surprising that ERA opponents who had wanted to let the people talk it to death now shifted course and decided to kill it themselves, and sat silent in seven languages including the Scandinavian, waiting for the kill which came with a vote of 26 to 24, followed by a clincher motion to prevent resurrection in the 1977 General Assembly, on the theory that all is fair in love and war, and this is both.

From his home in Morganton, Senator Ervin was reported in a telephone interview as saying for ERA opponents: "The Senate vote was a great victory for all North Carolinians who want to keep government at home instead of having it transferred to Washington. It was a great victory for good sense. I feel somewhat sorry for those who lost, but their loss was America's gain."

Throughout the state, ERA supporters were left with the consolation of the heartfelt rhyme:

For all sad words of tongue or pen,
The saddest are these: "It might have been."

And of an answering rhyme saying the same thing in different words:

But sadder than this, you often see,
It is, but hadn't ought to be.

There is the story of the little boy who was frightened by stories of the dinosaur, the brontosaurus, and other monstrous animals once walking on the earth. He confided his fears to his father that he might meet one of these animals on the way to school. His father was a very wise and understanding man and told him it was true that such animals once roamed the earth, but that through the centuries the climate

[164]

had changed and they had gradually disappeared.

There was such a change of climate over the woman's right to vote during the fifty years from the 1919–1920 years when the General Assembly of North Carolina refused to ratify the amendment giving women the right to vote—even though it already had been ratified by enough states to put it in the United States Constitution, and 1971 when the General Assembly ratified it unanimously in both House and the Senate. And so it may be with the woman's right to equal rights under the law in years to come.

THOUGHTS IN THE AFTERGLOW

I go along with this statement in a speech by Senator William Smith of New Hanover County on the Senate floor as the campaigns were coming to a head on Tuesday, March 1, 1977:

> I have no illusions that the Equal Rights Amendment is any panacea, and I am certain it will not accomplish all of the things that its proponents contend it will. I am equally certain that it does not harbor the evils which its opponents contend. It is rather a simple affirmation of faith that people ought not to be discriminated against because of sex, or for any other reason for that matter.
>
> Some thought has been given in recent days to a referendum, but in my opinion a referendum would tear this State apart. In my district there are probably 40 or 50 small unaffiliated churches and I think all of them have passed resolutions opposing ERA. They are absolutely convinced that God is on their side and that God opposes ERA. They have embarked upon what they conceive to be a holy crusade to defeat the Equal Rights Amendment. The main line churches on the other hand have adopted resolutions in support of the Equal Rights Amendment and they, too, are convinced that God is with them. A referendum would pit church against church, minister against minister, congregation against congregation, brothers and sisters against brothers and sisters, and parents against children, each side convinced that the well-being of the State was dependent upon the outcome.
>
> I do not know how a referendum would turn out, but I do not want to subject my State to the emotional turmoil that would surely be involved in a referendum. As much as I desire the passage of the Equal Rights Amendment, I would rather see this Senate defeat it today, here and now, than to see the inevitable chaos of a referendum.

[165]

Senator Smith wanted the question decided on the senate floor where the clash of differing opinions in the free and open discussion of joint debate could strike off sparks to light up the face of this amendment like matches struck in darkness. I believe that is the very essence of the legislative process, the heart of democracy, the hope of popular government. I believe that in this particular case, that essence was destroyed and that hope when glimmering when opponents of the Equal Rights Amendment refused to join in the Senate debate. I believe with Lincoln that it may be just as bad to do the right thing in the wrong way as it is to do the wrong thing. I believe that ERA opponents, in abdicating free and open discussion in the cross fire of joint debate threw away something that is far more precious to this state and the United States than the Equal Rights Amendment to the Constitution of the United States.

Senator Ervin never abdicated that responsibility of elected representatives of a free people while he served in the General Assembly of North Carolina in the 1920s. Nor when he served in the United States Senate in the 1950s and 60s. Nor when the merits and demerits of the Equal Rights Amendment were being tested in the cross fire of joint debate and cross examination on the floor of the United States Senate in 1972. He did not abdicate this responsibility in the public hearings in the Legislative Buildings in Raleigh in 1975. Or in the Dorton Arena mass meeting and the public hearing in February 1977. I do not believe he would have abdicated this responsibility on the floor of the North Carolina Senate on Tuesday, March 1, 1977.

CHARGES HURLED BY ERA OPPONENTS

Blanket charges have been hurled against ERA in North Carolina—in 1973, 1975, and again in 1977. They were hurled in public hearings and in private letters, such as this from a "worried constituent" who wrote for himself and others:

> We urge our legislators to vote "NO" on the Equal Rights Amendment because it will deprive the American woman of the privileges and rights she now possesses and every vote for "The So-Called Equal Rights Amendment of 1975" is a nail for the coffin of the American people. The women will be deprived of the right to be supported and provided with a home by her husband, and the right to be exempt from the draft, women and men will use the same restrooms on their jobs,

women when drafted into the service will sleep in the same barracks with the men, and use the same restrooms. Sex crimes will no longer be punishable, protective laws on working conditions will be abolished, family relationships destroyed, financial benefits for women will be jeopardized if this amendment is ratified. This may be the major step in establishing a brutal totalitarian police state over the American people.

If I believed that the Equal Rights Amendment would do these things, I, too, would vote against it.

If I believed that the men and women supporting ERA—including the twenty-four Senators and sixty-one House members—were anti-God, anti-Christ, anti-home, anti-family, communists, homosexuals, or rodents spreading immorality wherever they go, I, too, would vote against it.

If I believed, as one group of "Informed Christian Voters" believes, and said in a letter to a legislator, that a vote for the Equal Rights Amendment is "a blatant and conscious move to defy the Word of God and His instructions on the role of women in our society," and, in support of this proposition quoted *Genesis*—saying that "woman was created to serve man," the husband was created "to rule over woman"; quoted *I Timothy* as saying "let the woman learn in silence with all subjection"; "Suffer not a woman to teach, nor to usurp authority over the man, but to be in silence"; and quoted *Deuteronomy* as saying "women shall not wear men's clothing..."

If I believed ERA defied the will of God, I, too, would vote against it.

If I believed ERA would "put our legal system in chaos ... do horrible things to the men, women, and children who inhabit the earth ... destroy the constitutionality of every existing law—federal or state which makes any distinction between the legal rights and responsibilities of men and women, no matter how sensible and just that distinction is ... That wives, mothers, and widows would be robbed of their protection, and laws relating to rape and seduction and other sexual crimes would be annulled—if I believed ERA would do these things, I, too, would vote against it.

If I believed that "ERA is an invisible acid eating away at the moral ankle-irons of North Carolina Society" and that ERA supporters are "rodents spreading vice and immorality wherever they go," I, too, would vote against it.

I do not throw aside these charges as unworthy of a rational opposition, nor claim that they are foolish on their face. Years ago I was in Washington in the office of Congressman Graham Barden who had

[167]

been a college mate in Chapel Hill. He read me a letter from a constituent asking him to find out if bullfrogs would eat goldfish. "What a foolish question," I exclaimed, "to take up the time of the busy chairman of the House Education and Labor Committee." "Albert," he replied, "When you are running for office you don't get any foolish questions! As a matter of fact this is a sensible question. My constituent is a wealthy woman, living in New Bern, with a pool in her backyard filled with goldfish, which are her pride and joy. She wants to put in bullfrogs whose croaking will bring reminders of rural solitudes to an urban setting, and that is why she wants to know if bullfrogs will eat goldfish. I have called on all the resources of the Library of Congress and the Department of the Interior for an answer to this question, and this morning I got this letter: "Dear Mr. Congressman, we have been unable to find anything written on this question in the literature of the world, and we can only suggest that you advise your constituent that if the bullfrogs ever get hungry it might be well for the goldfish to be out of the way."

I do not believe that the Equal Rights Amendment would take away from men anything they ought to keep, or that it would take away from women anything they ought to have. I do not believe it would take away from Congress or the states anything but the power to discriminate for or against men or women. I believe it would hold up and affirm the ancient standard as old as this republic—the standard of equal rights to all and special privileges to none. I believe it simply says that sauce for the goose is sauce for the gander—at last.

I go along with the dissenting opinion of Mr. Justice Holmes in Abrams vs United States, saying:

> When men have realized that time has upset many fighting faiths, they may come to believe even more than they believe the very foundations of their own conduct that the ultimate good desired is better reached by free trade in ideas—that the best test of truth is the power of the thought to get itself accepted in the competition of the market, and that truth is the only ground upon which their wishes safely can be carried out. That at any rate is the theory of our Constitution. It is an experiment, as all life is an experiment. Every year if not every day we have to wager our salvation upon some prophecy based upon imperfect knowledge. While that experiment is part of our system I think that we should be eternally vigilant against attempts to check the expression of opinions that we loathe and believe to be fraught with death, unless they so imminently threaten immediate interference with the lawful and pressing purposes of the law that an immediate check is required to save the country.

[168]

It is obvious that ERA supporters have not yet met that test in North Carolina.

I believe in the Equal Rights Amendment. I support it with all my heart. I hope, that out of the thirteen states which have not considered it, three more will be found to ratify it and make it the 27th amendment to the Constitution of the United States. I believe that failure to ratify it will slow down, but not stop, the movement saying that "equality of rights under the law shall not be denied by the states or the United States on account of sex." But I do not believe with those supporters of ERA who claim that failure to ratify it by March 22, 1979, will "so immediately threaten immediate interference with the lawful and pressing purposes of the law—that it is required to save the country."

Nor do I believe with those opponents of ERA who are claiming that its defeat on or before that date "is required to save the country." Particularly when they are claiming that every disaster which will come to the country with ERA, is already coming by way of the 5th and 14th amendments, as attested by Supreme Court decisions since 1971.

WHERE DO WE GO FROM HERE?

The song of ERA may have ended here in North Carolina, but the melody lingers on. It will not come back in fullthroated chorus if three states ratify it before the cut off date in 1979, nor if enough states vote it down by 1979 to make a new confrontation useless. But if it is still an open question when the General Assembly of North Carolina convenes in 1979, I have no doubt that supporters and opponents will confront each other and the people of North Carolina once again.

If, as, and when, that time comes, supporters of the Equal Rights Amendment will have an uphill fight with a steeper hill to climb than they had in 1973, 1975, or 1977. They had one strike against them in 1975, two strikes against them in 1977, and they will start with three strikes against them in 1979 or anytime in the hereafter. And that there will be a hereafter I have no doubt. For I believe that women will continue this fight for equal rights under the law "until the last notes of Gabriel's horn trembles into silence"—to use Senator Ervin's colorful phrase.

There is only one chance, as I see it, that the fight will stop this side of that ultimate moment, and that chance is this: If the United States

[169]

Supreme Court continues to extend and expand its interpretation of the commerce clause and equal protection clause of the 14th amendment, and the due process clauses in the 5th and 14th amendments, and overworks them with double duty as it has done in recent years, and if their decisions in fact reach the point where as a matter of fact there is nothing left for an ERA to add and ERA supporters become convinced of that fact, then I believe the battle will come to a reluctant end—with both sides claiming victory. Then, and not till then, will the North Carolina General Assembly and aspirants for higher office be rid of what, to most of its members, has been a vexing question disturbing them with the "joys of elevated thought" between election days—as illustrated by the roses sent from the Senate to the House in 1975 and from the House to the Senate in 1977, after each had given the other a temporary consolation for a momentary victory. Then, and not till then, will the lion and the lamb lie down together, with the lamb—as always—inside the lion, with both sides claiming to be the lion, and with both sides swallowed up in victory. We must not forget that this sort of thing happened in 1971 on the 50th anniversary of the amendment giving women the right to vote, when North Carolina ratified a fifty year old *fait accompli,* and the sons and daughters of its supporters and opponents agreed that the woman's vote had not done as much damage, or as much good, as opponents and supporters had prophesied.

In the meantime, where do we go from here? For three sessions of the General Assembly people of North Carolina have lined up, squared off, and fought each other to a showdown so close that neither side could be sure of victory before the last vote was in and counted. Each side was sure that the other was spreading misinformation, with one side claiming it could prove it, and the other claiming that no proof was necessary. With each side claiming it had a trump card up its sleeve, and each side claiming that God had put it there.

"The partisan," said Socrates 2400 years ago, "when he is engaged in a dispute, cares nothing about the truth of the question, but is anxious only to convince his hearers of his own assertions." There is little difference between the partisan in 467 B.C. and 1977 A.D.

"What will happen when an irresistible force runs into an immovable object?" was a question in semantics put a century ago. The only answer I can think of to that question is: "An inconceivable catastrophe." We can avoid that catastrophe in our discussions of the Equal Rights Amendment here if we are willing to cut through phrases to the acts, and find the truth between the lines in the battle of slogans and competing claims of what ERA will, and will not, do. We can avoid it if we are willing to listen to the impassioned plea of Oliver Cromwell to the General Assembly of the Church of Scotland in a knock-down drag-out fight in 1650: "I beseech you, in the bowels of Christ, think it possible that you may be mistaken."

In that spirit I am trying to think my way through some of the basic issues dividing opponents and supporters of the Equal Rights Amendment here in North Carolina and throughout the country. I am trying to outline the case *for* and *against* ERA as it has been stated by people who ought to know what they are talking about, and then re-examine my own thinking on the issues involved, in the hope that others will re-examine their own views and make up their own minds, without the pressures of propaganda from either side. It is a drop in the bucket—but it is my drop and I want to put it there.

I want no part of a campaign to start or stop ERA. I want no part of a campaign to bury or resurrect it. I want no part of a raw and divisive struggle for political power growing out of it, at state or local levels.

THE CASE AGAINST THE
EQUAL RIGHTS AMENDMENT

The best reasoned statements against ERA, to my way of thinking, have come from Professor Paul Freund of the Harvard Law School and Senator Ervin of North Carolina.

Professor Freund

In opposing the Equal Rights Amendment Professor Paul Freund of the Harvard Law School argued in the *Harvard Civil Rights—Civil Liberties Law Review* for March 1971:

> The issue has always been over choice of means, not over ends. The objective is to nullify those vestigial laws that work an injustice to women, that are exploitative or impose oppressive discriminations on account of sex. Although such laws have been progressively superseded or held to be violative of equal protection, some of these laws still disfigure our legal codes. Beyond this, the Women's Rights Movement seeks to achieve equal opportunity and equal treatment for women in

[171]

business, professional, domestic, and political relationships, but unless equality is denied by a public agency or because of a law the Equal Rights Amendment by its terms has no application. If we want to see more women in the law firms, in the medical profession, in the Cabinet—and I, for one, do—we must turn elsewhere than to the proposed amendment. The point is not the smug argument that we must change hearts and minds and attitudes (though that too is involved) rather than look to law: the point is that within the realm of law we have to compare the effects and effectiveness of a constitutional amendment on the one hand and the mandate of congressional legislation and judicial decisions on the other.

The proposed amendment attempts to impose a single standard of sameness on the position of the sexes in all multifarious roles regulated by law—marital support, parental obligations, social security, industrial employment, activities in public schools, and military service—to mention the most prominent. It is necessary to try to analyze all these various applications of the single–standard formula in order to discern whether anomalies, uncertainties, and injustices would result. Unfortunately we have no definitive guide in such an exploration, for neither in the House nor in the Senate was there a committee report on the amendment, which might have focused attention on concrete issues rather than on a generalized slogan—"equal rights under the law"—which is intended to supplant "equal protection of the laws." The alternative legal course is to achieve changes in the relative position of women through paramount federal standards or to overcome invidious classifications on the ground that they are presently unconstitutional. The choice resembles that in medicine between a single broad–spectrum drug with uncertain and unwanted side–effects and a selection of specific pills for specific ills.

A doctrinaire equality, then, is apparently the theme of the amendment. And so women must be admitted to West Point on a parity with men; women must be conscripted for military service equally with men (though classification on an individual basis for assignment to duties would be valid, it is asserted); girls must be eligible for the same athletic teams as boys in the public schools and state universities; Boston Boy's Latin School and Girl's Latin School must merge (not simply be brought in parity); and life insurance commissioners may not continue to approve lower life insurance premiums for women (based on greater life expectancy)—all by command of the Federal Constitution.

I would not wish to leave the subject on a purely negative note. My concern, as I have said, is with the method proposed, which is too simplistic for the living issues at stake. It remains, then, to suggest alternative approaches. A great deal can be done through the regular legislative process in Congress. Concrete guidelines are set forth in an April 1970 *Report of the President's Task Force on Women's Rights and Responsibilities*. After recommending support of the proposed amendment, the *Report* urges that

Title VII of the Civil Rights Act of 1964 be amended to empower the EEOC to enforce the law, and to extend coverage to state and local governments and to teachers.

Titles IV and IX of the Civil Rights Act be amended to authorize the Attorney General to assist in cases involving discrimination against girls and women in access to public education, and to require the Office of Education to make a survey on the subject.

Title II of the Civil Rights Act be amended to prohibit discrimination because of sex in public accommodations.

—the jurisdiction of the Civil Rights Commission be extended to include denial of civil rights because of sex;

—the Fair Labor Standards Act be amended to extend coverage of its equal pay provisions to executive, administrative, and professional employees;

—liberalized provisions be made for child-care facilities . . .

an extensive, important, and thoughtful set of proposals. If a two-thirds majority can be found for the abstraction of the Equal Rights Amendment, it would be puzzling to know why a simple majority could not even more readily be found to approve this concrete program.

In addition, Congress would give a vigorous and valuable lead by enacting model laws for the District of Columbia in the fields of labor legislation and domestic relations.

The real issue is not the legal status of women. The issue is the integrity and responsibility of the law-making process itself.

SENATOR ERVIN

In opposing the Equal Rights Amendment, Senator Ervin argued in a letter to members of the North Carolina General Assembly in February, 1977:

Let me enumerate as briefly as possible the crucial objections to the Equal Rights Amendment:

1. *The Amendment is unrealistic because the demand for it is based on antiquated decisions of the Supreme Court of the United States upholding the constitutionality of laws which have since become obsolete.*

As a member of the United States Senate, I made a serious study of all the propaganda which has been issued by advocates of the Amendment since the Amendment originated more than 50 years ago. The study revealed that the demand for the amendment is based fundamentally upon antiquated decisions of the Supreme Court construing laws which have since become obsolete.

2. *The Equal Rights Amendment is unrealistic because it commands Congress and all State Legislatures to ignore sex when making laws.*

Laws are designed to regulate the conduct of men and women. Insofar as they engage in similar roles, they should have equal rights and responsibilities. It is otherwise, however, where they have incompatible functions. The Equal Rights Amendment is unrealistic because it constitutes an effort to convert men and women into identical legal beings having exactly the same rights and exactly the same responsibilities at all times and under all circumstances. In so doing, the Amendment emulates Procrustes, the fabled robber of ancient Greece who stretched or mutilated his victims to make them conform to the length of his bed. There is more than a modicum of truth in the assertion of Professor Philip Kurland, Prefessor of Constitutional Law at the University of Chicago, who asserts that the Equal Rights Amendment attempts to convert men and women into a unisex.

It is the height of folly to command legislative bodies to ignore sex in making laws. This is true because the continuation of life on earth is dependent upon sex. God gave men the capacity to beget children and women the capacity to bear them.

The strongest advocates for the ratification of the Equal Rights Amendment are business and professional women. While some of them can undoubtedly cite discriminations which they have suffered on account of the customs of society, none of them can cite any law which gives to a business or professional man any right which they do not enjoy. This is so simply because business and professional women enjoy every legal right which the law confers upon business and professional men. Why any of them should desire to rob those women who elect to become wives and mothers and unfortunately widows of necessary legal protections or to rob all women of protection against crimes which can only be committed by men is past comprehending.

The Procrustean attempt of the Amendment to solve the problems which life presents to men and women by conferring upon them exactly the same rights and exactly the same responsibilities at all times and under all circumstances, irrespective of differing roles in life, will raise more serious problems than it will solve. Moreover, it attempts to solve by law relationships which only can be solved satisfactorily by cooperation and religion.

3. *Recent decisions of the Supreme Court interpreting the Due Process Clause of the Fifth Amendment, the Due Process Clause and Equal Protection Clause of the Fourteenth Amendment, and other constitutional provisions and recent federal and state laws nullifying invidious legal discriminations against women make it manifest that the Equal Rights Amendment is totally unnecessary.*

Since 1971 the Supreme Court of the United States has made at least eight rulings which show that the ratification of the Equal Rights Amendment is totally unnecessary to remove any legal discriminations to which women may be subjected. Three of these decisions are based on the Due Process Clause of the Fifth Amendment which applies to the federal government.

The other five decisions are based on the Equal Protection Clause of the Fourteenth Amendment which applies to the states.

In these eight cases, the Supreme Court of the United States holds, in substance, that any law, federal or state, which makes any distinction whatever between the legal rights and responsibilities of men and women is unconstitutional unless the distinction is based upon reasonable grounds and is designed to protect women in some role they enact in life.

I respectfully submit that these holdings afford a far better way to satisfy the wishes of advocates of ratification of the Equal Rights Amendment, whose blunderbuss approach would invalidate any law making any legal distinction between the rights and responsibilities of men and women, no matter how reasonable the distinction might be, and no matter how necessary the distinction might be to protect women in roles which they may play in life.

The advocates of ERA persuaded politically-minded Senators to defeat each of several amendments offered by Senator Ervin and thereby to manifest the legislative intent that under the Amendment women will be compelled to render compulsory military service; to serve in combat units of the armed forces in times of war; that women in general shall not enjoy any legal protections or exemptions now granted to them; that wives, mothers, and widows shall not enjoy any legal protections or exemptions now granted to them; that fathers shall be freed from primary responsibility for the support of their children; that men and women and boys and girls shall not enjoy the privacy now secured to them by law; and that sexual offenses shall not be punishable as crimes. . . .

What has been said in respect to recent decisions of the United States Supreme Court applies with like force to the laws now appearing in the statute books of the nation and the states. They, too, make it evident that the Equal Rights Amendment is wholly unnecessary. . . .

I do affirm, however, with absolute conviction that using the blunderbuss Equal Rights Amendment to nullify any such remaining laws would be even more foolish than exploding an atomic bomb to eradicate a few mice.

4. *If it is ratified, the Equal Rights Amendment will transfer from the States to the Federal Government vast governmental powers which have been reserved to the States throughout our history. By so doing, the Amendment will*

[175]

substantially thwart the purpose of the Constitution to create "an indestructible union composed of indestructible States" and reduce the States in large measure to powerless zeroes on the nation's map.

When the Founding Fathers drafted and ratified the Constitution, they divided governmental powers between the Federal Government and the States, delegating to the Federal Government the powers necessary to enable it to operate as a national government for all the States and reserving to the States all other governmental powers.

The chief governmental power reserved to the States by the Constitution has been the power to make the laws governing the rights and responsibilities of the men and women living within their respective borders.

By virtue of this reserved power, the States have made throughout our history the laws regulating marriage, the support of the family, the property rights of married people, the care and custody of children, divorce, alimony and the myriad other aspects of relationships between men and women. As a consequence, each State has been able to conform its laws relating to these matters to the convictions of the people residing in its borders and to ignore the differing views entertained by people living in distant States.

Moreover, the power to interpret laws of this nature has resided in the state courts whose rulings concerning them have been exempt from reversal by the Supreme Court of the United States except in those comparatively rare instances where such laws deny individuals the equal protection of the laws or deprive them of due process of law in violation of the Fourteenth Amendment.

While its advocates may not so intend, all of these things will be drastically changed if the Equal Rights Amendment should be ratified. This is true because the Equal Rights Amendment will convert the States from sovereign authorities in the constitutional field now assigned to them into rather meaningless zeroes on the nation's map.

Let us look at the Equal Rights Amendment.

Section 1 provides that "equality of rights under the law shall not be denied or abridged by the United States or by any state on account of sex."

Section 2 specifies that "the Congress shall have the power to enforce, by appropriate legislation, the provisions" of Section 1.

Section 1 will vest in the Supreme Court of the United States complete and conclusive power to determine the validity of every law, federal or state, having any bearing on the legal rights and responsibilities of men and women. At the present time the Supreme Court bench is occupied by some Justices who are judicial activists, i.e., Judges who are bent on construing the Constitution of the United States to mean what it would have said if they rather than the Founding Fathers had written it.

As one who venerates government by laws, and abhors government by men, I am unwilling to vest in judicial activists the vastly expanded and multiplied judicial power which the Equal Rights Amendment would confer on the Supreme Court of the United States. . . .

If ratified, the Second Section of the Equal Rights Amendment will play havoc with the legislative powers of North Carolina and the other forty-nine States. This is so because this section will transfer from the legislatures of all the States to the Congress the ultimate power to pass binding laws regulating the rights and responsibilities of men and women.

After ratification, a State Legislature will be able to pass laws of this nature only by the forbearance of Congress, which can step in at any time and pass congressional acts nullifying and supplanting any and all State laws undertaking to regulate the rights and responsibilities of men and women.

Surely no intelligent person will gainsay the proposition that members of the North Carolina General Assembly are far better qualified to enact sound and acceptable laws governing the rights and responsibilities of men and women living in North Carolina than are those legislators to whom the Equal Rights Amendment would transfer that power, namely, the Congressmen from California, Indiana, New York, North Dakota, and the other forty-six States. . . .

The Case For the Equal Rights Amendment

The best reasoned statements of the case for ERA on the national level, to my way of thinking, have come from Professor Thomas Emerson of the Yale Law School and Professor William B. Aycock of the University of North Carolina Law School.

PROFESSOR EMERSON

In supporting the Equal Rights Amendment Professor Emerson argued in the Harvard Civil Rights—Civil Liberties Law Review for March 1971:

> The basic premise of the Equal Rights Amendment is that sex should not be a factor in determining the legal rights of women, or of men. Most of us, I think, agree with this fundamental proposition. For example, virtually everybody would consider it unjust and irrational to provide by law that a person could not go to law school or be admitted to the practice of law because of his or her sex. The reason is that admission to the bar ought to depend on legal training, competence in the law, moral character, and similar factors. Some women meet these qualifications and some do not; some men meet these qualifications and some do not. But the issue should be decided on an individual, not a group, basis.

[177]

The fact of maleness or femaleness should be irrelevant. This remains true whether or not there are more men than women who qualify. It likewise remains true even if there be no women who presently qualify, because women potentially qualify and might do so under different conditions of education and upbringing. The law, in short, owes an obligation to treat females as persons, not statistical abstracts.

What is true of admission to the bar is true of all legal rights. If we examine the various areas of the law one by one we will, I believe, reach the same conclusion in every case. Sex is an impermissible category by which to determine the right to a minimum wage, the custody of children, the obligation to refrain from taking the life of another, and so on. The law should be concerned with the right to a living wage for all, the welfare of the particular child, the protection of citizens from murder—that is, with the real issues—not with stereotypes about one or the other half of the human race.

The fundamental principle underlying the Equal Rights Amendment, then, is that the law must deal with the individual attributes of the particular person, rather than make broad classifications based upon the irrelevant factor of sex. The aim of the Equal Rights Amendment is simply to establish these philosophic truths as principles of law.

It should be noted at this point that there is one type of situation where the law may properly focus on a sexual characteristic. When the legal system deals directly with a physical characteristic that is unique to one sex, in a certain sense, the individual obtains a benefit or is subject to a restriction because he or she belongs to one or the other sex. Thus a law providing for payment of the medical costs of child–bearing would cover only women, and a law relating to sperm banks would apply only to men. Such legislation cannot be said to deny equal rights to the other sex. There is no basis here for seeking or achieving equality.

Instances of this kind, involving legislation directly concerned with physical differences found either in *all* women or in all men, are relatively rare. They may be distinguished from cases where the physical characteristic is not unique to one sex, and from cases of real or assumed psychological or social differences. A legislative distinction between sexes based on some physical characteristic not unique to one seems clearly inappropriate. Consider a determination that only men may be licensed to drive commercial vehicles because they are presumed to be stronger. Insofar as superior strength is not a characteristic of all men, such a determination unreasonably and thus unjustifiably discriminates against large numbers of women. Psychological and social differences between the sexes are similarly unjustifiable bases for discrimination since there is no clear evidence that such traits are unique to one sex or the other. Unless the difference is one that is characteristic of all women and no men, or all men and no women, it is not the sex factor but the individual factor which should be determinative.

The theoretical basis for prohibiting differential treatment in the law based upon sex is thus quite clear. The practical reasons for doing so are

[178]

equally compelling. History and experience have taught us that a legal system which undertakes to confer benefits or impose obligations on the basis of sex inevitably is repressive. It is perhaps too much to expect that the sex which wields the greater influence in formulating the law will not use its power to entrench its position at the expense of the other. At least this has been the outcome of sex differentiation in the American legal system. . . .

It is unnecessary to press these matters further. That our present legal system grossly discriminates against women cannot seriously be questioned. The major portion of that indictment is indeed admitted by most observers, and the critical need for substantial and immediate revisions in our legal structure is likewise conceded. The only remaining issue concerns the method which should be utilized to achieve reform.

There appear to be three basic methods by which discrimination against women can be eliminated from our legal system. The first, the legislative approach, must begin with the repeal or revision of each separate piece of existing legislation through action by the federal, state and local legislatures having jurisdiction, and change of each separate administrative rule or practice through similar action by every federal, state and local executive agency concerned with administration. It goes without saying that such a procedure would involve interminable delay. It is unlikely that proponents of women's rights will be able to eliminate all discriminatory statutes and practices when forced to fight over every separate issue on innumerable fronts. Even if such an effort were successful, it would have no prospective effect, and there would be no protection against future discriminatory legislation and practices. The legislative approach then lacks any guarantee of ultimate success. The struggle would be justified only if no other course of action were possible.

A second method is through court action under the equal protection clause of the fourteenth amendment and the comparable provision of the fifth. This procedure has the advantage of affording a more broad–scale attack upon the problem, with a single agency of government, the United States Supreme Court, playing the role. Moreover, some progress has already been made. It is of course recognized that women are "persons" within the embrace of the fourteenth and fifth amendments, and are entitled to "equal protection of the laws" under those provisions. Some state and lower federal courts have rendered important decisions upholding equality of rights for women under the existing constitutional provisions. I feel reasonably confident that in the long run the United States Supreme Court would reach a position very close to or identical with that of the proponents of the Equal Rights Amendment. Nevertheless, there are serious drawbacks to this approach.

In the first place there are some Supreme Court decisions and some lower court cases which move in the wrong direction. The task of overcoming or distinguishing these decisions could be a long and arduous one. There is, in short, a certain amount of legal deadwood which would

[179]

have to be cleared away before the courts could make clear–cut and rapid progress. In the second place the Supreme Court has been subjected over a period of time to powerful attack for moving too fast and too far in frontier areas of the law. The Court may consequently be somewhat reluctant to take the lead in bringing about another major social reform, regardless of how constitutionally justified that reform may appear to be. Hence it would be important for the courts, in performing such a task, to have the moral support of the other institutions of government and the people as a whole.

Thirdly, and most important, the problems involved in building a legislative framework assuring equality of rights to women are somewhat different from those which the courts have faced in other areas of equal protection law. In ordinary cases, when a claim is made that equal protection of the laws has been denied, the Supreme Court will apply the rule that differential treatment is valid providing there is a reasonable basis for the classification; and the Court will accept the legislative judgment that the classification is reasonable unless that judgment is beyond the pale of rationality. Yet such a legal doctrine is not appropriate where the differential treatment is based on sex. For reasons stated above, classification by sex, except where the law pertains to a unique physical characteristic of one sex, ought always to be regarded as unreasonable. It would be inappropriate, time consuming, and ultimately futile for the courts to investigate in each case whether a legislation or administrative practice favored women, disfavored women, benefited society as a whole, and so on. That decision–namely, that all discrimination is outlawed—must be fundamental and not subject to relitigation.

In cases where differential treatment is based upon race, the courts have developed a special rule under the equal protection clause. In racial cases the constitutional doctrine is that classification by race is a "suspect" classification, and the legislature has the burden of showing that it is not an "invidious" or harmful classification or that it is justified by the most compelling reasons. Yet, taken as a whole, the problems of race discrimination are somewhat different from those of sex discrimination. For example, questions of benevolent quotas, compensatory treatment, culture bias in psychological testing, separatism, and other issues may need differing treatment. The increasingly complex doctrines being developed in the field of race discrimination are therefore not necessarily applicable to the field of sex discrimination.

The same can be said of other areas of equal protection law. Discriminatory treatment on account of poverty or illegitimacy, classifications in economic regulatory legislation, denial of the right of franchise through malapportionment of legislative districts,—all these present issues peculiar to their own spheres. In short, the establishment of equal rights for women poses questions that are in important ways *sui generis*. An effective solution demands a separate constitutional doctrine that will be geared to the special character of the problem. Furthermore, as stated before, unless Congress and the states, through adoption of a

[180]

constitutional amendment, express the firm conviction that this reform must be promptly and vigorously undertaken, progress is bound to be slow and faltering.

We come then to the conclusion that the third method—a constitutional amendment—is by far the most appropriate form of legal remedy. The final question is whether the Equal Rights Amendment now before us furnishes a satisfactory constitutional framework upon which to achieve the goal of equal rights for women. I believe that it does.

The proposed amendment states clearly and simply the fundamental objective: "Equality of rights under the law shall not be denied or abridged by the United States or by any State on account of sex." In this respect it follows the tradition of the great provisions of the Constitution guaranteeing freedom of religion, freedom of speech, due process of law, protection against cruel and inhuman punishment, and other rights.

The word "rights," it seems clear, includes not only rights in the narrow sense of the term, but all forms of rights, privileges, immunities, duties and responsibilities. Thus service on juries, whether it be looked upon as a "right" or a "duty," plainly falls within the scope of the amendment.

The term "equality," interpreted in light of the basic philosophy of the amendment, means that women must be treated by the law in the same way as other persons: their rights must be determined on the basis of the same factors that apply to men. The factor of femaleness or maleness is irrelevant. This principle is subject to the proposition, already noted, that laws may deal with physical characteristics that exclusively pertain to one sex or the other without infringing upon equality of rights. As previously stated, such instances would only rarely occur.

The phrase "shall not be denied or abridged" constitutes an unqualified prohibition. It means that differentiation on account of sex is totally precluded, regardless of whether a legislature or administrative agency may consider such a classification to be "reasonable," to be beneficial rather than "invidious," or to be justified by "compelling reasons." Furthermore, for much the same reasons as in the racial area, the clause would not sanction "separate but equal" treatment. Power to deny equality of rights on account of sex is wholly foreclosed.

The Equal Rights Amendment applies only to governmental conduct, federal or state. It does not affect conduct in the private, nongovernmental sector of society. The problems of "state action" raised here are similar to those the courts have dealt with under the fourteenth and fifteenth amendments. The basic legal doctrines that govern are the same, though they may have somewhat different application in the area of sex discrimination.

Finally, it should be noted that the Equal Rights Amendment fits into the total framework of the Constitution and should be construed to mesh with the remainder of the constitutional structure. One particular aspect of this is worth brief attention. It concerns the constitutional right to privacy.

In Griswold v. Connecticut the Supreme Court recognized an independent constitutional right of privacy, derived from a combination of various more specific constitutional guarantees. The scope and implications of the right to privacy have not yet been fully developed by the courts. But I think it correct to say that the central idea behind the concept is the existence of an inner core of personal life which is protected against invasion by the laws and rules of the society, no matter how valid such laws and rules may be outside the protected sphere. If this is true, the constitutional right of privacy would prevail over other portions of the Constitution embodying the laws of society in its collective capacity. This principle would have an important impact, at some points, in the operation of the Equal Rights Amendment. Thus I think the constitutional right of privacy would justify police practices by which a search of a woman could be performed only by another woman and search of a man, by another man. Similarly the right of privacy would permit, perhaps require, the separation of the sexes in public rest rooms, segregation by sex in sleeping quarters of prisons or similar public institutions, and a certain segregation of living conditions in the armed forces. The concern over these issues expressed by opponents of the Equal Rights Amendment seems to me to have been magnified beyond all proportion, and to have failed to take into account the young, but fully recognized, constitutional right of privacy.

I will not undertake to consider in detail how the Equal Rights Amendment would affect various existing laws, regulations and practices. It seems useful, however, to state without elaboration what the three essential points at issue seem to be:

First, the courts are entirely capable of laying down the rules for a transitional period in a manner which will not create excessive uncertainty or undue disruption. The courts face similar problems every time they hold that part of a statute is unconstitutional, and they have developed detailed rules for handling these issues under the concept of "separability" (or "severability"). The essential question is whether the legislature would have intended the statute to stand in its modified form. In making this decision the courts have the aid of legislative history where available. There is no reason to suppose, therefore, that formulation of a coherent legal theory applicable to the Equal Rights Amendment is too complex or too difficult for the legal system to cope with.

Second, there has been a great deal of speculation that passage of the Equal Rights Amendment would cause vast changes in many features of our national life. I am inclined to feel that the alarms and warnings are, as usual, overplayed. Such great changes will occur, however, only if they are necessary. Opponents of the measure who stress this aspect of the amendment are acknowledging that widespread discrimination against women persists throughout our society.

Third, it has been argued that adoption of a constitutional amendment will bring about drastic alterations in important institutions of society almost inadvertently, before there has been time to work out the major policy changes required by the new provision. The example most frequently given is the Selective Service System. But one need not conclude that, in those few areas where major new policy must be formulated, there is not adequate time in which to do it. If Congress adopts the Equal Rights Amendment it will surely have full opportunity during the period of ratification by the states to take up amendments to the Selective Service Act. Other areas of our law, such as the marriage and divorce laws, may need similar attention from state legislatures. It is not a weakness but a strength of the amendment that it will force prompt consideration of some changes that are long overdue.

My conclusion from this survey of the legal problems raised by the Equal Rights Amendment is that the method chosen is the proper one and the instrument proposed is constitutionally and legally sound.

PROFESSOR AYCOCK

In ~~opposing~~ _supporting_ the Equal Rights Amendment, Professor William B. Aycock said at a public hearing in 1977 sponsored by the North Carolina Senate Committee on Constitutional Amendment:

At the moment of my birth in Wilson County the Fourteenth Amendment made me a citizen of North Carolina and a citizen of the United States. However, it was not until I attended the public schools in Johnston County that I knew anything about the Fourteenth Amendment. It was not until I started teaching history in the public schools of Guilford County that I began thinking about equality of rights under the law between the sexes. My classes were composed of girls and boys. I tried to instill in both the hopes and aspirations the founding fathers had for this nation. Some day, it was inevitable that increasing numbers of women would expect to have equal opportunity with men under the law. Thus, laws predicated on the assumption that women outside the home were inferior to men were bound to be reexamined. Progress has been made in changing these laws. But there is unfinished business.

Today the issue is whether or not the ERA is a desirable way to get on with this unfinished business. On this issue there is a sharp division of opinion. There are those who have faith in the ERA as an appropriate next step in the process. On the other hand, there are those who have strong fears about the ERA. I understand the power of fear and I respect my fellow citizens whose fears are stronger than their faith on this issue. But having weighed my own fears against my own faith, I have chosen to go with my faith. My purpose today, as a citizen of North Carolina and a citizen of the United States, is to share with you my reasons for making this choice.

I discern that the foremost fear has to do with Section 2 of ERA. Sec-

[183]

tion 2 provides: "The Congress shall have the power to enforce, by appropriate legislation, the provisions of this article." Will this section transfer to Congress vast powers now reserved to the states? I do not think so because I am unable to envision any new type of law that Congress would pass under Section 2 that it is not authorized to enact now. May I explain how I arrived at this conclusion? First, beginning in 1971 the Supreme Court of the United States consistently has held that the Equal Protection Clause in the Fourteenth Amendment is applicable to sex discrimination by the states. Second, Section 5 of the Fourteenth Amendment provides: "The Congress shall have power to enforce, by appropriate legislation, the provisions of this article." The sum of these two facts is that Congress *now* has power to legislate on sex discrimination. I have no basis to fear that Section 2 of the ERA will transfer vast new power now residing in the states because Congress already has the power. Congress has already exercised its power under the Commerce Clause to legislate on sex discriminaton. The Equal Pay Act of 1963 and Title VII of the Civil Rights Act of 1964 are two examples of such legislation. Congress is not required to utilize its Fourteenth Amendment power but it can. Congress would not be required to utilize the same power in Section 2 of the ERA but it could.

Fears have been expressed because Section 1 of ERA, "Equality of rights under the law shall not be denied or abridged by the United States or any State on account of sex," is a generalized expression. So it is. Our state constitution and the federal constitution contain many generalized expressions. This is especially true of the Bill of Rights. For example, what about freedom of speech? There are no exceptions set forth in the first amendment to freedom of speech. Instead of littering the Constitution with exceptions to generalized expressions, courts, both state and federal, define generalized expressions in the context of the facts of cases that come before them. We know that freedom of speech is not absolute. In its exercise one is subject to the laws of libel and slander; one cannot maliciously shout fire in a crowded building; and one cannot threaten to murder the President of the United States. Even more precisely on point are the "Equal Protection Clause" of the Fourteenth Amendment and the "Due Process Clause" of the Fifth Amendment because it is under these clauses that sex discrimination cases have been adjudicated. I have studied each of these cases decided by the Supreme Court of the United States. I am favorably impressed with the common sense manner in which the Court has decided these cases. The Court has not condemned out of hand every law that discriminates between the sexes. Instead, it examines the facts to ascertain if there is adequate justification for a continuation of the discrimination. For example, in *Kahn v. Shevin* the Court upheld a Florida Statute providing a property tax exemption for widows even though there was none for widowers. This discrimination in favor of women was found to be justified because it was shown that the earnings of women were only 59 percent of those of men. When the differential in earning power is eliminated, this discriminatory statute will either have to be repealed or amended to apply equally to widowers. The most recent case decided by the United States Supreme Court under the Equal Protection Clause on sex discrimination involved an Oklahoma law. This law permitted 18 year old girls to buy beer but prohibited purchase by boys under age 21. The Court considered the evidence offered in justification for this difference in sex treatment and found it to be insufficient..Oklahoma now has to decide on the age it prefers to apply equally to both sexes.

I have faith that the Supreme Court will deal with Section 1 of the ERA in the same common sense way it has applied the Equal Protection Clause. The ERA will not repeal common sense, the right of privacy, or disregard the obvious biological differences between men and women. For example, abortion laws will not be wiped out on the ground that they do not apply to men. I have no fear about the prediction that the ERA will repeal the laws of nature.

I do not fear the possibility that some litigant will bring a frivolous law suit under ERA. The reason I do not fear it is because I *know* it will happen. I know it will happen because it has happened. In the past a suit was instituted to contest the constitutionality of a local law prohibiting motorists to turn right on red on the ground it interfered with interstate commerce. Prisoners have sued a warden who evicted their cat. They alleged they were entitled to notice and a hearing. It would not surprise me if a male prisoner sued to enjoin the warden from separating him from women prisoners. He will lose for the same reason that he would not prevail were he to argue that *incarceration* itself deprives him of "liberty" guaranteed by Section 1, Article 1 of the North Carolina Constitution.

I do not fear the possibility that some bureaucrat will make some silly ruling. This has already occurred under existing law. It will occur again with or without ERA. The saving grace is that there is someone in authority with enough common sense to set matters aright.

Because lawsuits testing state and federal laws on sex discrimination can be brought under existing provisions of the Constitution, it is appropriate to inquire—is there any need for ERA? The test of strict legal necessity is to narrow. The ERA has values beyond this narrow test. The principle of equality of rights under the law between the sexes, to be found now only in a number of court decisions, is only dimly perceived by most of us. It simply is not feasible for most people to study each of these cases. Justice Cardozo explained it this way: "Cases do not unfold their principles for the asking. They yield up their kernel slowly and painfully." To this law students will concur and to this most experienced lawyers will attest. The ERA offers us an opportunity to join in a national commitment for equality of rights under the law between the sexes. Our forefathers in North Carolina insisted that a Bill of Rights should be expressed in the Constitution. For the same reason the ERA should be enshrined in the Constitution. The ERA would surely be a shining star among our constitutional freedoms. It would affirm the dignity of women as the Declaration of Independence affirmed the dignity of men. It would serve as beacon for every school child and for all the world to see. From it would radiate a constant reminder that so long as there is inequality of rights under the law in this land of freedom between men and women, there is work yet to be done. During the two year period between the adoption of ERA and its effective date, the process of eliminating discriminatory laws will be accelerated. Further, the ERA would serve as visible standard by which to measure the validity of new laws for all time to come.

As I close, I am reminded of our forefathers who assembled at Halifax in the East and at Mecklenburg in the West. They had to choose between their faith in freedom and their fear of death. North Carolina could not lay claim to "first in freedom" if they had not chosen faith over fear. Today, with no danger to our lives to fear, we, too, have a choice. I have chosen to support the ERA because I believe it to be consistent with the heritage with which I am privileged to be endowed.

My Own Thinking

Why do ERA Supporters Seek the Goal by Way of an Amendment to the United States Constitution Rather than Amendments to the Constitutions of Fifty States?

It is the shortest distance from where they are to where they want to go. Let me illustrate my reasoning:

Women started fighting for the right to vote by seeking amendments to the separate state constitutions. Studies show that from 1870 to 1910 they fought four hundred eighty campaigns in thirty-three states to get the issue submitted to the voters and only seventeen resulted in referendum votes. It was a slow, tedious, expensive, unproductive, and frustrating process.

Women turned to the federal road as the shortest distance between two points by proposing an amendment to the United States Constitution, saying: "The rights of citizens of the United States to vote shall not be denied or abridged on account of sex." It was submitted by Congress to the states, three-fourths of these ratified it quickly, and it became the 19th amendment to the Constitution of the United States in 1920.

In the first session of the 68th Congress of the United States, in 1923, Miss Mabel Vernon, Executive Secretary of the National Woman's Party, testified before the Judiciary Committee of the House of Representatives, saying:

As we were working for the National Suffrage Amendment it was borne in very emphatically on us that we were not going thereby to gain full equality for the women of this country, but that we were merely taking a step, but a very important step, it seemed to us, for the gaining of this equality....

She was testifying in favor of the first version of an equal rights amendment to the United States Constitution which had been proposed that year for women on all fronts throughout the United States.

Women continued to introduce it in changing forms, year after year, until Congress approved it and submitted it to the states for approval in 1972.

Would ERA do Away with Laws Requiring Husbands to Support Wives and Children?

I do not believe it would, and here is why:

Nothing in the Constitution prevents the state legislatures or the federal Congress from adding to, or taking from, the laws on the books providing for the support of wives and children now, if they want to.

The state legislature could have done this at any time in the last two hundred years if it had wanted to. It can do it now if it wants to without the existence of ERA. ERA does not add to, or take away, the powers or the choice from the General Assembly, which is no more likely to require it in the future than it has in the past.

ERA will not take away the right of the wife to support from her husband if he is able to support her and she is not able to support herself.

It will require her to support him if she is able to support him and he is not able to support himself.

ERA would not prevent the passage of laws requiring the husband and wife to contribute to the support of their children in proportion to their ability to do so, nor would it prevent the passage of laws requiring the husband or wife to support the children if one could do so and the other could not.

And, before or after ERA, neither state legislatures nor the federal congress can require husband or wife to support each other or their children if they are unable to do so.

Under ERA, sex discrimination benefits will be extended to the previously excluded sex, and sex discrimination burdens will be eliminated for both sexes.

[187]

In other words where the laws discriminate in favor of women, the benefits of this discrimination will be extended to men.

Where the laws discriminate in favor of men, the benefits of this discrimination will be extended to women.

The burdens of discrimination are eliminated from men and women.

Would ERA Degrade Women and Destroy the Home?

I do not believe it would, and here is why:

Suppose we start our discussion with women who are married and living with their families, with husbands able, willing and anxious to provide adequate support for them and their children.

These families are miniature governmental units in themselves. The parents are the lawmakers and the law enforcers in these units. They prescribe the rules and regulations and guidelines for bringing up the children in the way they should go. They are allowed by the law of the land to exercise more power over the members of these family units in the formative years of their lives, than the heads of city, county, state or federal governmental units. State and federal governments come to the aid of these family units with supporting programs to hold them together as going concerns, just as they come to the aid of counties, cities, and towns. These home and family units are the most significant governmental units in the country because they are the wellsprings of all the citizens of all the governmental units in the land. We cannot destroy these homes and degrade these families without pulling out the underpinnings from every city, county, state, and federal governmental unit in the land. Who would want to do that?

I do not believe that purpose was in the minds of the members of the United States Congress who in 1972 voted overwhelmingly to submit the Equal Rights Amendment to the fifty states to be ratified as the 27th amendment to the Constitution of the United States.

I do not believe that destroying the home or degrading the family was in the minds of the members of the North Carolina General Assembly who voted to ratify the Equal Rights Amendment in 1977 in numbers roughly equal to those who opposed it.

I do not believe that the men and women who are supporting the Equal Rights Amendment in North Carolina and who come from homes and families in the state and the same communities as their opponents—I do not believe that they are supporting the Equal Rights

Amendment for the purpose of fouling their own nests.

Look at the homes and families where the husbands are not making enough money to support their families, and the wives have to put their children in day-care centers and go out of their homes to get a job to make ends meet. Should they be denied equality of rights under the law on account of sex?

Look at the homes where the husband is dead, or divorced, and the woman is the head of the home and family and the sole support of herself and her children, and she has to go out of the household to get a job in order to provide food and shelter and clothing and schooling for her children. Should she be denied equality of rights under the law on account of sex?

Look at the homes and families where the husband has "flown the coop"—deserted his home and family, and cannot be found to pay alimony to his wife, or contribute to the support of his children, even if he could be found. Should the wife and mother be denied equality of rights under the law, on account of sex?

Look at the homes and families where the husband is out of a job, and cannot find work. And at the families where he is sick and unable to work. Should the wife and mother be denied equality of rights under the law on account of sex?

Look at the homes and families where the children are grown and self-supporting, and the wife is not fully occupied with housekeeping responsibilities, and doesn't want to sit around twiddling her thumbs? Should she be denied equality of rights under the law on account of sex?

Look at the women who per choice or per chance are unmarried and have to make homes and livings for themselves on their own. Should they be denied equality of rights under the law on account of sex?

It was once claimed that women would be degraded and the home destroyed: If married women were allowed to own and control property, go into business, and keep their earnings for themselves.

If women were allowed to acquire education beyond the high school as an avenue to opening new jobs, employments, and professions.

If women were allowed to organize women's clubs and other voluntary associations and participate in community activities outside their homes.

If women were allowed to serve on juries, as trustees of public educational institutions, to vote and hold office in city, county, state, or federal governmental units, or even to put a notary's seal on a legal

[189]

document.

It is fair to ask all of us to look around in our own communities to find how many women have been degraded and how many homes have been destroyed by these activities.

Would ERA Require Men and Women to Use the Same Restrooms, Toilets, and Sleeping Quarters?

I do not believe it would, and here is why:

> There is little or no reason to believe that this would happen and just about every reason to believe it would not.
>
> The Supreme Court of the United States has ruled in the case of Griswold v. Connecticut 389 U.S. (1965) and in other cases, that there is a constitutional right of privacy in situations involving disrobing, sleeping, or performing personal bodily functions.
>
> States have the power to require a reasonable separation of sexes with respect to such facilities as sleeping quarters at coeducational colleges, prisons, and military barracks.
>
> Several states have added Equal Rights Amendments to their state constitutions in the last two years and in no state where an ERA has been adopted are men and women required to use the same restrooms, baths, and toilet facilties.

Even Professor Paul Freund of the Harvard Law School, who opposes ERA, wrote in January, 1974, "I have no fear Courts would apply to ERA to require opening up restrooms and jail cells regardless of sex, on the analogy of race."

North Carolina has not only never required it in the last two hundred years or more of her history—she has never permitted it. The federal Congress has not only never required it in the hundred eighty nine years of its history—is has never permitted it. It would involve such a cataclysmic change in the habits, customs, and traditions of the people that no legislative body elected by the people could survive it.

Would ERA Defy the Laws of God?

I do not believe it would, and here is why:

I have no quarrel with the "Informed Christian Voters" who wrote a letter to a member of the 1975 General Assembly, saying that his vote for the Equal Rights Amendment "was a blatant and conscious move to defy the will of God and His instructions on the role of women in society." They quote scripture to prove (1) that women are not equal to men, (2) that they were created to be the servants of men, (3) that they ought not to have authority over men, (4) that "women shall not wear men's clothing," and so on.

I would only say that this argument, literally applied, would play havoc in our society as it is organized today:

(1) It would completely wreck the public school system which has an overwhelming number of women teaching boys as well as girls.

(2) It would throw out of jobs the growing numbers of women in colleges and universities who are teaching young men as well as young women.

(3) It would remove from public and private employment countless women who have worked their way into positions where they are controlling and directing the activities of grown men as well as women.

(4) It would prevent presidents from appointing women to their cabinets and governors from appointing women as department heads.

(5) It would prevent the people from electing women to the General Assembly, to city councils, or to boards of county commissioners.

(6) It would destroy those parts of the clothing industry now making trousers for women.

I believe it was St. Paul, and not God, who claimed that the word of God would be "blasphemed" if women were allowed to teach, or to be put in authority over men, or to speak out in church. I believe it was the writer of Deuteronomy, and not God, who wrote: "women shall not wear men's clothing." These statements are hearsay testimony at best and opinionated statements at worst.

St. Paul said to his fellow Christians: "There is neither Jew nor Greek, there is neither slave nor free, there is neither male nor female, for you are all one in Christ Jesus." Was he not then going back to the old time religion as set forth in Genesis where it is said that "God created man in his own image; in the image of God created He him; male and female created He them." Both for his own purposes, with one purpose as good as another, with no reference to one being inferior to another, and with one being equal to the other in the sight of God.

I would add that the idea expressed in the first sentence of the Book of Genesis, "In the beginning God," is so big that trying to put it in the average person's head is like trying to cram the ocean into a quart pot. I would add that according to the Old Testament and the New, God is a living, breathing, growing God, and is on record as changing His mind many times. He would like to see His sons, and daughters too, growing in wisdom and in stature and in favor with God and man. He might even have had a hand in the changes in our society which has outgrown old customs as normally and naturally as growing boys and girls outgrow old clothes.

We must not forget that He did have a hand in this process on one memorable occasion two thousand years ago when Jesus broke with the custom of stoning the woman taken in adultery while letting the man go free. The men of that day's establishment tried to trap him into a position of defying the Law by asking him what He would do with this woman. He out-thought, out-figured, and out-smarted them with the devastating answer: "Let him who is without sin among you cast the first stone." His victory became conclusive as, one by one, the questioners dropped their stones and silently stole away, and Jesus turned to the woman and said: "Woman where are thine accusers?" I have no doubt that this was one occasion on which His Father in Heaven looked down upon him and said again: "This is my beloved son in whom I am well pleased."

I think I would be less than candid with my readers if I did not observe that Jesus' victory did not permanently change the custom of the times. That it is only within the last fifty years that the General Assembly of North Carolina began to feel its way toward His position by changing the "law of the land" so as to mete out equal treatment to the man and the woman caught in fornication and adultery.

SECTION 2 OF THE EQUAL RIGHTS AMENDMENT

Many objections to ERA are rooted in Section 2 which states: "Congress shall have the power to enforce, by appropriate legislation, the provisions of this article."

Let us look at a variety of situations in which fears of this provision have been expressed:

1.

Would ERA Send Women to War?

There are many facets to this question:

[192]

First the Equal Rights Amendment does not give Congress the power to send women to war, for the simple reason that Congress has that power now, and has had it for two hundred years. It was given to it in Article 1, Section 8 of the United States Constitution which says that Congress shall have the power "to raise and support armies . . . to provide and maintain a navy . . . to provide for organizing, arming, and disciplining the militia." If the life or death of the country had been at stake at any time within that period, and drafting women into the armed services would have been the final act that could save it, I have no doubt that Congress could, and would, have done it, and that under such circumstances Congress could, and would, have done it, and that under such circumstances Congress could, and would, do it now, without the Equal Rights Amendment.

Second, ERA would make this difference: If, as, and when, Congress drafts men into the armed forces, it will have to draft women, too. But it should be pointed out that in the 1971 draft call, only those men classified as 1-A were ever called to serve. Only 5% of the eligible males were inducted into the army. Less than 1% were assigned to combat duty. Fathers, sons, brothers, 18–26, with a child, or one whose absence would "cause hardships" were deferred to class III-A.

I do not believe that Congress will knowingly cut off its nose to spite its face. I do not believe it will treat women and mothers more harshly than it has treated men and fathers. I believe it will classify women in the armed services, as it has been classifying men in the armed services, and assign them to the tasks for which they are best fitted.

And let me point out that the balance of fighting weapons has shifted throughout the centuries from the heavy broadsword of Richard the Lionhearted, whose tremendous physical strength could cut a bar of iron in two with one blow, to the nuclear bomb which laid waste to Hiroshima and Nagasaki, and can be set in motion by a single finger pressing a button.

Third. Three hundred fifty thousand women served in the armed forces in World War II—volunteering of their own free will.

In hearings of the Eightieth Congress in 1948, General Eisenhower had this to say about women in the armed services:

Like most old soldiers, I was violently against women soldiers. I thought a tremendous number of difficulties would occur, not only of an administrative nature . . . but others of a more personal type that would get us into trouble. None of that occurred . . . in the disciplinary field . . . they were a model for the Army. More than this, their influence throughout the whole command was good. I am convinced that in another war, they have got to be drafted just like men.

Fourth. Near the end of World War II, Congress was in the process of enacting a law to draft "unmarried, unemployed women into the services in preference to drafting men away from their families." The Nurses Selective Service Act of 1945 passed the House and was reported out favorably by the Senate Military Affairs Committee when the war ended. In most if not all of the supportive services women can serve as effectively as men. All men draftees are classified and assigned to the work they can do best. There is no reason why the same policy would not be followed for women draftees.

One ERA opponent has said: "When I saw how that small militant group of women lobbyists for ERA scared male members of Congress nearly to death, I said to myself, if we could just draft them in time of war . . . they would scare the enemy so bad that the enemy would hoist the white flag without a single shot ever being fired." I would go along with him in drafting all women who could have this effect upon the enemy.

Fifth. Combat service. In opposing ERA in the 1975 General Assembly, Representative Kitchin Josey drew the most graphic picture of draftee training and combat service I have ever read:

> For the draftee, whether sailor, airman, marine or plain dough foot soldier, being inducted is anything but glamorous. Months of boot training is degrading and a dog's life. Weeks of war games and maneuvers are uncivilized and demoralizing. Combat is a stinking, dirty, living hell, where young men often act like brave fools, cry like little babies, bleed like stuck pigs and die like yellow dogs and many of those who return are more of a shock to their families than those who remain . . . .

Within weeks after the 38th state ratifies ERA, the Congress will, as it must, change that law to read: "Persons instead of males." And immediately thereafter, my daughter, and other parents' daughters will be going to the draft boards to register . . . . The thought of this brings gripping fear to my very innards . . . ."

And so it does to me—for sons as well as daughters. But we must not forget that within the last thirty years the most terrible dangers of warfare have shifted from the front line trenches and hand-to-hand combat to the private homes of men and women and children. And no

[194]

woman, married or unmarried, young or old, with or without children, is exempt from this draft. No parents' daughter, within or without draft age, is exempt from this sort of warfare, with or without a draft, and with or without the Equal Rights Amendment. Every horror of draftee training and hand-to-hand combat is multiplied ten-fold by the horrors of Hiroshima and Nagasaki.

If, as, and when, the chips are down, and the life or death of the country is on the line, and the only way to save it is to send women into the hell of mortal combat at its worst, I have no doubt that the only way in which men could beat women to the fighting front would be to outrun them, and that no more women than men would start running in the opposite direction. I believe this includes the women who are out to *Stop ERA* today as well as those who are out to start it.

I believe that the blood of heroes flows in the veins of women no less than in the veins of their brothers. I believe there are as many women as there are men who would "give their lives for a piece of paper when that paper means freedom; for a murmured prayer when that prayer means truth; for a flower when that flower means love; and for a trifle of flag when that flag means home."

I believe that women would go as unflinchingly as men into the living hell of combat so vividly and convincingly described by Representative Kitchin Josey who had been there and knew whereof he spoke. And I believe as many women as men would go in the spirit put in the poet's words:

What all our lives to save thee?
We reck not what we give thee.
We will not dare to doubt thee.
But ask what ever else, and we will dare.

2.
Would ERA "Command Congress and All State Legislatures to Ignore Sex when Making Laws"?

I do not believe it would, and here is why:

Laws arè made to regulate the activities of people—men and women who have more to them than sex. To "command Congress and the State Legislatures to ignore sex when making laws" would paralyze both, and do away with legislative bodies altogether. I do not believe that supporters of ERA have this in mind. I do not believe that eighty-four United States Senators who voted to submit ERA to the states to ratify had this in mind. I do not believe that three hundred fifty-four members of the House of Representatives who voted to submit it to the states had this in mind. I do not believe that sixty-one members of the House and twenty-four members of the Senate in the North Carolina General Assembly who voted to ratify it had this in mind.

I *do not* agree with opponents of ERA who say: "The Equal Rights Amendment... constitutes an effort to convert men and women into identical legal beings having exactly the same rights and exactly the same responsibilities at all times and under all circumstances. In so doing the Amendment emulates Procrustes, the fabled robber of ancient Greece who stretched or mutilated his victims to make them conform to the length of his bed. There is more than a modicum of truth in the assertion that the Equal Rights Amendment attempts to convert men and women into a unisex."

I *do* agree with them when they say: "It is the height of folly to command legislative bodies to ignore sex in making laws. This is true because the continuation of life on earth is dependent on sex. God gave men the capacity to beget children and women the capacity to bear them."

Look at the claim that ERA "constitutes an effort to convert men and women into identical legal beings having exactly the same rights and exactly the same responsibilities at all times and under all circumstances."

I do not believe that supporters of ERA in the Congress of the United States, or in the General Assembly of North Carolina, or in the rank and file of people in North Carolina, ever visualized a homosexual world in which men marry men, and women marry women, and men and women quit marrying each other. If that should happen for the life or lives of persons now in being, or twenty-one years thereafter, as the rule against perpetuities runs, there would be nobody around to share the experience of homosexual embrace, and for that reason if for no other it would be foolish to permit them to adopt children, for there would be no children to adopt. I believe that no legislator would ever think of introducing legislation to start it, and that if he did he would be sent to the insane asylum by his fellow legislators before he had a chance to run for re-election. But if any legislature were foolish enough to enact such a law, and the Equal Rights Amendment were in force, I can conceive of a court saying that if you are going to give a man the right to marry a man, you would have to give a woman the

[196]

right to marry a woman.

Let's examine the notion that ERA is "an effort to convert men and women into identical legal beings." ERA has nothing to say about "equal identities," it has everything to say about "equal rights." There is a difference between *identity* and *equality*.

Professor Emerson puts it this way: "When the legal system deals directly with a physical characteristic that is unique to one sex, in a certain sense, the individual obtains a benefit or is subject to a restriction because he or she belongs to one or the other sex. Thus a law providing for payment of the medical costs of child-bearing would cover only women, and a law relating to sperm banks would apply only to men. Such legislation cannot be said to deny equal rights to the other sex. There is no basis for seeking or achieving equality."

In his article on Equality Under the Law Between sexes, Professor William B. Aycock quotes the late Justice Brogden of the Supreme Court of North Carolina as saying: "Common sense is older than common law, statutory law, or equality, and this saving grace of human experience must be reckoned with in determining the application of technical rules of behavior." I believe with him that the Equal Rights Amendment would not require the federal congress or the state legislatures to pass laws reaching farfetched conclusions or absurd results.

3.

Would the Equal Rights Amendment Transfer to Congress Vast Legislative Powers which have been Reserved to the States throughout Our History?

I do not believe it would, and here is why:

I go along with Professor William B. Aycock's thinking when he says:

> I do not think Section 2 of ERA will transfer to Congress vast powers now reserved to the states. I do not think so because I am unable to envision any new type of law that Congress would pass under Section 2 that it is not authorized to enact now. May I explain how I arrived at this conclusion? First, beginning in 1971, the United States Supreme Court consistently has held that the Equal Protection Clause in the Fourteenth Amendment is applicable to sex discrimination by the states. Second, Section 5 of the Fourteenth Amendment provides: "The Congress shall have power to enforce, by appropriate legislation, the provision of this article. The sum of these two facts is that Congress now has power to

legislate on sex discrimination. I have no basis to fear that Section 2 of ERA will transfer vast power residing in the states, because Congress already has that power."

Congress has already exercised its power—under the Commerce Clause—to legislate on sex discrimination. The Equal Pay Act of 1963 and Title VII of the Civil Rights Act of 1964, are two examples of such legislation. Congress is not required to use its Fourteenth Amendment power, but it can. Congress would not be required to utilize the same power in Section 2 of ERA but it could.

It seems to me that opponents of ERA are in substantial agreement with Professor Aycock's conclusion, when they say that "recent decisions of the Supreme Court interpreting the Due Process Clause of the Fourteenth Amendment, and other constitutional provisions and recent federal and state laws nullifying insidious legal discrimination against women make it manifest that the Equal Rights Amendment is totally unnecessary."

And they go on to buttress this conclusion by saying: "Since 1971 the Supreme Court of the United States has made at least eight rulings which show that the ratification of the Equal Rights Amendment is totally unnecessary to remove any legal discriminations to which women may be subjected. Three of these decisions ... are based on the Due Process Clause of the Fifth Amendment which applies to the federal government. The other five decisions ... are based on the Equal Protection Clause of the Fourteenth Amendment which applies to the states."

If Professor Aycock and these opponents are correct in their conclusions, what becomes of the statement:

If it is ratified, the Equal Rights Amendment will transfer from the States to the Federal Government vast governmental powers which have been reserved to the States throughout history.

The Equal Rights Amendment will convert the States from sovereign authorities in the Constitutional field now assigned to them into rather meaningless zeroes on the nation's map.

If these powers have already been transferred from the States to the Federal Government by the Fifth and Fourteenth Amendments, what is left for the Equal Rights Amendment to transfer?

I agree with the observation of ERA opponents that "members of the North Carolina General Assembly are far better qualified to enact sound and acceptable laws governing the rights and responsibilities

[198]

of men and women living in North Carolina than are those legislators to whom the Equal Rights Amendment would transfer that power, namely, the congressmen from California, Indiana, New York, North Dakota, and the other forty-six states." And so are members of the General Assemblies of every other state. I think that the supporters of ERA will agree with this.

I think that is why Section 3 of the Equal Rights Amendment says : "This amendment shall take effect two years after the date of ratification." I think that section is not trying to beat the states to the draw in making laws in this field. It is saying to the states: You are invited, urged, and given time—two years—to eliminate discriminations under the laws of your particular states on account of sex. Congress doesn't want to do it for you—it wants you to do it for yourselves. At any time during those two years, or at any time thereafter, the states can keep on making all the laws they want to about men and women without let or hindrance, with one limitation: they cannot deny equal rights under the law to men or women.

I believe with Professor William B. Aycock that the Equal Rights Amendment does not in itself change a single specific law now on the books, nor does it eliminate a single discrimination or inequality between men and women. It simply sets up a standard to guide the legislatures and the courts in eliminating discriminations and inequalities. In the words of Professor Aycock, "it will shine like a beacon on the path ahead, lighting the way for legislatures, courts, and litigants alike, compared to the narrow shafts of light cast by single and separate statutes and decisions correcting isolated inequalities."

If, as, and when the Equal Rights Amendment is ratified and goes into effect, the Supreme Court of the United States is authorized to do absolutely nothing, unless and until some man or woman, of his own free will and accord, complains that some law, enacted by a state or by Congress, or pronounced by a court, denies him "equal rights under the laws—on account of sex."

At that point the Supreme Court of the United States will hear all parties to the complaint in open court, and decide whether such violation exists. The several states can keep on making all the laws they want to make in the fields "reserved to the states throughout our history" under the Constitution of the United States, subject to the one overriding provision that they must not violate the "supreme law of the land." I believe that the Supreme Court of the United States is better qualified to decide this question than any one State Court or state legislature.

By way of summary: What do we have to fear from Section 2 of the Equal Rights Amendment, saying: "Congress shall have the power, by appropriate legislation, to enforce the provisions of this article"? These same words appear in the 13th Amendment to the United States Constitution, in the 14th, the 15th, the 19th, the 24th, and the 26th. Those amendments took away from the states, and the United States, the power to impose "slavery or involuntary servitude"; the power to deny to any person . . . the equal protection of the laws"; the power to deny "the right of citizens to vote . . . on account of race, color, or previous condition of servitude"; the power to deny the right of citizens to vote . . . on account of sex"; the power to deny the right of eighteen-year-old citizens to vote.

In each case Congress is authorized in the same words to carry out these national commitments—no more and no less. In like fashion ERA would take away the power of the states, and the United States, to deny "equal rights under the law on account of sex"—no more and no less. I do not believe that the Equal Rights Amendment, including Section 2, is any more likely to ruin the country than the amendments which have come before it.

4.

Should ERA be Rejected as a Separate Amendment to the Constitution because of the Claim that the Due Process Clause of the Fifth Amendment and the Equal Protection Clause of the Fourteenth Amendment Already Give the Supreme Court All the Power ERA would Give It to Eliminate Discrimination under the Law on Account of Sex?

I do not believe it should, and here is why:

The due process clause of the 5th amendment was put in the United States Constitution in 1791. It was a hundred sixty years later in 1971, before the United States Supreme Court extended it to forbid the denial of "equal rights under the law on account of sex."

The equal protection clause of the 14th amendment was put in the United States Constitution in 1868. It was put there for the specific purpose of outlawing discrimination on account of race. It was a hundred and three years in 1971, before the United States Supreme Court extended it to forbid the denial of "equal rights under the law on account of sex."

The commerce clause was put in the United States Constitution in 1787. It was not until a hundred fifty-one years later in 1938, that it was invoked as the underpinning of the Fair Labor Standards Act prescribing identical hours of labor and equal minimum wages for men and women, and sustained by the Supreme Court of the United States. It was not until a hundred eighty-seven years later in 1964, that it was invoked as the underpinning of the Civil Rights Act prohibiting discrimination against women by employers with fifteen or more employees engaged in any activity affecting interstate commerce.

The United States Supreme Court sidled into these extensions of the 5th and 14th amendments—they are doing double duty now. How far and how fast the court will go in further extensions in specific cases, or whether it will hedge, slow down, or backtrack, will depend on surrounding circumstances, as suggested by Professor Emerson when he says:

> In the first place there are some Supreme Court decisions and some lower court cases which move in the wrong direction. The task of overcoming or distinguishing these decisions could be a long and arduous one. There is, in short, a certain amount of legal deadwood which would have to be cleared away before the courts could make clear-cut and rapid progress. In the second place the Supreme Court has been subjected over a period of time to powerful attack for moving too fast and too far in frontier areas of the law. The Court may consequently be somewhat reluctant to take the lead in bringing about another major social reform, regardless of how constitutionally justified that reform may appear to be. Hence it would be important for the courts, in performing such a task, to have the moral support of the other institutions of government and the people as a whole.

Ratifying the Equal Rights Amendment would give the Supreme Court a solid base for a frontal advance on the problem of giving equal rights to women under the law, instead of a sidling extension of amendments ratified for other purposes.

If it is true, as opponents claim, that "recent decisions of the Supreme Court of the United States interpreting the due process clause of the Fifth Amendment, and the due process clause and equal protection clause of the Fourteenth Amendment . . . make it manifest that the Equal Rights Amendment is totally unnecessary—if this is true, and "equal rights under the law" are already on the way, why not speed up the process and let them come a generation sooner rather than a generation later? Is it not true that in this situation, too, justice delayed is justice denied?

We wrote the white man into the constitution in 1787. We wrote the black man into the constitution in 1868. Why not write the woman, white and black, into the constitution by or before 1979?

5.

Should the Equal Rights Amendment be Rejected because of the Claim that "At the Present Time the Supreme Court Bench is occupied by Some Justices who are Judicial Activists, i.e., Judges who are Bent on Construing the Constitution of the United States to Mean what It Would have Said if They rather than the Founding Fathers had Written It."

I do not think so, and here is why:

Judicial activists, "it is said by ERA opponents, are judges who are bent on construing the constitution of the United States to mean what it would have said if they rather than the Founding Fathers had written it . . . I am unwilling to vest in judicial activisits the vastly expanded power which the Equal Rights Amendment would confer on the Supreme Court of the United States."

I have no doubt that Thomas Jefferson felt the same way about the decisions of the United States Supreme Court in the early 1800s and so did his political party associates and most of the State Court judges, when Mabury v. Madison, McCulloch v. Maryland, Gibbons v. Ogden, and Martin v. Hunter's Lessee from 1803 to 1825, laid the basis for an "indestructible union" of the people of the United States. John Marshall and his associates were the "judicial activists" of these years.

I have no doubt that Justices Sutherland, McReynold's, Vandevanter and Butler in the middle 1900s felt the same way about Holmes and Brandeis and Cardoza who were "judicial activists" on the Supreme Court of the United States when "we, the people" were struggling against the outworn philosophy which prevented the levy of a federal income tax, held on with grim determination to the exploitation of child labor, hindered the efforts of working men to come together into unions for their own protection, and fought limitations on the working day with the claim that "a man couldn't do a day's work" in eleven hours, or ten.

It is a matter of record that in the 1930s, Franklin D. Roosevelt felt the same way about the justices on the Supreme Court of the United States

[202]

who in the 1930s handed down their decisions crippling and destroying new deal legislation giving the national government power to grapple with problems which could not be handled by the separate states acting separately.

It is a matter of record that Richard Nixon felt the same way about decisions of the United States Supreme Court handed down by Warren, Black, Fortas, and Douglas, judicial activists in the 1950s and 60s, and that is why he put "strict constructionists" as his appointees on the court.

In a hundred seventy-five years—from the early 1800s to the 1970s—I have no doubt that Supreme Court Justices, activists and non-activists alike, have been "bent on construing the constitution of the United States to mean what (in their opinions) it would have said if they rather than the Founding Fathers had written it."

I think that there is something to be said for "judicial activists" and the part they have played as catalysts between reaction and revolution throughout our history. "Law must be stable," said Roscoe Pound, "but it cannot stand still."

We must not forget that Thomas Jefferson, John Adams, George Washington, James Madison, Alexander Hamilton and their associates were "political activists" who wrung the Declaration of Independence, the Constitution of the United States, and the American Bill of Rights from the status quo of the latter 1700s. That Abraham Lincoln and his followers were "political activists" who wrung the freedom of the slaves from the status quo of the 1860s and made it stick in the 13th, 14th, and 15th amendments. That Theodore Roosevelt with his Square Deal at the turn of the century, Woodrow Wilson with his New Freedom in 1914, Franklin Roosevelt with his New Deal in the 1930s, Harry Truman with his Fair Deal in the 1940s, John Kennedy with his New Frontier and Lyndon Johnson with his Great Society in the 1960s—all of these men were "political activists" in the 20th Century, and who will say that the United States of America in the 1970s is not the better for them?

And so with political activists among women. Abigail Adams was a political activist in the 1700s. Lucretia Mott, Elizabeth Cady Stanton, Susan B. Anthony in the 1800s, and Carrie Chapman Catt and their associates in the 1900s—all of these women were political activists who bridged the gaps from one status quo to another—fast enough at least to avoid stagnation and revolution in the American way of life.

And so of the political activists among women in North Carolina, women who spearheaded efforts to remove the shackles of medieval common law and statutes and restore to married women the control of property they had surrendered on their wedding day. Women who spearheaded efforts to break the rigor mortis of customs, traditions and laws which frowned on women who wanted to go to college, join women's clubs, or vote and hold office in any city, county, state, and federal governmental units. Women who are now spearheading the fight for equal rights under the laws of North Carolina, in the effort to bring about a world for which women throughout the generations have dreamed and planned and worked and fought and died and scarcely dared to hope.

There is more truth than poetry in the observation that the "political activist" of one generation becomes the "political conservative" of the next—witness the late Mr. Justice Frankfurter. Remember also his answer to the question whether going on the Supreme Court of the United States ever changed a lawyer's views on social and economic questions: "If he is any good, it does."

I believe it is the normal, natural, and sometimes reasonable fear of the unknown and what might happen to the status quo which prompted men to hold on to the "whiphand" over the property and person of their wives. Which prompted most men and some women to hold on to the customs and traditions denying women the privilege of joining women's clubs, going to college, and voting and holding office.

I believe it is fear of the unknown and what might happen to the status quo which is prompting opposition to the Equal Rights Amendment and inviting the collaboration of the John Birch Society, the conservative political courses, and other extremist right wing groups.

I go along with the thinking of Franklin D. Roosevelt when he said in his inaugural address:

> This great nation will endure as it has endured, will revive and will prosper. So, first of all, let me assert my firm belief that the only thing we have to fear is fear itself—nameless, unreasoning, unjustified terror which paralyze needed efforts to convert, retreat into advance.

6.

Are the Native Abilities of Women Equal to the Native Abilities of Men?

Running through many of these arguments, in a *sotto voce* sort of

ay, is the conviction that somehow or other, in the very nature of
things, women are not the equals of men and do not have the standing
to ask for equal rights in our society. Where did that notion come
from?

Like many men I am largely a product of the environment and
traditions in which I have lived and moved and had my being. In most
of the forward movements of my time I have been little, if any, better
than a middle of the roader—though, I must confess, there have been
times when I have tried to move "the middle of the road" in the
direction I wanted to go. Sometimes I have succeeded—more often I
have failed. I was not an aggressive fighter in the early 1900s for the
right of women to vote and hold office. I have not been, and am not
now, an aggressive fighter for the Equal Rights Amendment. But
through the fifty years from the 1920s to the 1970s I have slowly, all too
slowly, changed the current of my thinking about woman's place in
the world. Let me outline the successive experiences which have
changed my thinking:

First. I was raised in a family of seven girls and two boys. No one in
that family thought for a moment that the girls did not have abilities
equal to the boys, or that they could not learn as fast, or that they were
in any way inferior. In fact, my brother and I agreed that our oldest
sister had the best brain in the family, that our middle sister had the
best business head in the family, and that all of our other sisters had
fully as much sense as we had. And yet all of us without question
accepted inherited customs and traditions fencing women in.

There were some jobs on the family farm that women *didn't do* and
men did; from this starting point it was easy to arrive at the conclusion
that the reason women *didn't* do these things was that women *couldn't*
do them. This habit of thought continued in later years. There were
some occupations and professions that *men went into and women did
not*; and by the same inverted logic people came to think that the
reason was that women *couldn't* do the work required in these professions and men *could*. It was an easy step to the conclusion that women
didn't have as much sense as men. I am afraid that in the early 1900s
our family, boys and girls, accepted this sort of thinking as in the
nature of things.

Second. It is no credit to the boys in my class in the public schools
from the first to the eleventh grade that the inbred notion of masculine
superiority persisted while a girl was leading our class in grades—she

[205]

led it every year for eleven years—despite the fact that we knew she had fully as much common sense, if not more, than any boy in the class; despite the fact that we could see for ourselves that she had as good judgment in extra–curricular activities as any boy in the class.

This girl has done as good a job as any man in the routine of daily life in the two communities where she has lived, where she has become one of those "confident, effective, and happy people who know how to live ordinary lives in extraordinary ways" and have the "ability to saturate efficiency in making a good living with the ideals of living a good life." Let me illustrate my meaning:

She attended North Carolina College for Women in Greensboro and summer schools at the University of North Carolina at Chapel Hill and the University of California at Berkeley.

She taught the first grade in Smithfield Public Schools for years married and moved to Goldsboro, and there through the years worked with the County Board of Elections, the District Office of the State Board of Probation, the local Radio Station, the Wayne County Hospital Women's Auxiliary, and the Salvation Army.

She took an active part in church work: serving as President of Church Women, Circle Chairman, member of the Musical Pulpit Committee, playing the piano in Sunday School and Church Services, and singing in the Church Choir.

She organized the Community Concert Association, brought the North Carolina Symphony Orchestra to her hometown, organized local groups to attend statewide concerts in the state capital, and served on the North Carolina Arts Council.

"I'm not a fence-sitter," she says. "I am a participant. I have to pull for someone." She always pulled for her husband and their home "We bought this house during the depression," she says, "and when we finally got it paid for we were so happy we decided never to move. have such a happy and meaningful life here in Goldsboro," she exclaims, and her friends have no doubt that that is the sort of life she would lead wherever she lived.

Today, age finds her with a heart so young and a life so full of affection and praise that every one who knows her loves to be around her.

I knew her in Smithfield as Irene Myatt, and in Goldsboro as Mrs. John R. Morris.

Third. There was another girl I knew briefly when she came to

Chapel Hill for her junior year, with interest in the romance languages. She took front rank in her classes as a Phi Beta Kappa student, became president of the Women Students' Association in her senior year, and led the fight which persuaded the General Assembly of North Carolina to erect the first women's dormitory on the University campus.

She did not start out to be a "career woman"—she became a wife. Things did not work out as she had expected, and around her thirty–fourth birthday she realized that in all likelihood her survival would soon depend on her ability to provide food, shelter, and clothing through her own efforts.

She took a job in the personal shopping and export department of R. H. Macy in New York at a salary of $21 a week. She burned the midnight oil, or, rather, as she says, "fell asleep from fatigue, pouring over books I took home from the Macy library, and after two years learned the retail business in 'the world's biggest store.' She took a job in a department store in Greensboro as personnel and training director under the direction of a merchandise manager whom she called "second to none," and who was willing to give her all the responsibility she thought she could handle—"personnel management, training, customer relations, buying, shipping problems, the works, a heavy load and good for me."

During World War II she became acquainted with a young English Naval liaison officer stationed at Charleston. After the war, his merchant banking firm in England organized a corporation in New York to promote the sale of British goods—importing and exporting, and acquired ownership of the famous old Mark Cross Company noted as wholesaler and retailer of fine leather goods since the middle of the nineteenth century.

This girl had impressed the English businessman to the point that he visited her and her husband on their farm near Greensboro to discuss serious management problems in the Mark Cross Company, and he invited her to come to New York to study their problems and help them choose a general manager for the company. To make a long story short, the company was so impressed with her work that in 1955 the shareholders invited her to become a consultant and member of the board of directors. In 1956, she became chief executive of the company with the title of chairman of the board and continued until 1961 when the business became sufficiently profitable that the owners could sell it to advantage.

In 1958, she became a director of the Drake America Corporation, another American investment of the English firm—a combination export agency acting for thirty–five major manufacturers, doing the complete export job from the selling of the products to the financing of the purchases. "This was a new field for me, both in nature and scope," she writes. "It was interesting to begin dealing with the whole world. Fortunately the six years I spent with Drake America proved to be highly profitable, and I was able to enjoy the satisfaction of knowing that the shareholders felt that their confidence had been justified."

In the years from 1952 to 1957, she was visiting lecturer on merchandising in the economics department of the Woman's College of the University of North Carolina at Greensboro, teaching these courses each semester; she did her job with such distinction that when she went to New York the College offered to reschedule her classes on the three days she was in Greensboro.

She returned home in the spring of 1968. Her visit to advise and counsel with a friend in New York City in the early 1950s had led to a fourteen year vigil in the business world. For twelve years she had caught the Sunday night train in Greensboro every week and started to work in New York on Monday morning and caught the Wednesday night train and returned to her husband, home, and farm on Thursday morning, for she had never thought of giving them up or short–changing them. At the end of her final ride back home in 1968, Southern Railway officials were waiting for her in Greensboro with arms full of flowers. And shareholders of Drake America, for whom she had been working, voted her a fabulous going–away gift, her husband called it the "golden handshake."

Step by step she had "worked her way through school" in a man's world, giving evidence, more substantial than intuition, of a know-how that delivered the goods before the next promotion came. Becoming no less of a woman, no less of a wife, and no less feminine and home–loving in the process because she knew her business responsibilities and tended to them—attested by the fact that she was adored by her husband with the adoration of the magi for thirty–three years of married life.

"A part of your curiosity about my good fortune," she writes me, "stems, you have confessed, from the fact that I am a woman. I have always chosen not to consider it a handicap and consider that fact incidental. I believe that women forge their own chains and don them of their own accord. I am not interested in chains and chips on shoulders, and I have not found barriers because I have not looked for them."

' She lives near Summerfield today and her name is May Belle Penn Jones.

Fourth. In the 1940s and 50s, I saw women coming to schools at the Institute of Government as public officials—elected and appointed. They knew their business as well as the men. They caught on to the problems as quickly as men. They held their own in the give and take of open discussions with men. They won the confidence and respect of those men, overcoming any notion they may have had about feminine inferiority.

I recall their names and faces as I write these lines. There were county accountants, auditors, and finance officers: Stella Spencer of Lenoir in Caldwell County, Mary Covington of Rockingham in Richmond County, Maida Jenkins of Carthage in Moore County, Flora Wyche of Sanford in Jones County, Katie Cobb of Kinston in Lenoir County, Lilian Ross of Morganton in Burke County, and so on. They won their appointments or elections and were re–appointed and re–elected on their merits for successive terms of office ranging from twenty–five to thirty years. Stella Spencer became President of the State Association of County Accountants, President of the National Association of County Finance Officers, and was chosen Finance Officer of the Year by her fellow members in the National Association.

There were the registers of deeds, including Eunice Ayers of Forsyth County, Christine Williams of Duplin County, Rubye Rhyne of Gaston County, Margaret Moore of Caldwell County, Betty June Hayes of Orange County. They held their standing among men colleagues to the point that through the years each of the first three became president of the State Association of Registers of Deeds. They have been elected for successive terms adding up to thirty years and more.

Eunice Ayers went on to become president of the National Association of Recorders and Clerks, and in 1971–72 received the award of Clerk of the Year from the National Association of County Commissioners. Betty June Hayes received this award at the meeting of the National Association of County Commissioners in 1976.

[209]

There were clerks of the Superior Court, including Martha Comer of Surry County, Frances Rufty of Rowan County, Eunice Manney of Catawba County. There was Lib Denny of Winston–Salem, Deputy Sheriff of Forsyth County, who knew her business, loved it, and tended to it so well for a quarter of a century that she became assistant sheriff.

Other men can call the roll of women they have known who have held their own in competition and standards of performance. These are women I have known and observed at their work on the job.

Fifth. There are the women who were denied the right to vote and hold office in North Carolina from 1663 to 1920, and who in the last fifty years have slowly climbed and fought their way to equal membership on the state and county executive committees of the Democratic and Republican parties, to co–chairmanship of these committees, and in some places have been chosen to head the county executive committees on the basis of superior performance. And this year a woman, Betty McCain, was unanimously elected chairman of the State Democratic Executive Committee. I do not believe that candidates for office in either political party in any county in the state would choose a woman as county chairman unless he believed she was the best "man" for the place.

The myth of women being inherently inferior to men in ability has died a natural death in my mind from my observations of women in action—beginning with my mother and sisters, continuing with the others I have observed through the years, and culminating in forty–eight years of life and work with the woman to whom this book is dedicated.

7.

Should ERA be Rejected because It would Apply to No Discriminations except Those Created by Law–in the Public Sector, and Would Not in Any Way Effect Discriminations Resulting from Habits, Customs, and Traditions in the Free Enterprise System in the Private Sector?

I do not believe it should, and here is why:
One opponent of ERA notes this fact, without comment, saying:

> discrimination may be created by law or by the customs of society or by nature. The Equal Rights Amendment would apply to no discriminations except those created by law. It would not effect in any way dis-

crimination created by the customs of society or by nature.

Professor Freund makes this observation: The Women's Rights Movement seeks to achieve equal opportunity and equal treatment for women in business, professional, domestic, and political relationships, but unless equality is denied by a public agency or because of the law the Equal Rights Amendment by its terms has no application. If we want to see more women in the law firms, in the medical profession, in the Cabinet—and I, for one, do—we must turn elsewhere than to the proposed amendment. The point is not the smug argument that we must change hearts and minds and attitudes (though that too is involved) rather than look to law: the point is that within the realm of law we have to compare the effects and effectiveness of a constitutional amendment on the one hand and the mandate of a congressional legislation and judicial decision on the other.

I look on the fact that the ERA goes so far but no farther, as a reason for going at least that far and not as a reason for going no farther.

It is commonly accepted that public discussion generated the pressure of public opinion on the United States Supreme Court to the point that the Court relaxed its virulent opposition to New Deal legislation, and President Roosevelt could, and did, claim that though he had lost the battle—he had won the war.

There is little doubt that public discussion and judicial consideration of the cases involving discrimination on account of race led to public discussion and judicial consideration of cases involving discrimination on account of sex, and that this led to the judicial extension of the due process and the equal protection clauses of the 5th and 14th amendments to forbid discriminations under the laws on account of sex—extensions which have moved opponents to argue that ERA is "totally unnecessary" for this reason.

There is little doubt that public discussion of the Equal Rights Amendment since 1972 has speeded up legislative efforts to eliminate discriminations on account of sex under the laws of North Carolina.

Fifty-seven bills to eliminate sex discrimination were introduced in the 1973 General Assembly—one was ratified.

Nineteen bills were introduced to eliminate sex discrimination in the 1974 General Assembly—two were ratified.

Six bills were introduced to eliminate sex discrimination in the 1975 General Assembly—three were ratified.

After defeat of ERA in 1975 the 1975 General Assembly directed the Legislative Research Commission to "examine North Carolina laws and practices . . . as they relate to a specific sex, as they may deny

[211]

equality of rights under the laws of this state, and as they might be modified by the possible passage of the Equal Rights Amendment to the Constitution of the United States . . . ."

Thirty bills to eliminate discriminations on account of sex had been introduced in the first forty-five days of the General Assembly—most if not all of them based on the recommendations of this Commission, and more bills are being prepared for introduction.

There is little doubt that public discussion of cases involving sex discrimination *under the laws* will spill over into and affect the habits, customs, and traditions now tolerating discrimination on account of sex in private occupations, employments and professions *beyond the reaches of the law.*

This will come slowly enough at best. Let me illustrate my meaning:

A Snail's Pace

The Equal Rights Amendment will not be so much the end of woman's fight for equal rights nor the beginning of the end, as it will be the end of the beginning. The changing status of women in our society in an up–grading sense is likely to go slowly enough to satisfy the most ardent critics of the woman's liberation movement, and to dampen the fears of men who fear her competition in the marketplace. Let me illustrate my meaning:

In high school days I read Caesar's description in his Gallic wars of the "river flowing through the Sedui and the Sequanii into the Rhone with such incredible slowness that no one could discern the direction of its current." And so of the movement of women for "equal rights" for centuries under the common law and statutes of England.

Some years ago when I was lying in a hospital bed recovering from what the doctors called "a stroke with cardiac complications," it seemed to me that the improvement of my condition was as slow and indiscernible as the flow of Caesar's river into the Rhone. I could not see it by the hour, or by the day, barely by the week—only in months and years did it become apparent. In those transition days I had plenty of time to look at the clock on the wall. I could not see the hour hand moving, no matter how intently and fixedly I looked at it. But with my own eyes I could see the minute hand moving, and at the end of an hour I could see that the hour hand had moved an hour's space. And this observation assured me that my condition was improving, albeit so slowly that I couldn't see it.

[212]

As one observes Caesar's river, so, too, one could discern the current in North Carolina for nearly two hundred years after the common law and statutes took root in our soil and grew with the early settlers coming to North Carolina in the 1660s. Perhaps the air was stirring ever so slightly in those years, but the first straws in the wind were visible in three nibbling changes in the statutes of 1837, followed by a fourth nibbling change in the statutes of 1848—giving women a toehold; followed by a great forward thrust in Article X, section 6 of the Constitution of 1868—giving women a foothold; followed by one step forward after another with increasing momentum for a hundred years and more to this day when they are fighting to consolidate their gains in the Equal Rights Amendment which will give them a beach-head from which they can go forward with their efforts to eliminate all inequalities and discriminations on all fronts where they are based on sex. I think that is a reasonable hope and belief.

Most if not all women know that the Equal Rights Amendment— if, as, and when it is ratified—will signal a new beginning in their long unbroken struggle which has brought them from where they were to where they are. Here in North Carolina they have lived to learn that all the little nibbling changes in the laws have won them toeholds, footholds, and beachheads for a new advance and all of them together have helped to change the climate in which today they live and move and have their being. They know all too well the rocks in the road ahead of them. This knowledge and insight is reflected in two articles: one by a woman I have been privileged to observe in action at intervals since her college days in the 1920s, the other by a woman I have never seen nor had heard tell of until I read a speech she made in the summer of 1976.

Women in Business: May Belle Penn Jones

At the end of an unusually successful career as a business management executive on local, national, and international fronts, May Belle Penn Jones wrote a revealing statement to her fellow alumni and students in the October 1975 issue of the *Alumni News* of the University of North Carolina at Greensboro.

There are at present more than twenty–six million women workers in the United States, about one–third of the work force. These women are for the most part working for economic reasons, to support themselves, sometimes to support their families, to supplement the earnings of the husband, and sometimes, though not in a majority of cases, in search of self fulfillment or escape from what they consider a humdrum or non–challenging existence of idleness or of unwelcome domestic duties. Since the economic reason is the paramount one, the first question to ask concerns how they fare in the work world, "how well are they paid compared with the male worker?" A look at the figures prepared by the U.S. Department of Commerce Census Bureau and presented on these pages, gives the very brief answer—"not well."

Since financial compensation and recognition by one's peers are important measures of success, women chafe under the fact that there is a major difference in the pay received by the man and the woman doing the same job. They complain of the difficulty of gaining the opportunity to secure interesting and challenging jobs and they miss the stimulation of the recognition of their abilities on the part of their peers.

In our present discussion we are limiting ourselves to the problem of the woman seeking or holding a position in management.

In 1956 an article in *Fortune* magazine estimated that of a probable quarter of a million "real executives" in the United States, there were almost certainly not over 5,000 of these who were women. Even though the number in 1970 is undoubtedly greater, it is doubtful that the percentage has changed much—this in spite of Title VII of the Civil Rights Act recognizing that all persons be treated without regard to sex in all

INCOME OF YEAR-ROUND WORKERS–BY SEX, 1955-68

Year	Median Wage or Salary Income		Women's Median Income as Percent of Men's
	Women	Men	
1955	$2,719	$4,252	63.9
1956	2,827	4,466	63.3
1957	3,008	4,713	63.8
1958	3,102	4,927	63.0
1959	3,193	5,209	61.3
1960	3,293	5,417	60.8
1961	3,351	5,644	59.4
1962	3,446	5,794	59.5
1963	3,561	5,978	59.6
1964	3,690	6,195	59.6
1965	3,823	6,375	60.0
1966	3,973	6,848	58.0
1967	4,150	7,182	57.8
1968	4,457	7,664	58.2

INCOME BY SEX AND MAJOR OCCUPATION, 1968

Major Occupation Group	Median Wage or Salary Income		Women's Median Income as Percent of Men's
	Women	Men	
Professional, Technical Workers	$6,691	$10,151	65.9
Nonfarm Managers, Officials	5,635	10,340	54.5
Clerical Workers	4,789	7,351	65.1
Sales Workers	3,461	8,549	40.5
Operatives	3,991	6,738	59.2
Service Workers (except Private Household)	3,332	6,058	55.0

Source: U.S. Department of Commerce, Bureau of the Census: Current Population Reports, P-60, No. 66.

[215]

phases of employment, including hiring, promotion, firing, apprenticeship and other training programs and job assignments. At a time when at least one–third of the work force is composed of women, why do so few attain executive or managerial status? How do those fare who do reach this status?

I do not believe that there is any substance to a view that women are unsuited to business at any level consistent with their intelligence, education, temperament and, most important, their motivation. For a good many years women have proven that they can fully compete with men in intellectual attainment, that they can reach the same levels of education, that they have fully as great sense of responsibility in the discharge of duty, that they do not lack moral or physical stamina—yet women have not in great numbers found a place in the executive and management levels of business. Why?

The barriers to advancement are numerous, but in my view, one of the most significant of these barriers is that she is barred from stepping on the first rung of the advancement ladder. Women do not often find themselves sought for or accepted into executive training programs. In short, they are not employed with advancement in mind. They are usually expected to be prepared for a specific job, either because they have a mechanical skill, such as stenographic, machine operation or clerical chores. From the word go a woman is expected to pay her way now—not in the future.

When management is charged with discrimination in excluding women from executive training, the glib answer is that training programs are expensive and attrition is costly; that women trainees are lost through marriage, following the husband, time out for childbearing, home responsibility, etc., etc. I believe that the attrition in training men is also substantial—without any of the foregoing reasons. I think the real reason for denying the training opportunity to women is that as long as enough male recruits are available, management traditionally prefers them and sees no valid reason not to prefer them.

But the fault does not lie exclusively with management. By far the greater number of women entering the business world do so believing that this will be a temporary phase. Most women and most men go into business for economic reasons. When the economic reasons become less pressing (if they do), more women than men are glad to call it quits. How many times young women have said to me "I am living for the day when I can stay at home!" This does not by any means apply to all women in business. There are those who find the business activity a rewarding means of self fulfillment. Many times this discovery, and the serious desire to meet the challenges of business, come late enough that the battle to get out of the ranks of the routine worker into the ranks of those slated for advancement is rough and requires not only better than average ability but a lot of luck.

With a third of the work force composed of women the phrase "a woman's place is in the home" sounds silly. But a woman has to decide, and reasonably soon, where her place is and has to be able to determine whether that place is reasonably consistent, not only with her abilities, but also with her assessment of the rewards in terms of their price.

In the zeal for "liberation" and the rebellion against the limitations and "prison walls" of a traditional role, it seems to me that many women forget with what starry eyes they may have viewed the orange blossoms and bridle veil that generations have pictured as the "open sesame" to happiness. If, or when, a woman concludes that the management of the home and the bearing and rearing of children are not fully and permanently satisfying, she may already have entered an age group no longer considered as profitable promotion material since there is too much catching up to do. For whatever reason the woman enters the work force late, the fact remains that she is at a disadvantage from the standpoint of equal pay and equal access to advancement opportunity. I remember all too well a flat turndown at Macy's with the cold reminder that I was "too old" when I expressed interest in taking executive training in merchandising. In order to get this training, I borrowed a mimeographed course from a young colleague and burned the proverbial midnight oil working out lessons without benefit of an instructor. Later I was lucky enough to find an employer whose criterion was more favorable to my ambitions.

Many successful women have demonstrated that home responsibility and business executive responsibility are not mutually exclusive. If this be the case, and a woman is willing to have a go at it, a much earlier beginning may make the road to advancement easier. The married woman, however, is faced to a greater degree than the married man with problems arising out of the need to balance the responsibilities of home and the responsibilities of the job—executive or otherwise, but especially with the demands made on the executive. This is true largely because of the traditional concept of her domestic duties—a concept of such enduring strength that, consciously or unconsciously, she has accepted it—which insures a trace, at least, of a feeling of guilt if such duties are shunned or neglected. She faces also family resistance to claims on her time when they at times supersede family claims. Happy is the woman executive whose husband is able to accept with pride her double role as wife and business woman in the same way that he expects her to respect the demands of his own career which may limit his family life! It is, as a matter of fact, estimated that more than two out of every five women in the work force are not married and this conflict does not apply.

Harvard Business Review in reporting on a survey made in 1965 of the attitudes of 2,000 executives (one–half male, one–half female), noted that there was general agreement by both sexes that "a woman has to be exceptional, indeed over–qualified, to succeed in management today." In thinking about this brief summary of the attitude of the respondents in this survey, I find that I am in agreement almost more with the word "exceptional" than with "over–qualified." I see such a woman as exceptional in the sense that what she wants from life is not confined to what the average woman has chosen in the past; I see her as exceptional in having found the opportunity in an exceptional situation to advance in spite of the traditional prejudices and other barriers standing in her way; I see her as exceptional in that she accepts the necessity of the personal sacrifices demanded in terms of long hours, high pressure and the limitations on family life that are almost universal in executive life.

I trust that I will not be considered a traitor to my sex when I express the opinion that ambitious women might think and act (as many of them do) more constructively if concentration on discrimination were subordinated to concentration on the opportunities and challenges of the job at hand. As attitudes become more receptive to the woman executive, she will be able to lessen her defensiveness.

True, it takes considerable self confidence and maturity on the part of a woman not to be somewhat influenced by the "after all, she is a woman" attitude of the business community; but, to the extent that she can clearly see the barriers to her advancement without allowing them to become obsessions, she is able to apply herself to the positive aspects of her job rather than dwelling on what she must overcome in competing with men. In fact, from the considerable number of highly successful women executives I have known and worked with, I have heard almost nothing about competing with men but a great deal about competing against tough business facts, situations and problems. The effective woman executive is an executive *person*, not an executive woman. If a woman executive, when faced with opposition or conflict, tends to think that "it is because I am a woman," she is disqualified as an effective executive person in my opinion.

There appears to be general agreement that women are special people. Nowhere have I heard it argued that *as people* there are no fundamental differences in point of view. A problem arises then from the fact that the business world—and very specially the business executive world has been set up to reflect what men are not, not what women are. Does this not mean then that if women are to be treated as Title VII says they must be treated, "without regard to sex in every phase of employment," women must think and act under the rules and philosophy of the business man, thus, at least to some degree altering their women personality? In most cases, I believe, in which women have been successful in management roles, they have adjusted themselves to male tenets. I do not say that this is necessarily desirable—merely that this is the way it appears to be at this stage. It is for this reason that business men believe that they give high praise to a woman executive when they say "she thinks like a man." This is food for thought.

How do business men believe an executive would think if she—or he—thought like a woman? What, in fact, does it mean to think like a woman? Would "woman thinking" be clouded, illogical, fallacious, emotional? Or would it be thinking at all in the view of the businessman who is quite sincere in his praise of thinking like a man—he means to say in essence that this is superior thinking. I am sure that he is right in believing that if a woman manager thinks like a man, she is less apt to rock the boat of established patterns. Might it not be most interesting to see whether a special contribution might be made if a manager could think like a man and like a woman at the same time? I should think it quite possible that greater balance might result in the management group—or we might even see another Dorothy Shaver, the great late President of Lord & Taylor.

If we are to take seriously today's questions of the whole "establishment," including business, we would treat in a much broader context the question as to whether women have the capabilities and traits that would serve the best interests of business. Should not the whole field of what the establishment considers suitability for executive responsiblity be re–examined? Up to the present women striving for management responsibility and status have been judged suitable or not suitable, both as candidates and in performance by the standards of the establishment, and the business establishment is obviously male. If criteria are critically and dispassionately re–examined in the light of current and future needs in a society in which business will unquestionably play, and is already consciously preparing for a new and enlarged role in the society, it may very well be that some of the traits peculiarly emphasized in women,and formerly scorned as such, may be seen as ingredients distinctly required in the new role of business.

As an example, there are those who speak a good word for intuition at the top level of decision making. Women have long been charged with considerable reliance on intuition in making judgments. Women are criticized for viewing situations and people too subjectively—a major criticism of business today has been that it is too impersonal, too little concerned with the individual. Perhaps management might benefit by striving for a point of view of greater sensitivity, greater intuitiveness. In other words, it is possible that a change in evaluation of the suitability of a woman now praised if she "thinks like a man" might encompass the thought that to "think like a woman" could be an asset.

I am inclined to suspect that putting these male and female labels on thinking is largely bunk. Men and women go about things differently. This is more a matter of personality than of the thinking machine. The thinking that produces a decision is one thing, the route to the goal may be quite different, but is this not equally true in any group action, regardless of sex? Personality differences are not exclusively sex differences! Not all women executives are paragons of logical thinking—nor are all men executives. Not all women have emotional control—nor have all men. Men are people, women are people—even executives are people!

In the same survey referred to above, as many as 61% of the men and 47% of the women were of the opinion that the business community will never wholly accept women executives, no matter how many laws are passed. I believe that "never" is too big a word. I think that acceptance will not be realized as a result of law; but it may *possibly* come about through a change in values, or by a change in the supply and demand of potential management material. It might result from the increased need in the business community of tomorrow for the special qualities or temperament thought to exist to a greater extent in women than in men. If the brain drain away from interest in a business career that many observers predict as they listen to our "bright young men," materializes, "bright young women" may be needed to fill the management gaps. Such a change is not yet visible, but it would be rash to assume that it cannot develop.

In the end I do not believe that pressure will revolutionize the present resistance to the business opportunities and advancement of women managers; but I think that changes in society may bring about a fundamental change in attitude toward the woman in the business community. It is such changes in society over the years at a much slower pace than that of today's upheavals that have brought about the moderate opportunity existing for women now as compared, let us say, with the virtually no opportunity of fifty years ago. In any case, if women are to be in demand in management, it must be because their contribution is equal to, identical to, superior to or complementary to man's capabilities, or, it will come about through a scarcity of management material. In other words, it will not come through aggressive campaigns or through legislation that women will come into their own in the business community.

What do I see as the future of the woman business executive? I see that her numbers will increase as her desire increases to enlarge her world in this direction, as society changes and as the role of business in society broadens. I believe that the likelihood of improving her comparative pay is good. I think her numbers may continue to be a drop in the bucket of the total executive world, not because she cannot produce but because she will continue to be exceptional if this is the sphere in which she believes her greatest opportunity for self fulfillment lies. I am optimistic enough to believe that the choice will eventually be hers. But today, the business world is still a man's world.

A HUSBAND, CHILDREN, AND TWO CAREERS

Marilyn Siegel Smith comes from the state of Washington, but her speech at commencement exercises upon her graduation from Harvard Law School are worthy of inclusion in this saga of women in North Carolina. Her remarks were published in *Harvard Today*, special commencement issue, 1976.

When I entered Radcliffe ten years ago, the lives of Cliffies were hedged by restrictions. At dormitory meetings we debated how to allocate our twenty–five hours a week of parietal hours. We signed out and in at night. We had a curfew, with penalties for being late. We were not supposed to wear pants to class. For lunch we had to go to the Graduate Center, back to Radcliffe, or to the basement of Memorial Church with our sack lunches. Although men were admitted to the new Hilles Library, women were not allowed in Lamont Library. With an hour between classes, we could not drop into Lamont for a book on reserve.

Little by little the social atmosphere relaxed. Parietal hours multiplied and then disappeared; we wore whatever we wanted; dormitories became co–educational; and women were admitted to Lamont and to the Harvard Band.

When I graduated in June, 1970, in the first joint Radcliffe–Harvard commencement, we were beginning to care about the issues raised by the women's movement. We had not before then realized the significance of our Harvard experience—the grumblings about Cliffies who never washed but who studied too hard (and therefore got the grades the more brilliant Harvard men deserved), the lack of women on the faculty, the lack of career counselling. A woman who was Phi Beta Kappa and magna cum laude was greeted with surprise by her thesis advisor when she expressed an interest in going on for a Ph.D. Spurred on by the common experience of being the only woman in a section and feeling very, very conspicuous, we hoped for equal admissions.

I cannot speak of the changes that have come over Radcliffe and Harvard since I graduated, but I can and will address myself to the changes that have come over me and my friends, and what they tell me about the future of Radcliffe and Harvard students in the real world. Last year, at my fifth reunion, the problem on everyone's mind was that of career versus family. Could one have a loving husband, children, and *two* successful and fulfilling careers? This question must be considered in view of the kind of man a Radcliffe woman is likely to marry—a man who has been and expects to continue to be "successful," who intends to enjoy his work, work hard at it, and derive his ego satisfactions from it. Such a man—a doctor or lawyer, for example—does not work a forty–hour week.

I stand before you today, law degree practically in hand, mother of two glorious children, and I bring you bad news. It will be a long time before the needs of family and career will be comfortably wed.

Child–raising is important work. It has its moments of unequalled joy. It is also difficult and time–consuming. Yet, child–raising is not a respected profession. If it were, men as well as women would want to do it. The corollary of this is that by taking a few years out to raise your children you will inevitably hurt your career. Having those years on your resumé, explicitly or by omission, will put you at a competitive disadvantage with anyone who has been "working," studying, or travelling during those years. That you are a mother may also hurt because of the stereotype to

[221]

which, I think, we are all susceptible—that mommies are—dumb.

You will be working with men and women without family commitments, who will expect you to work long hours with them. You will *want* to work those hours. If you cannot, you may not be hired, or you may lose a promotion or be fired. If you *do* work the long hours, you will have guilt feelings. You *should* have guilt feelings. The professions are filled with men who do not see enough of their children; to imitate them is no solution.

Day care centers are cited as one solution to the problem. As I know from experience, there *are* good day care centers; they are, deservedly, expensive. There are also *bad* day care centers. No day care center can resolve the practical problems engendered by long working hours, week–end work, vacations, and sickness. No day care center is a replacement for a parent or a home.

Part–time work is another solution. There are not, and will not be, many part–time jobs with adequate compensation, responsibility, status, and truly part–time hours, as long as part–time work is women's work only.

I look forward to the day when men will share not only vacuuming but child–raising, when career patterns will be flexible enough to accommodate people who want to spend their time with their families.

But I am pessimistic. Although I see an increased acceptance of a woman's right to her own career, I see little corresponding desire on the part of men to raise their children and little encouragement to do so from our social institutions. What I fear is that, like our mothers and our grandmothers, we will become two kinds of women—women with children and women with careers. The women's movement, it is true, has increased the career options for women, so that childless women can now be lawyers and welders, as well as school–teachers. If women only must choose, however, we have not come so far at all.

If my own experience means anything, I cannot overstate how difficult it is to do justice to both children and a career. It is a constant battle. It does have its rewards. I remember when my three–year–old daughter learned the Davy Crockett song in school. She asked me what "Kilt him a bar when he was only three" meant. I told her it meant that he had killed a bear when he was only three years old.

She said, "His mother must have helped him."

I was thrilled that my daughter would assume it was the mother who would help kill the bear. Later, it occurred to me that she was speaking from her own observation. Who was likely to be *with* a three–year–old when a bear came along? His mother, of course. Later still, it occurred to me that, although I am not a pioneer like Davy Crockett's mother, in my own way, and in my own time, I too am knocking down bars, to protect myself and my children.

Some day, some time, you, too, may need to fight. I hope that you will do so.

Pioneers

May Belle Penn Jones and Marilyn Siegel Smith are symbols of women by the tens of thousands in North Carolina and all over the United States—women who have faced and are facing what are commonly called "the facts of life"—facing them with courage, with candor, and with conscience. I think their statements show that they have heard "the still, sad music of humanity, nor harsh nor grating, though of ample power to chasten and subdue." They understand the meaning of the Greek playwright when, twenty–five hundred years ago he wrote of the law of God that "Knowledge comes through suffering—sorrow falls drop by drop upon the heart until, against our will, and even in our own despite, comes wisdom to us by the awful grace of God."

They are the symbols of women here and there and everywhere who are facing the future, feeling their way and stumbling forward toward the sort of world for which women throughout the centuries have fought and dreamed and died, but scarcely dared to hope. "Although," says Marilyn Siegel Smith, "I am not a pioneer like Davy Crockett's mother, in my own way, and in my own time, I too am knocking down the bars, to protect myself and my children. Some day, some time, you, too, may need to fight. I hope that you will do so."

I do not know how she will come out, and I doubt if she knows. But I think I do know that this is the sort of spirit which has brought women to where they are, and is more than likely to take them where they want to go.

VIII
Four Women in North Carolina

CORNELIA PHILLIPS SPENCER

If I had to pick one woman who represented the women of North
Carolina at their best in the years from the 1860s to the 1880s, I would
pick Cornelia Phillips Spencer. She was born in 1825, came to Chapel
Hill when she was one year old, grew up in the University of North
Carolina where her father was professor of mathematics, became Cor-

nelia Phillips Spencer in 1855, went to live in Alabama, became a widow in 1861, returned to live in her father's house in Chapel Hill in 1862, lived there through the days of Civil War and Reconstruction, went to live with her daughter and son-in-law in Cambridge, Massachusetts in 1894, and died there at the age of 83 in 1908.

In an introduction to *Selected Papers of Cornelia Phillips Spencer* in 1953, Dr. L. R. Wilson wrote:

> From 1865 to 1900, she was known as the author of *The Last Ninety Days of the War* (1866), of "Pen and Ink Sketches of the University" (1869) in the *Raleigh Sentinel*, of "The Young Ladies Column" (1870—76) in the *North Carolina Presbyterian*, of daily and weekly "Reports of the University Normal Schools" in the *State Press*, of *First Steps in North Carolina History* (1888), and of "Old Times in Chapel Hill" (1884—90) in the *University Magazine*.
>
> She was recognized as one of the principal advocates of the day of better common schools and as the champion of the cause of higher education for women, which resulted in the establishment of the [State Normal and Industrial College in 1891—later the North Carolina College for Women, the Woman's College of the University of North Carolina, and now the University of North Carolina at Greensboro]. The epigrammatic quip made about her by life-long friend and confidant, Governor Zeb Vance, aptly described the high place she held in the public's mind. When someone declared she was the smartest woman in North Carolina, he added, "And the smartest man, too."

These *Selected Papers* included her writings on education: the Function of Education, the Common Schools, Vocational Education, Physical Education, the Education of Woman, Teachers and Their Training, the University Normal School, Schools and Colleges.

The University: the University of Caldwell and Swain, the Tragic Years of Degradation and Eclipse, the Reopening and After.

These *Selected Papers,* continues Dr. Wilson, "give only a limited though direct impression of the total range of her interests and of the impact of her thought upon the public officials, college and university presidents, editors, publishers, ministers, educators, and other leaders who continually turned to her for information and guidance, particularly in matters relating to education, books, and manuscripts, and the social and religious problems of the day."

Dr. Wilson writes: These papers "show the resolution of one woman, who, alone, and armed only with her pen, formulated a plan of action and determinedly stuck to it until the nightmare was ended and

[225]

a new day could be ushered in. No finer chapter of endeavor in behalf of the public good of North Carolina has been written by any other of the State's sons and daughters."

Her "Pen and Ink Sketches of the University," appearing in the *Raleigh Sentinel* from April 26 to July 6, 1869, sounded the call for the reopening of the University of North Carolina, closed in the aftermath of Civil War. The last of these sketches closed with these words: "To the Alumni must the University look for her restoration. To the Alumni have I addressed these desultory papers, in the hope of kindling their attachment and awakening their interest."

Living and growing up in Chapel Hill during the 1830s, 40s, and early 50s, she had known them as students—David Lowrie Swain, President of the University from the 1830s to the Civil War, Zeb Vance, student in the 1850s, and others who had come to prominence and influence throughout the state. They rallied to her call and began the long fight which led to a bill for the financial reorganization and support of the University. It passed its first reading by a single vote, but the support increased rapidly and it passed unanimously on the second and third readings.

The part she had played in the fight was recognized by the action of the authorities in telegraphing the news to her on March 20, 1875. Hope Summerall Chamberlain tells what she did in *Old Days in Chapel Hill:* "March 20, 1875, was Mrs. Spencer's fiftieth birthday. It was on that day that the news was telegraphed to her, a few minutes after the bill was safe. She called her few young girls, her scholars, her neighbors' children, and with them mounted the stairs to the belfry [in Smith Building]. It was no funeral peal which waked the echoes when for half an hour she told the hills and the falls, and the living souls left within the joyful sound, that the days of silence and defeat were over."

SALLIE SOUTHALL COTTEN

If I had to pick one woman as symbolic of the best in all forward-looking women in North Carolina at the turn of the century, it would be Sallie Southall. She was born in 1846, grew up in Murfreesboro, attended Wesleyan Female College and graduated from Greensboro Female College at the age of 17, taught school during the Civil War, became Sallie Southall Cotten in 1866, raised six children, and or-

ganized and directed North Carolina's exhibit at the World's Fair in
Chicago in 1893. Throughout the 1890s she worked with women of all
races—"teaching them and encouraging them to form clubs or study
groups for self-improvement and for proper child care, and to promote
actions to influence the economic aspects of family and community
life." She helped to organize the National Conference in 1897,
forerunner of the Congress of Parents and Teachers.

In the early 1900s Sallie Southall Cotten wrote:

> Without knowing *why*, woman has started on the adventure of
> self-development, facing with courage past race habits and tra-
> ditions, masculine ridicule—once so hard to bear—and all the
> handicaps incidental to the attainment of an acknowledged
> equality with man. Man, while leading and dominating the ani-
> mal kingdom yet continues to belong to it, yet nowhere else in
> the animal kingdom is the female subservient to the male, and
> the inconsistency is beginning to dawn upon him. So when the
> Divine Discontent, like a spirituous ferment, stirred the souls of
> many women and urged to action, the result became organized
> womanhood. The great need for strength and cooperation led to

the forming of many organizations among women, all of them being for the benefit of humanity. The demand for suffrage, long ridiculed into obscurity, finally began to receive respect until Justice prevailed.

She was the leading spirit in bringing together at Salem College in Winston-Salem in May, 1902, the Sorosis and Round Table and Embroidery Clubs of Winston-Salem, the Sorosis Club of Wilmington, the Woman's Club of Goldsboro, the Circulating Book Club of Salisbury, and the Alphen Club of Statesville, and in organizing the North Carolina Federation of Women's Clubs.

The number of federated clubs grew from seven to 17 by the first regular convention held in Winston-Salem in October, with 29 delegates attending; to 20 by the second convention in Concord, with 440 members; to 29 by the third convention in Goldsboro, with 550 members. It continued to grow by steady and rapid degrees throughout the years until the North Carolina Federation included 307 Women's Clubs with a membership of 13,000 in 1975.

ELLEN BLACK WINSTON

If I had to pick one woman who represented the women of North Carolina at their best in appointive public office in the 1940s, 50s, 60s, I would pick Ellen Black Winston.

She was born in Bryson City, graduated from the public schools, from Converse College with the A.B. degree in 1924, and from the University of Chicago with a master's degree in 1928 and a Ph.D. in 1930.

She taught social science and served as Dean of Girls in Raleigh high schools, headed the Department of Sociology at Meredith College (1940–44), served as Visiting Professor at the University of North Carolina at Chapel Hill, became Commissioner of Public Welfare in North Carolina in 1944 and continued in that office until 1963.

I saw her at work on this job throughout the years from 1944 to 1963 as she reorganized the department, lifted its sights, expanded its operations, increased its services, and became an efficient and effective departmental administrator and an inspiring leader to her associates in the state organization and her co-workers in a hundred county welfare organizations—without a superior and with few equals in state

and county government. During these years she served as President of the North Carolina Conference for Social Service, President of the Legislative Council, Senior Social Scientist of the Farm Security Administration, and Chief Training Officer for WPA in North Carolina. She did the research for authoritative articles and brochures influencing the course of government in the field of her activity.

Her work attracted attention throughout the nation and she was chosen President of the American Public Welfare Association for 1957–59, President of the National Conference for Social Service for 1965–66, and served as member, adviser, and counselor of a multiplicity of national boards and commissions dealing with public welfare and social services.

She became Commissioner of Public Welfare in the United States Department of Health, Education, and Welfare in 1963 and received the Distinguished Service Award for her work there in 1967. Thereafter she served as the U.S. representative on a nine-member United Nations Preparatory Committee for the International Conference of Ministers of Social Welfare, and was one of the six members appointed to the U.S. delegation for that meeting in New York.

SUSIE MARSHALL SHARP

If I had to pick one woman in elective office who has represented the women of North Carolina at their best in the 1940s, 50s, and 60s, and still represents them at their best in the 1970s, I would pick Susie Marshall Sharp.

She was born in Reidsville, graduated from the public schools, from Woman's College of the University of North Carolina at Greensboro, and from the Law School of the University of North Carolina at Chapel Hill. She was the only woman in her law class, was in the front rank of students, and became student editor of the *North Carolina Law Review*.

She went to practice law with her father in Reidsville. At first the clients of the office would come to consult her father before she got to the office in the morning, or while she was out to lunch, or after she had left in the afternoon—to avoid the embarrassment of talking to a woman lawyer about legal matters which were a man's business. In the years that followed, the situation was gradually reversed—clients were coming to the office to consult with her while her father was out, to avoid embarrassing him. One large business corporation retained the firm on the express condition that she would personally attend to all its legal business.

She was the only woman lawyer in the state to be chosen city attorney. She was the first woman to be appointed Judge of the Superior Court where she handled judicial business as effectively as any man on the bench and was regularly elected thereafter. She was appointed, and then elected, Justice of the Supreme Court of North Carolina where she has served as effectively as any man. She was a candidate for the office of Chief Justice in 1974 with the approval of working colleagues who hold on to the tradition of inherent masculine superiority by claiming she is the "best man on the bench." She was elected by the largest voting majority on the state Democratic ticket, and became the first woman to be elected Chief Justice of a state supreme court in any state in the United States.